# THE RESURGENCE OF
# SATYAM
The Global IT Giant

# THE RESURGENCE OF
# SATYAM
## The Global IT Giant

Zafar Anjum

RANDOM HOUSE INDIA

Published by Random House India in 2012
1

Copyright © Zafar Anjum 2012

Random House Publishers India Private Limited
Windsor IT Park, 7th Floor, Tower-B
A-1, Sector-125, Noida-201301, UP

Random House Group Limited
20 Vauxhall Bridge Road
London SW1V 2SA
United Kingdom

978 81 8400 075 7

This book is sold subject to the condition that it shall not, by way of trade or otherwise, be lent, resold, hired out, or otherwise circulated without the publisher's prior consent in any form of binding or cover other than that in which it is published and without a similar condition including this condition being imposed on the subsequent purchaser.

Typeset in Dante MT by Eleven Arts

Printed and bound in India by Replika Press Private Limited

*For*
*Ma, Papa, Shabana, Zara*
*and*
*the people at Satyam who embodied
and demonstrated the 'Spirit of Satyam'*

# CONTENTS

*Prologue: In Search of Satyam (Truth)*   1

1. The Birth of a Scandal   27
2. Shock, Anger, and Betrayal   43
3. A Bomb Explodes in New Delhi   59
4. Hyderabad Blues   79
5. The League of Extraordinary Gentlemen   91
6. The Healing Begins   107
7. An Unlikely CEO   127
8. A Marriage Made in Heaven   141
9. The Camel Rider   157
10. Turning the Tide   187
11. Back in the Big Boys' Club   209

*Epilogue*   227
*Afterword*   241
*Acknowledgements*   245
*Notes*   247
*A Note on the Author*   267
*A Note on the Type*   268

# PROLOGUE
# IN SEARCH OF SATYAM (TRUTH)

*A Journey of Discovery*

*When one man can create Satyam as an organization of 53,000 people, why can't 53,000 committed people rebuild one SATYAM?*
—Mirza Faizan, a Satyam employee in 2009

I chanced upon the Satyam story in an unusually casual manner. It was January 7, 2009 and I was back in my Singapore office after the Christmas holidays. As I was settling down into my routine and browsing the Internet, there was this curious piece of news about Satyam's Founder and Chairman, Ramalinga Raju, having admitted to cooking the books of his own company to the tune of US$1 billion.[1]

The story seemed incredible. Was it a bad New Year joke?

I read one story, then another, and another. The piece of news was as far from being a joke as possible. It was in the newspapers, on TV, and all over the Internet. It was everywhere.

The news of Raju's fraud sent shockwaves throughout India's corporate sector. Satyam, India's fourth-largest outsourcing services provider, was a big name, a big brand in the country's IT sector. It counted 185 of the Fortune 500 companies among its portfolio of around 600 clients, which included international brands such as General Electric and Nestlé.

In the next few days, the Satyam scandal snowballed into a global story and it was dubbed as India's Enron.[2] Like all scandals that feed media frenzy and stoke popular imagination, people had burning questions about this one too that needed answering. Why would an iconic entrepreneur like Ramalinga Raju do something like this, and then admit his crime? What forced his hand into making such a confession at that particular time? Was it political pressure brought on him that forced him to confess? Or was it a cover to hide something ever bigger? Nobody had the answers. All the public had was a letter of confession written by Raju and a lot of speculation and gossip.

In the backdrop of the global financial crisis and the schadenfreude owing to the success of the Indian outsourcing industry, there was tremendous interest in the story. As the online editor of four of Asia's top technology magazines (*CIO Asia, MIS Asia, Computerworld Singapore, and Computerworld Malaysia*), I immediately knew that my readers too would want to know what travails awaited this beleaguered giant.

I remember running a few blog posts and hosting a special podcast on this topic. I called some of the top outsourcing analysts in the region and asked them what they thought of the scandal and how they saw the future of Satyam. That podcast became one of the most popular downloads on our website and remained popular for about two years, indicating people's interest in this extraordinary story of corporate misbehaviour.

## WHY SATYAM'S FALL WAS A BIG STORY

Satyam's fall was a big story because it had serious implications for the entire Indian IT services industry. It was not just about Satyam's 53,000 employees who faced uncertainty. India's image was at stake. The world was questioning India's ability to handle a crisis like this. Doubts were also raised over India's judicial system—the suspicion was that Ramalinga Raju would be let off the hook with light punishment.

The air was rent with negativity and questions about Satyam. Most outsourcing trade pundits agreed that Satyam had no chance of surviving as a company. Satyam had hit an iceberg and, like a shipwrecked vessel, its assets were likely to be bought over by different companies—piece by piece.

Even after the government appointed a board to stop the haemorrhage at Satyam, the company's fate seemed bleak.

Ironically, before the scandal, Satyam faced the danger of corporate takeover.[3] Post-scandal, however, as the auditors scrutinized Satyam's cooked books, no corporate house showed interest in touching

Satyam even with a barge pole. Not even Tech Mahindra initially, which went on to make a successful bid for the company.[4]

Internally, the challenge for Satyam as a company was to keep its spirit alive amid a severe cash crunch and loss of market confidence. The Satyam leadership was struggling to retain employees and customers. There were all kinds of rumours going around to make things worse for them.

Unfortunately, I was not in India where the main story was developing. However, since Satyam had a presence in Singapore, I began to cover the company's affairs from an Asia Pacific (APAC) perspective. Though I too had my doubts about Satyam surviving the crisis, I was nevertheless impressed by the resilience of the company's staff. The image of the handprints that Satyam's employees had put on a wall poster—with the slogan 'The Spirit of Satyam'—acted like a beacon of hope in my mind. That image seemed to draw me to the Satyam story more and more.

In Singapore, Rohit Gandhi, the company's APAC chief, used to brief the media on all matters related to Satyam after Tech Mahindra acquired it. Over the months and years after the acquisition, I followed the developments at Satyam—the company's restructuring and rebranding, the institutionalizing of the Shadow Board, the winning back of old customers and bagging of new deals, Satyam's coming out party at the 2010 FIFA World Cup held in South Africa, and so on.

Within a year-and-a-half of being acquired by Tech Mahindra, Satyam, now christened Mahindra Satyam, had staggered back to life. By the third quarter in 2010, it was back in good shape.[5] Though it still had some battle scars owing to the mortal blows delivered by the scandal, the company began to display the swagger of a boxer who had come out a winner in round one, and was raring to go for round two.

When I met Rohit in early 2011, I expressed my desire to do a book on Satyam's amazing turnaround. He enthusiastically backed my idea. He told me that Harvard Business School was also interested in doing a case study on the company.

In the next few quarters, more good news flowed from Satyam. The company's turnaround—from a scandal-hit organization with an uncertain future to one that reported a ten-time increase in its year-on-year profits—took many watchers by surprise. One Indian commentator wondered if Mahindra Satyam was the next dark horse of the Indian IT industry. With a hefty dose of good luck, he wrote, this company could become the next Cognizant—the US-based company that beat Wipro in 2011 to become the third-biggest IT services company.

This kind of performance by Satyam had me hooked to the idea of doing a book on the company's revival, mainly to satisfy my own curiosity. How did it get a second life? How did a shipwrecked vessel pick up its splinters and set sail with new fervour—that's what I wanted to know. In a time of unprecedented crisis, how did the 'Spirit of Satyam' stay alive? Who were the stand-up guys when the chips fell? How did they save the day? How did this phoenix raise itself up from the ashes to take flight? And where was Satyam now headed? I wanted answers to all these questions and wanted to convey them to my readers. If I succeeded, I thought it might shed some light on this fascinating chapter in the corporate history of India.

On September 1, 2011, when I first met Mahindra Satyam's CEO, C.P. Gurnani, at Tangling Club in Singapore, he was kind enough to express his support for my project. At the meeting, Gurnani told the gathering how Satyam's success had silenced its critics. Satyam's turnaround was a slap across the faces of all those, including some from the media, who had doubted the company's survival. After hearing him, I was more than sure that I had to do this book.

## A FLIGHT TO HYDERABAD

On January 9, 2012, I boarded a SilkAir flight for Hyderabad. The four-and-a-half-hour journey ended with SQ5376 landing at Rajiv

Gandhi International Airport in Hyderabad at 10.15 pm local time. There was some major turbulence mid-flight, but I was too excited to worry about it as I was going to meet some of the courageous folks who were involved in turning Satyam around.

During the flight, I slept for a while and for the rest of the time, immersed myself in a collection of British short stories edited by A.S. Byatt. I loved a story by Ian McEwan, titled 'Solid Geometry'. In the mysterious story set in England, a much-nagged husband makes his chuntering wife disappear by practising a secret method of folding her limbs. In a wicked way, it reminded me of Satyam's erstwhile chairman B. Ramalinga Raju and how he had blindfolded his company's employees and shareholders and led them down the garden path by conjuring 'non-existent' profits on the company's balance sheet. The crux of both the narratives, if you will, lay in a trick, however malevolent, that worked for the perpetrator. Also, McEwan's story gave me more pleasure than the basmati rice-and-fish dinner that was served on board or the inane TV shows (*Mr Bean, Just for Laughs*) that the passengers were subjected to as in-flight entertainment.

It took less than ten minutes to clear immigration at the airport and another five minutes to collect my checked-in suitcase. I was pleasantly surprised at the speed at which things moved.

Hussain, a young man working with Mahindra Satyam's travel desk, was waiting for me at the arrival hall's exit, holding an A-4 sheet with my name printed on it. He brought me to a Skoda Octavia which would transport me to my hotel.

The car's driver, Krishnamurthy, a chubby fellow of average built, one of the nine drivers employed by Satyam, was dressed in a safari suit. He reminded me of a babu from a government office.

It was early January and I had expected a nip in the air, as North India was grappling with a severe cold wave. Further up north, it was snowing in Jammu and Kashmir and the state was suffering from a blackout. I had packed in a few items of warm clothing, but looking at the weather, I knew I was going to be disappointed. I had missed the Hyderabad winter.

'It was a bit chilly last night but it is not so cold tonight, sir,' Krishnamurthy said. Like most Indian chauffeurs, he liked to speak with a 'yes sir, no sir' suffix to every sentence. Only last week, he informed me, he had ferried C.P. sir (C.P. Gurnani) from the airport to his bungalow. I consequently checked on his story and found it to be true. Mahindra Satyam did have a sales conference at its corporate headquarters in the first week of January. The conference had culminated in a concert at the newly-inaugurated amphitheatre in a rock garden in the Satyam campus.

My conversation with Krishnamurthy revealed that he had been with Satyam for quite a few years. He had also driven Raju around when he was still at the helm of the company.

On our way to HITEC City,[6] Krishnamurthy drove the car through a four-lane highway. The road was smooth and traffic was thin at that time. A signboard announced that Mumbai was some 622 kilometres away. It struck me then that Hyderabad was situated at the tip of the Deccan Plateau and Mumbai couldn't be that far after all. Another thing that struck me was the direct relationship between Hyderabad and Mumbai. The Mahindra group, which is based out of Mumbai (and Pune in Maharashtra), had acquired Satyam.

Both cities have different cultures and it would be reflected in the way an old Satyam would transform into a new Mahindra Satyam—a culture of lesser hierarchy, more openness, and greater camaraderie.[7]

In the semi-darkness of the night, as the car kept on cruising, I could see patches of barren land and huge rocks skirting the road, punctuated with shrubs and trees standing in a medley of natural disharmony. Either the builders had hacked away at the boulders and the earth, leaving little space for plants to grow, or nature had simply moved her attention elsewhere.

When we reached the hotel in HITEC City, a security guard checked the car for explosives at the main entrance. After a minute, we were allowed to enter the hotel compound. It seemed as if I was back at the airport. My bags were screened and I was personally frisked with a metal detector at the hotel's door. I didn't mind the process, though. In India, security had been stepped up everywhere after the Mumbai terror attacks in 2008 and rightly so.

I asked Krishnamurthy to come back at 9.30 am the next morning. He had to take me to Mahindra Satyam's corporate office for meetings.

## ONE MORNING IN HYDERABAD

The next morning's *Times of India* greeted me with a top story on Satyam. 'Satyam sues Raju and Co for fraud', the headline shrieked.

Was it a coincidence? My first morning in Hyderabad and Satyam makes the headlines. I was bemused.

I read the report with great interest. Exactly three years after the Raju scam had come to light, Mahindra Satyam had decided to drag Raju to court along with the company's former Board of Directors, some former Satyam employees, as well as auditing firm PricewaterhouseCoopers and its affiliates and partners for perpetrating fraud, breach of fiduciary responsibilities, obligations, and negligence in performance of duties.

The report said that Mahindra Satyam had filed a suit in the city civil court of Hyderabad, seeking undisclosed damages. The company had sued nearly 123 PwC partners across the US and India offices along with its various affiliates, including Lovelock & Lewes. While the company did not specify the quantum of damages it was seeking from the accused parties, Mahindra Satyam Chairman Vineet Nayyar told the newspaper that 'figure would definitely be much in excess of the US$210 million that the company had to cough up to settle its legal liabilities'. This included the US$125 million US class action suit settlement, US$70 million Upaid lawsuit settlement, and US$10 million settlement with the US markets watchdog—the US Securities and Exchange Commission.

When I reached the Satyam corporate headquarters in Madhapur at 9.30 am that day, it didn't quite look the place that was on a newspaper's front page. Or maybe Satyam had gotten used to being in the news.

Hari T., who wore the twin hats of being Satyam's chief people officer and chief marketing officer, and my main point of contact at the Satyam headquarters, was on leave. He had been working non stop for months and had taken a much-needed break, something which he had shared that with me in an email beforehand. I had been asked to look for Hari babu who was in the human resources department or Indraneel Ganguly who is senior vice president of marketing and communications. Neither of them had arrived in office by that time. Indraneel came to office around noon, I was told. Two security guards on duty helped me locate Sahu Uday Kumar from the administrative office. Uday had been instrumental in helping me with the accommodation and transportation arrangements in Hyderabad.

A tall young man with hair cropped short and a prominent moustache, Uday appeared at level 4 of the building where I was waiting for him. He took me to the fifth floor, where Raju's office was previously located. We sat in the waiting lounge on a white leather sofa and had coffee.

'The coffee is good,' I complimented him.

'It's from our kitchen, sir,' he said.

Uday comes from a hospitality background. He had worked with the Oberoi Group of Hotels and was working in a resort in the Middle East prior to joining Satyam in 2007. On the day the Raju scandal broke out, he was in Satyam's Secunderabad office. He rushed to the HITEC City corporate office after hearing the news of Raju's resignation. 'It was a scene of total confusion,' he remembered. 'We didn't know what would happen next.'

For the next three months, he told me, the fifth floor became the epicentre of crisis management, and the small corporate kitchen that tended to Raju and members of the board, played its role in keeping Satyam going—as far as keeping everyone fed and sated was concerned. 'There were the new board members, officials from SEBI, and law enforcement agencies. They had to be served breakfast, lunch, and dinner. The new board met almost eighteen times in three months. All the top Satyam officials were camped in there. There were around 70 to 100 people who were being fed from the small kitchen,' he told me with pride.

All this was not budgeted. Soon, they ran out of the money allocated for kitchen expenses and no one knew where the money they needed to feed the investigators and the board members was going to come from. Banks and suppliers had frozen their credit lines. But the kitchen had to go on serving the people who were camping at the Satyam headquarters in those critical days. At that time, everyone pitched in—Uday, his colleague Vikram, and even the chef of the kitchen. They bought groceries with their own money to keep the kitchen running, without a thought or without any hope of getting reimbursed. I found their dedication to service and devotion to the company touching.

Arranging transportation for the guests was another challenge. That same morning, Uday introduced me to his colleague Vikram. Vikram told me how they were left with only two company cars—not enough to ferry so many people from the airport to the campus. Apart from one travel company, all other companies had pulled the plug on them. Some employees used their own cars to ferry guests from the airport to office and back. Similarly, for boarding arrangements, employees had to file personal bonds to let hotels accommodate the board members and other guests.

Standing by the window in the waiting lounge, Uday explained the view to me. Right in front of the building was a rock garden with an amphitheatre. It had just been inaugurated, but some finishing work still remained. Across the garden was one of Satyam's offices, which has a capacity to seat four to five thousand people. Adjacent to it, yet another building was under construction. Next to the construction site was the Satyam Learning Lab.

The building I was in with Uday was connected to the building which housed the Satyam's Centre of Excellence. A corridor that connected these two buildings had Raju and his brother's penthouse offices on it.

While waiting for Indraneel and Hari, I got a chance to look at Raju's erstwhile office.

From his room, Raju had an open view of both sides. Outside his room was a Zen garden, with a variety of pebbles and plants. Inside, his room was fairly big, with a wooden table and brown-and-white leather chairs placed in a corner. Facing the big work desk was another table with a few chairs and a teleconferencing monitor. Next to the work table was a showcase. One could imagine it loaded with gift items and memorabilia when Raju occupied the office. When I saw the room, the shelves were empty except for a small item which was a gift from the Government of Perak in Malaysia.

What was interesting about the room was that it had a concealed antechamber. When you entered the little room, you could see a small bed, a few chairs, a coffee table, and a few shelves. There was a small door attached to the room from where the boys could enter to bring food for Raju. During the days when the Maytas acquisition by Satyam was underway, the room was also used for meetings, Vikram told me.

I didn't know what to think of such offices, but I remembered a report which had this to say: '...the penthouse has showers, bedrooms, and a Japanese garden, but an expert in vastu shastra—India's version of feng shui—has declared its design a disaster.'

I have no idea which vastu shastra expert pronounced that verdict, but looking at what happened in 2009, maybe Raju's Zen garden was jinxed. Even three years after the scandal, as the reporter had quipped, the new management had not been able to deal with his legacy.

Uday told me about Satyam's other campus some 25 kilometres from the headquarters. That campus even has a zoo (now I knew where the tiger's metaphor came from in Raju's letter). It has dormitories for Satyam's associates and Satyamites go there to relax with their families.

Uday then showed me the boardroom where all board meetings used to take place—a spacious rectangular room with more than twenty white leather chairs parked around a big wooden table. There was a screen in front and projectors were mounted on the ceiling. There were also videoconferencing facilities. 'This is where Satyam's most important decisions were taken,' Uday told me. 'This must be one of the best boardrooms in the country.'

'You should also write your book's prologue sitting in this room,' he joked.

Uday then took me to the dining area on the fifth floor, which was attached to a small kitchen. There were half a dozen tables in the room which gave the impression of a mini restaurant. Uday called out to two cooks who were inside the kitchen. 'He liked your coffee,' Uday told them. They grinned innocently.

One of the cooks had served Raju during his time. I asked him what Raju liked to eat. 'He would change his food habits every six months,' he said. 'For six months, he would eat foreign-style food. For the next six months, he would eat Indian food.' Raju liked to drink green tea. His favourite foods were salad (lettuce), keema biryani, and Chicken 65, the cook informed me.

When we emerged from the kitchen, we were told Indraneel was headed to meet us. Soon, I saw a burly Bengali man, wearing an elbow support that peeked out of his white half-sleeved cotton shirt, walking towards us. 'Tennis elbow,' he said in a booming voice when Uday asked him about the support.

We talked for about thirty minutes over coffee in the waiting lounge. Then Indraneel took me to his office on the fourth floor.

IG's (that's how he is addressed by his colleagues) room must be one of the most tastefully decorated office rooms I have ever seen. It was full of posters, collaterals, advertising campaigns, and interesting photos. There was a large framed poster of the Academy Awards statuette and a small framed poster of *Casablanca*. There were many posters of 'RISE' too, a campaign run in 2011 to energize the associates of the company.[8]

As we discussed the intent of my visit to Hyderabad, IG suggested using the picture of a rock as a metaphor for the book cover on Satyam. Rocks were a common sight in the HITEC city. Satyam as a company was like a Hyderabadi rock, he said—rock solid, Satyam was here to stay.

IG introduced me to his colleague, Upasana and through her, I met Ashish and Shruti. Over the next two days, these energetic young people helped me meet a slew of senior Satyam executives who shared their experiences of Satyam's turnaround with me. Some of the people I met there were A.S. Murthy, Chief Technology Officer, Mahindra Satyam; Rakesh Soni, Chief Operating Officer, Mahindra Satyam; B.K. Mishra, Senior Vice President, Energy and Utilities; and Dr Renu Khanna, Assistant Vice President, Leadership Development, Mahindra Satyam Learning World, to name a few.

I had met the chairman of Mahindra Satyam, Vineet Nayyar, in Singapore three years ago and had briefly met C.P. Gurnani in September last year. I wanted to meet him again for a longer discussion to get a high-level view of Satyam's turnaround strategy. I finally met him on April 19 this year when he flew down to Singapore for an event, Futurescapes 2012. I interviewed him for about an hour over breakfast at the Marina Bay Sands. When I met him, some Satyam associates were setting up the tables for the day-long event; others were busy in conversation. C.P. pointed to them and said, 'Meet these young people; they are Satyam's leaders and they are the ones who have turned the company around.'

I also got an opportunity to spend some time with Hari T., who had arrived along with C.P., the same day. Hari is one of those few leaders at Mahindra Satyam who was also part of the leadership in the Satyam of the Raju era. He spoke very candidly and I could see a variety of emotions flit across his face when he narrated his life and times at Satyam, especially during the period of crisis after Raju's resignation.

Towards the end of the conversation, we spoke about the merger of Mahindra Satyam and Tech Mahindra. When the two companies finally merged after the government clearance, Mahindra Satyam would be rechristened. It was sad to realize, as the conversation flowed, that the name Satyam would most probably be dropped from the Mahindra Satyam brand. An air of poignancy filled the room when we were done with the discussion.

After four years of surviving a crash, Satyam, the company that Raju had founded, was going to lose its identity. That is a sad thing to happen to a brand, but it also signifies that Satyam had got a new lease of life with a totally new brand name, and it had a future to claim. That is the law of the world. Nothing remains the same—ever. Things change, people change, and organizations go through transformations to stay in business. You can't quarrel with that.

## A TALE OF TWO EMPLOYEES

As I look back at Satyam's turnaround, two stories spring forth to my mind: in my opinion, these two stories of two ordinary Satyam employees illustrate why Satyam survived the ordeal.

One is the story of Mirza Faizan, who was working at a client's office when the scandal happened, and the other is the story of Hari Babu, who works in Satyam's human resources department at the company's headquarters. First, Faizan's story.

Mirza Faizan, 32, is a software engineer from Bihar. After receiving his engineering degree, he worked in Defence Research and Development Organization (DRDO), an agency of the Indian government responsible for the development of technology for use by the military, for some time. Then he joined Satyam Computers in 2006.

Faizan was posted at a client location in Bengaluru when news about Raju's letter became public.

'Two days had passed since Raju's resignation from Satyam, and Satyam's collapse seemed imminent,' Faizan recalled as he spoke to me. The media had whipped up a frenzy around the company's fall. Faizan was having a cup of tea in the cafeteria of his client company when one of his co-workers, also deputed with the same client through some lesser-known company, began to talk sarcastically about Satyam in front of the entire team.

'So, Satyam is gone,' he said. 'What are you guys planning to do now?'

The bite in his sarcasm did not go unnoticed. Faizan could barely gulp down the tea that suddenly tasted bitter to him. He wouldn't have reacted to a comment like this in normal circumstances. Coming from Patna, as a middle-class boy, his parents had taught him self control and moderation in the face of provocation. But the question had now been lobbed like a grenade in his direction. It was a taunt, one made in front of his entire team. Faizan thought he needed to defuse the situation and also fix the guy's thought process.

Taking inspiration from his military training that had instilled in him the habit to fight till the last breath, he said, 'Who says Satyam is gone when I am very much alive here and committed to create value on behalf of my company?'

'Hello mister!' The interloper shot back, 'Your chairman has resigned, you guys are facing financial turbulence, and you still have the face to say that Satyam is not gone!'

*This is a full-on attack, bordering on virulent animosity*, Faizan reckoned. *I just have to reply to him in his own language*, he thought.

'Tell me, what will you do and where will you go if our country India was not there?' he asked him.

The attacker did not expect a googly like this from an aerospace electronics and aircraft display systems engineer. But Faizan wanted to engage his combatant at a deeper level.

'What a stupid question!' the guy said, his tone rising. 'How can India be gone? It is a country!'

'Country! What makes a country?' Faizan retorted. 'Land? Economy? Our prime minister? Our president? Our geography? Or the *people*?' He paused and then continued, 'If our PM resigns, will you say India is gone? If our economy faces a slowdown, will you say India is gone? But if the people of a country are lost for any reason, then yes, we will say that the country has no meaning. Who cares about the vast land of Antarctica today, which has just one permanent resident, Father Georgy? Which country does it belong to? Why does it not have any government? Why does it not have an economy? Or, how many countries were there when humans used to hunt for food in prehistoric times? Countries, wealth, infrastructure, and booming economies are nothing but products of *people's* effort; they do not have any existence on their own.'

The man had fallen silent. But the final blow was yet to come. 'When one man can create Satyam as an organization of 53,000 people, why can't 53,000 committed people rebuild one *Satyam*?' Faizan argued.

Dazzled, the guy stood up, shook hands with Faizan and murmured, 'Yaar, when I used to hear from my roommate who works in Satyam that "every Satyamite is a leader", I used to laugh it off. Now, I know why!'

What a beautiful, inspiring story, isn't it? We will talk in detail about it later. First, let's hear Hari Babu's story.

Hari Babu is a lead manager of operations in the human resources department at the Satyam headquarters. He has been working with Satyam since May 2000.

On January 7, when the story of Raju's resignation broke, Hari was devastated like most other Satyam employees. 'That day when we came to office, the news suddenly broke on CNBC TV18 that the stocks were sliding,' he remembered. 'We never knew what was happening. It was like an earthquake. We were in complete panic mode. Even as the main head of HR, we didn't know what was happening. That was the kind of confusion. After the end of the day, we came to know what had come to pass. Ramalinga Raju had surrendered and confessed.'

'There was no direction about whether we had to come to office the next day or not,' he said. Then he slipped into hero-worship mode for Raju. 'To my mind, Raju is a very respectable person, and everybody sees a role model and leader in him,' he said. 'Everybody sees Raju as God, especially in Andhra Pradesh where he has adopted 600 villages in the rural areas, supplying water to them and generally working towards their upliftment, and suddenly this was happening to him. It was hard to digest. When he confessed, some guys were saying that he had done the right thing; others were saying that he had done a bad thing. The question is: for whom had he done all this? For the employees. They have a soft corner for him. People are accepting what he has done. I am also in the same category. We have enriched our careers, we have grown our roots here, and whatever he may have done, he has done only good for me. There is nothing bad for me (in what he has done) as an individual. It is sad to know what he has done, but the fact that he has been identified as a thief—that is the saddest part.'

Now that his hero had fallen and the company's fate was in doldrums, Hari was not sure as to what to do. But there was one thing that he was sure about, and that was his loyalty to the company. 'Definitely, at this moment, I will not jump to another company,' he said, recalling the days after January 7. 'I should be here as a responsible person in HR. Even if my salary is not paid for the next couple of months, I should be here, I thought.'

And that's what he did, even when it meant endless troubles for him. Being in HR, the investigative agencies were hitting him really hard for all kinds of data. 'I was in the CBI office for almost ten days, sitting there, and there were five inspectors asking me different questions,' he said. 'It was difficult for us to provide the information and they were forcing us to. We didn't have anybody's support—neither from the leaders, nor the management. I spoke to my leaders, spoke to the CEO of my company, and told them about my challenges. The CBI was threatening me that even if I left the company, they were going to catch me. What's my mistake? Being in HR? Being in a responsible job? Is that my mistake? Where shall I go? There was a lot of trauma. Few of the guys fell sick. Their blood pressure went down. A few got heart attacks also. Because there was no support and they were being threatened.'

All those months, before Tech Mahindra took over Satyam, were horrible for Hari and other employees like him. 'I carried a lot of things in my head,' he said. 'I lost my sleep for almost two years. I am still suffering from insomnia.'

Now, all of that is in the past. Hari, like all Satyam old timers, is proud of what he has gone through. 'We have made history and now we stand on a solid footing,' he says. 'We have seen the hard times, and now the rest seems like a cakewalk for us. God is testing us. He has given us hard times as well as opportunities.'

I was moved by Hari's story too—he spoke with so much passion and conviction about Satyam and Raju, and yet he was able to move on.

India is Indira and Indira is India—that's what was said when Mrs Indira Gandhi was the country's prime minister. Same was the case with Satyam and Raju—Satyam is Raju and Raju is Satyam. Raju had built Satyam (which incidentally, means truth in Sanskrit) into one of India's biggest software and outsourcing companies.

When Satyam employees were compiling a film to introduce the company to its new owners, Tech Mahindra, in June 2009, they had to deal with this dilemma: how can you talk about Satyam without repeated photos and quotes of its disgraced founder? In the end, they used only two photos of Raju. At that time, Hari T., Hari Babu's boss, told the employees, 'You don't have to feel guilty, but you don't have to hero worship him either.'[9]

One reason the Satyamites kept on going was because they could distinguish between Raju and Satyam. Raju was gone but Satyam as a company could go on, survive.

Once that dissociation had happened, Satyam employees, like Hari, were ready to move on. They were ready to fight for the company's future and their own.

Hidden in these two stories is the secret of Satyam's survival and revival. If a company's rank-and-file employees, like Faizan and Hari, can show such devotion for the company and such confidence as professionals, displaying a never-say-die attitude in circumstances beyond their control, nothing can stop such a company from achieving success. There was something in Satyam's culture that had planted this courage and determination in the DNA of their employees.

This is true not only for Satyam's ordinary staff; I have seen the same attitude in Satyam's leadership. Add to it a new governance model and a sense of informality brought into the company by Tech Mahindra, and you have a glimpse of the secret behind Satyam's resurgence.

It is stories like these—stories of courage, defiance, and wisdom that went into rewriting the history of Satyam—that I want to tell in this book. I hope you like it.

Zafar Anjum  
Singapore  
May 2012

## THE CAST OF CHARACTERS

### THE RAJU FAMILY
(Male lineage)

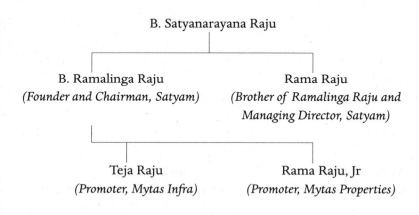

B. Satyanarayana Raju

- B. Ramalinga Raju *(Founder and Chairman, Satyam)*
  - Teja Raju *(Promoter, Mytas Infra)*
  - Rama Raju, Jr *(Promoter, Mytas Properties)*
- Rama Raju *(Brother of Ramalinga Raju and Managing Director, Satyam)*

### OTHERS

| | |
|---|---|
| Srini Raju | Ramalinga Raju's brother-in-law and Chief Operating Officer, Satyam |
| Vadlamani Srinivas | Chief Financial Officer, Satyam |
| Mangalam Srinivasan | Non Executive Director, Satyam board |
| Vinod K. Dham | Non Executive Director, Satyam board |
| Krishna G. Palepu | Non Executive Director, Satyam board |
| M. Rammohan Rao | Non Executive Director, Satyam board |
| T.R. Prasad | Former Cabinet Secretary and Non Executive Director, Satyam board |
| Hari T. | Chief Marketing Officer, Satyam (currently, also the Chief People's Officer at Mahindra Satyam) |
| A.S. Murthy | Chief Delivery Officer, Satyam (now Chief Operating Officer, Mahindra Satyam) |
| Som Mittal | President, NASSCOM |

| | |
|---|---|
| Dr Renu Khanna | Global Head of Leadership Development, Mahindra Satyam |
| Priscilla Nelson | Global Director of People Leadership, Satyam |
| Ed Cohen | Chief Learning Officer, Satyam School of Leadership |
| Ram Mynampati | Interim CEO, Satyam, and member, Satyam board |
| Anurag Goel | Secretary, Ministry of Corporate Affairs, Government of India |
| C.V. Bhave | Chairman, Securities and Exchange Board of India (SEBI) |
| Prem Chand Gupta | Cabinet Minister, Ministry of Corporate Affairs, India |
| Anand Mahindra | VC and MD, Mahindra & Mahindra |
| Kiran Karnik | Former President, NASSCOM and chairman of the government-appointed board of Satyam |
| S. Balasubramaniam | Chairman, Company Law Board |
| Deepak Parekh | Chairman, HDFC Bank and member, government-appointed board of Satyam |
| C. Achuthan | Lawyer and former head of the SEBI, and member, government-appointed board of Satyam |
| Tarun Das | Chief mentor of the Confederation of Indian Industry (CII) and member, government-appointed board of Satyam |
| T.N. Manoharan | Member, government-appointed board of Satyam |
| Suryakanth Balakrishnan Mainak | Member, government-appointed board of Satyam |
| B.K. Mishra | Senior Vice President, Energy and Utilities, Mahindra Satyam |
| C.P. Gurnani | CEO, Mahindra Satyam |

| | |
|---|---|
| Vineet Nayyar | Vice Chairman and Managing Director, Tech Mahindra and Chairman, Mahindra Satyam |
| Rohit Gandhi | Senior Vice President, Mahindra Satyam (Asia Pacific, India, Middle East, and Africa) |
| Indraneel Ganguly | Senior Vice President, Marketing and Communications, Mahindra Satyam |

## THE SATYAM SAGA—A TIMELINE

Dec. 16, 2008: On getting the board's approval, Satyam announces a plan to acquire 100 percent of Maytas Properties for Rs 6,240 crore (US$1.3 billion) and 51 percent of Maytas Infra for Rs 1,440 crore (US$300 million) despite the fact that the two acquisitions would 'punch a hole of Rs 7,680 (US$1.6 billion) in Satyam's books'. Shareholders reject the move. Raju changes his decision on December 17.

Dec. 18, 2008: Satyam announces that its board would meet ten days later on December 29 to consider a share buy back, and possibly announce dividends for the shareholders to restore confidence.

Dec. 23, 2008: World Bank bans Satyam as a service provider for eight years for providing bank staff with 'improper benefits'.

Dec. 26, 2008: Mangalam Srinivasan, an independent director, resigns after the Maytas deal falls through.

Dec. 29, 2008: Three more directors quit the Satyam board: M. Rammohan Rao, Vinod Dham, and Krishna Paleppu.

Jan. 7, 2009: Ramalinga Raju resigns, admits to fraud. He says he falsified the company's cash and bank balance sheet to the tune of Rs 5,040 crore.

Jan. 8, 2009: Satyam's Chief Financial Officer (CFO) Vadlamani Srinivas resigns.

Jan. 9, 2009: The Ministry of Corporate Affairs moves the Company Law Board (CLB) to remove the Satyam directors and auditors. It requests for appointing ten new directors to take charge of the company. The request is granted on the same day.

Jan. 10, 2009: Raju, his brother, and former company Managing Director, B. Rama Raju surrender to Andhra Pradesh police; they are taken into custody and sent to the Chanchalguda prison on charges of cheating and forgery.

Jan. 11, 2009: Satyam's Chief Financial Officer (CFO) Vadlamani Srinivas is arrested.

Jan. 11, 2009: The central government reconstitutes the Satyam board. Kiran Karnik, Deepak Parekh, and C. Achuthan are appointed as the new board members.

Jan. 14, 2009: Deloitte and KPMG named new joint auditors for Satyam; Satyam's former auditor, PricewaterhouseCoopers (PwC), says its opinion on the IT firm's financials may be rendered 'inaccurate and unreliable'.

Jan. 19, 2009: Probe ordered into possible nexus between Satyam and Maytas Properties and Maytas Infra.

Jan. 21, 2009: Ramalinga Raju confesses diverting Satyam funds to the Maytas firms.

Jan. 23, 2009: The Raju brothers and former CFO Srinivas sent to judicial custody till January 31; court rejects SEBI plea to record statements of the Raju brothers.

Jan. 24, 2009: Former Satyam auditor PwC's S. Gopalakrishnan and Srinivas Talluri arrested.

Jan. 27, 2009: The board appoints Goldman Sachs and Avendus, an Indian investment bank, to identify strategic investors.

Jan. 31, 2009: Judicial custody of all accused extended to February 7.

Feb. 3, 2009: The Supreme Court permits SEBI to interrogate the Rajus.

Feb. 5, 2009: Satyam gets Rs 600 crore (US $130 million) from banks to meet working capital requirements. A.S. Murthy is appointed interim CEO.

Feb. 6, 2009: Former NASSCOM Chairman and member of the newly reconfigured Satyam board, Kiran Karnik, appointed as Satyam Chairman.

Feb. 7, 2009: Court extends the judicial custody of Ramalinga Raju and four other accused to February 21.

Feb. 13, 2009: SEBI relaxes takeover norms for Satyam, giving their reconstituted boards the power to lower the target price for open offers.

Feb. 14, 2009: The Serious Fraud Investigation Office (SFIO) joins probe.

Feb. 16, 2009: The central government hands over investigation to the CBI.

Feb. 21, 2009: The government-appointed board, meeting for the seventh time, decides to invite strategic investors.

Mar. 6, 2009: Satyam gets permission from SEBI to sell 51 percent majority stake.

Mar. 9, 2009: The court allows CBI to take custody of Raju brothers, Srinivas, and sacked PwC auditors Gopalakrishnan and Talluri Srinivas.

Mar. 13, 2009: Satyam appoints former Chief Justice S.P. Bharucha to oversee the bidding, selection process.

Mar. 20, 2009: The Satyam board receives bids. Initially, 149 companies registered themselves to acquire Satyam. Out of these only ten submitted their expressions of interest.

Apr. 7, 2009: CBI files a 2,315-page charge sheet against the Raju brothers and seven other accused.

Apr. 13, 2009: Venturbay Consultants Private Limited (Venturbay), a 100 percent subsidiary of Tech Mahindra, is announced as the new owner of Satyam.

May 22, 2009: Four nominee directors of Tech Mahindra, including its Chief Executive Officer, Vineet Nayyar, join the Satyam board. The other three nominees are C.P. Gurnani, Sanjay Kalra, and Ulhas N. Yargop.

Jun. 21, 2009: Satyam is rebranded as Mahindra Satyam. The company says the new name will only be a go-to-market brand while the company's name stays the same.

Jun. 24, 2009: C.P. Gurnani, who headed Tech Mahindra's global operations, is inducted as the new CEO of Mahindra Satyam and S. Durgashankar as the new CFO.

Dec. 9, 2009: Mahindra Satyam agrees to a US$70 million legal settlement with British firm Upaid Systems Ltd to end all outstanding disputes.

Sept. 29, 2010: Satyam Computer Services (now Mahindra Satyam) announces the audited financial results for the financial year 2009 (year ended March 31, 2009) and 2010 (year ended March 31, 2010). This is a major milestone for the new management.

Mar. 21, 2012: Mahindra Satyam announces that Satyam Computer Services is to be merged with Tech Mahindra. The merger will result in the creation of a new offshore services leader with revenue of approximately US$2.4 billion, over 75,000 workers, and over 350 active clients.

# THE BIRTH OF A SCANDAL
## Confessions of a Dangerous Mind

*It was like riding a tiger, not knowing how to get off without being eaten.*
—Ramalinga Raju, Founder and Chairman, Satyam,
(1987–2009)

*January 6, 2009*
*Hyderabad*

How does it feel to be on your way to hell?

Most of us would have trouble imagining it, but B. Ramalinga Raju, the founder and chairman of Hyderabad-headquartered Satyam Computer Services, was already feeling the heat of that fiery place of perdition. He knew he was destined to burn and he knew exactly why—there was a dark and dangerous streak in his personality that he had successfully camouflaged from his employees, shareholders, and clients for over twenty years. And this darkness in him was about to eclipse the halo he had so carefully created around himself with hard work, business acumen, and acts of charity.

The only thing in his control was the timing of his descent to darkness. And that chosen moment for him was now.

It was the end of the rope for this IT czar of Hyderabad. In a sense, he was much like Ken Lay, the CEO and chairman of Enron. Lay's career in the energy business began and ended in Houston, Texas. Raju's career began in Hyderabad in the IT business and was going to end in the same city.

Hyderabad, the city of Nizams, owed its transition from the old economy—of pearls and diamonds—to the new—of processors and data centres—in part to Raju and his company, Satyam. A company that was a Rs 11,276 crore IT bellwether and India's fourth-largest outsourcing company. It was the first Indian IT services company to be listed on NASDAQ,[1] ahead of Infosys, India's second-largest IT services company. But all that glory was soon going to be relegated to the past.

Raju's troubles had started about three weeks ago, when he had announced his plan to merge Satyam with two of his family-run real estate and construction businesses—Maytas Properties[2] and Maytas Infra.[3] The Satyam board had approved the merger on December 16, 2008. The approval had opened a can of worms. Shareholders of Satyam revolted—they saw the acquisitions as an attempt to transfer more than a billion dollars from Satyam into the Raju family's considerably deep pockets. Now the shit had hit the fan and he had no place to hide his face.

A dreadful communication from Merril Lynch stared back at him from his desk. He didn't want to take another look at it. He had already gone through it many times. He could hear the letter's contents echoing in his mind, hammering his head inside out: 'We, DSP Merril Lynch, have terminated our advisory engagement with Satyam Computer Services Ltd for considering various strategic options on January 6, 2009... In the course of such engagement; we came to understand that there were material accounting irregularities, which prompted our aforesaid decisions.'[4]

Merril Lynch had smelt the rat in his closet. *From here, it could only get worse*, he figured.

Outside his office, there was a crisp chill in the air that afternoon. But Raju felt a chill far worse in his bones. His frail frame shivered in his navy blue suit. He took off his glasses, took a deep breath, and gazed up at the ceiling.

*How did I reach here?* Raju asked himself, as he began to pace the room. He looked outside and saw the road and the crawling traffic. There were huge rocks on the left side of the road and residential flats and office buildings across it. *It's the end of the road for me*, he thought. *All my plans have gone awry. Now, admitting my crime—a crime that I have committed over the years—is the only path open to me.*

In the last few weeks, things had taken a turn for the worse for him. From being hailed a hero he was going to plummet to zero, even garner hatred from those who worshipped him like a god. In 2000, when US President Bill Clinton visited Hyderabad, the then chief minister of Andhra Pradesh, N. Chandrababu Naidu, had showcased Raju as a first-generation entrepreneur and the face of India's IT prowess.[5] Among the big-brand IT companies, his company enjoyed a place of pride in Hyderabad. For one, it was a home-grown success—the shining jewel in the crown of a new Hyderabad, and secondly, Raju himself was a proud son of the soil, feted and awarded at home and abroad. If Charminar was the old symbol of Hyderabad, Satyam was its new icon.

That icon was now going to collapse.

Sitting in his plush office in Hyderabad's HITEC City, if Raju had looked out, he would have enjoyed a panoramic view of the tech metropolis—this is where more than 1,300 IT firms operated from; this is where global IT giants such as Microsoft, Google, CA Technologies, Amazon.com, and Facebook have found their homes in India.

In HITEC City itself, Satyam was spread over three campuses: in Gachibowli, InfoCity, and GateWay. Satyam was the largest IT employer in Hyderabad. The company employed 10 percent of the 275,000 IT workers in the city[6] and contributed handsomely to Hyderabad's US$ 4.7-billion IT exports.[7]

Enjoying the vista from his penthouse office, Raju should have felt proud of his achievements that day. On the contrary, he could not have felt worse. He found himself at the nadir of his business career. Being a player in many fields, he had really struck gold with Satyam, making a name for himself. Now it was all going to be over.

He felt cornered, lonely, and at the end of the ball game. He was about to part ways with the company he had so painstakingly built over twenty-one years.

Raju's decision wavered for a moment. His mind went back to the better times which seemed elusive now.

Things were so different just a year ago. Satyam was at its peak and many companies wooed him to strike a takeover deal. The list of suitors for Satyam included HCL Technologies, Wipro, IBM, Hewlett-Packard, Larsen & Toubro Infotech, Cognizant, Cap

Gemini, and private equity players KKR and TPG.[8] Even Anand Mahindra of Tech Mahindra had spoken to him personally to work out a deal.[9] But he had said no to all of them—he had cancelled two meeting with Mahindra after confirming the dates. He still had hopes of getting away.

### THE MAN BEHIND SATYAM

Byrraju Ramalinga Raju was born on September 16, 1954 in a family of farmers in the Garagaparru village of West Godavari, Andhra Pradesh. He was the eldest of four siblings. From his early days, Raju talked about doing something impactful for the society, something for the larger public good.[10] His grandfather owned several rice mills but later on, lost all his money in an ailing sugar factory.[11] Raju's father, Satyanarayana, did not give up farming completely but moved to Hyderabad in the 1960s to start a textile business.

Raju completed BCom from Andhra Loyola College at Vijayawada and subsequently did his MBA from Ohio University, USA.[12] From his teachers to his friends and relatives, everyone thought and spoke well of Raju—that he was honest, polite, and obliging.[13] His teachers at Loyola College thought that he was an obedient, well-mannered, and soft-spoken student. He showed great respect towards his teachers. He was popular among his fellow students because of his 'caring and obliging nature'.[14] He was generous, humble, and always ready to help others—traits that he was to carry forward to his working life as a businessman and executive.

After returning to India in 1977, Raju married at the age of twenty two. He then started many business ventures 'with the confidence that he could always fall back on the 100 acres of farmland and 20 acres of vineyards his family owned'.[15] He started Dhanunjaya Hotels and later forayed into cotton spinning. He set up a spinning and weaving mill named Sri Satyam Spinning with an investment of Rs 8 crore. This business was made possible with the help of the Andhra Pradesh Industrial Development Corporation (APIDC). The business failed but Raju subsequently moved to the real estate sector and started a construction company called Satyam Constructions. His unusual interest in real estate and construction would eventually cost him dearly, but more on that later.

In June 1987, Ramalinga Raju, with his elder brother Rama Raju and brother-in-law D.V.S. Raju, founded Satyam Computer Services at P&T colony in Secunderabad. He had just enough money to hire 20 employees.[16] Raju and his brother Rama Raju incorporated Satyam on June 24, 1987 as a private company. In 1991, Satyam became a public company after a special resolution was passed in July.[17] The same year, Satyam bagged its first Fortune 500 client—John Deere and Co. The company went public in 1992 with IPO shares. In 1993, Raju's company formed a joint venture with Dun and Bradstreet for IT services. In 1999, Satyam Infoway (Sify)—Satyam's Internet subsidiary—was listed on the NASDAQ. Sify was also one of the first to enter the Indian Internet service market.

Raju steered the company to greater heights in the next decade. Satyam snapped up joint ventures with General Electric, US defence, and auto parts firm TRW Inc, which was acquired in 2002 by Northrop Grumman. Raju was among the first Indian entrepreneurs to sense the outsourcing opportunities of the Y2K computer problem, which resulted in the 'coming-of-age of Indian outsourcers', including Infosys Technologies and Wipro.[18]

Once Satyam had got a toehold in the international IT services market, it grew at a fast clip in the new millennium. By 2000, Satyam's staff strength reached 2,000 and in 2001, made

> its debut on the New York Stock Exchange. By 2006, Satyam's revenues crossed the US$1 billion mark and by 2008, it had crossed the US$2 billion mark. The company now employed more than 53,000 associates working in software facilities in India and overseas.

In his early fifties, Raju had already climbed the pinnacle of glory in the world of business. With success had come numerous awards such as the Golden Peacock Award for Excellence in Corporate Governance, 2008; the Asian Most Admired Knowledge Enterprise Award, 2008; Dataquest IT Man of the Year in 2000; and CNBC's Asian Business Leader—Corporate Citizen of the Year award in 2002, among several others.

At the same time, he was also garnering praise for his non-profit work through the Emergency Management Research Institute (EMRI). This was Raju's corporate social responsibility initiative, which provided free medical services to people in Andhra Pradesh and eight other states including Gujarat, Tamil Nadu, Karnataka, Goa, Rajasthan, Uttarakhand, and Assam.[19] The service had logged over six lakh calls, handled 14,683 emergencies, and saved 1,000 lives with an average response time of less than thirty minutes—all within less than six months of the launch of its operations. 'Launched on August 15, 2005, "108", the trademark EMRI, has become a model which every State is trying to replicate', wrote *The Hindu* in a report. 'In a short span of time, the most recent initiative of the Byrraju Foundation and Satyam Foundation with Satyam Group's Founder and Chairman, B. Ramalinga Raju, has become the most comprehensive, integrated and successful emergency management system in the country.'[20]

Raju also received the prestigious Ernst & Young Entrepreneur of the Year award in 2007 'for his business acumen and efforts to service the community'.

The success of EMRI buttressed Raju's reputation at the state and national level. The people of Andhra loved him for this.[21] In his native village, Garagaparru, the villagers hailed the development work undertaken by the Byrraju Foundation. They considered Raju a good man; some even treated him as a modern-day God.

This, however, does not mean that Raju or his company, Satyam, had faced no controversies over the years.

One of the minor controversies that hogged the limelight happened in 1999–2000. Raju's company, Satyam Infoway (a subsidiary of Satyam, later known as Sify), had agreed to acquire an Internet company called India World in November, 1999 for US$115 million (Rs 499 crore). It was a huge deal in terms of money in those days, which led to many raised eyebrows. 'The deal was curious, considering the fact that for the financial year 1998–99, IndiaWorld had reported a measly profit of Rs 27 lakh on a turnover of Rs 1.3 crore.'[22] The promoter on IndiaWorld, Rajesh Jain, was to be paid the full acquisition money in cash in two installments. In the first installment, he was paid Rs 122 crore for 24.5 percent. The second installment was to be paid by June 30, 2000. A deposit of Rs 51.3 crore was made, which was to be forfeited if payment for the second lot of shares was not made. Raju's company later changed the terms of the deal and made partial payment of the second installment in stock to Jain. 'This was the first time Ramalinga Raju had shocked the world'.[23]

Satyam also attracted controversy in September 1999, when Satyam's Chief Operating Officer, Srini Raju (Ramalinga Raju's brother-in-law), suddenly left the company and sold off his 8 million shares in the market. Many wondered why he would leave a family business and start his own venture capital firm, iLabs Capital (later Peepul Capital).

In June 2002, S. Padamja, the then deputy director (Investigations) at the Income Tax office in Mumbai alleged that 'Satyam executives tried to block a probe into financial misdemeanours.'[24]

In July 2002, a newspaper report alleged that the Department of Company Affairs was prosecuting Satyam for violations of Companies Act in its 2000–01 accounts. Satyam refuted all those charges.[25]

These were, however, minor controversies that hardly unsettled Raju. They did not take the shine away from his name. Satyam's reputation stood intact and its business flourished unhindered.

His unravelling started in August 2008 when Maytas Infra won the 71-kilometre Hyderabad metro rail project. This was a project worth Rs 12,500 crore. In a unique move, Maytas offered the government money for the project (Rs 30,300 crore over 35 years) and also denied to accept the government subsidy (Viability Gap Funding). No company had ever offered this kind of a deal to the government. This was a welcome—albeit stunning—proposal for the government. Only E. Sreedharan from the Delhi Metro Rail Corporation (DMRC) who was advising the state government on the project, raised the red flag.

Sreedharan, a man of impeccable credentials and the man behind the Delhi metro, wrote a strong letter to Montek Singh Ahluwalia, the deputy chairman of the Planning Commission. He said that the 296 acres of land allotted to Maytas Infra Consortium for commercial use was a big political scandal in the making. 'It is apparent the operator has a hidden agenda which appears to be to extend the metro network to a large tract of his private landholdings so as to reap a windfall profit four to five times the land price,' he wrote.[26] This warning was not heeded. Not only that, DMRC was removed as advisor on the project.

However, Sreedharan's reading into Raju's mind was spot on. Raju's plan was to make a killing through property development around the length of the railway route, and he needed to buy land around the proposed route. His other plan was to petition the government to get the route extended to areas where he already owned land.[27]

To buy more land, Raju tried to raise money from the market, but the market was already dry because of the global financial crisis. He was not one to give up easily though. His scheming mind cooked up a plan to merge his two family-owned concerns—Maytas Properties and Maytas Infra.

Apparently, he wanted to sell the merger as a diversification move for Satyam. That's why, in December 2008, he announced that Satyam was to acquire these two companies. He justified it by saying that real estate business and infrastructure development would drive the growth of Satyam's business. 'There are two bullocks that would draw the cart', he told investors.[28] Both the acquisitions would be wrapped up in two to three months, he said. Satyam's CFO, Vadlamani Srinivas, added that the company's IT model had become risky and it was expecting a flat performance in 2009–10.[29] The acquisition of the two companies, he said, would raise revenues by 20 percent in 2009–10 and by 50 percent in 2011–12.

The real strategy behind this was something else though. Raju wanted to 'cover up the missing cash of Satyam', the profits he had been cooking up in Satyam's accounts and paying real income tax on those non-existent figures, 'with the real assets of Maytas'. The money from Satyam to Maytas would be transferred only on paper but nobody would know, as Maytas was a family-owned business.[30]

Satyam's board had been convinced of the move and the board had approved the proposal on December 16 to acquire 100 percent of Maytas Properties for Rs 6,240 crore (US$1.3 billion) and 51 percent of Maytas Infra for Rs 1,440 crore (US$300 million) despite the fact that the two acquisitions would 'punch a hole of Rs 7,680 (US$1.6 billion) in Satyam's books'.[31]

The market reacted furiously to this news. Some called the move 'daylight robbery'. They perceived the acquisitions as an attempt to enrich the Raju family at the expense of the company, amid grim global market conditions.[32] 'We don't need Satyam to buy Maytas Infra,' said one of the investors, Templeton. 'We are willing to go to any length to prevent this from happening.'[33] The investors 'cited corporate governance issues given the implied transfer of cash to founders', UBS analyst Govind Agarwal wrote in a research note. Management's intent to not subject the acquisition plan to a shareholder vote also sparked investor wrath. Citigroup, JP Morgan, and Merrill Lynch downgraded Satyam and slashed their share price estimates by up to half.[34]

As a result, Satyam's shares fell 55 percent on the New York Stock Exchange on December 16, wiping out nearly US$2 billion of the company's market capitalization. This was immediately followed with Satyam's stock falling 26.8 percent in Mumbai on December 17.

Raju was surprised at the stock market reaction. Given the situation, he announced the abandonment of the plan 'in deference to the views expressed by many investors' on December 17. There were other factors at work too. The possibility of government intervention helped doom the deal. The government said it would review the move, if it occurred, under the Companies Act.[35]

On December 19, Satyam announced that its board would meet ten days later to consider a share buy-back, and possibly announce dividends for the shareholders. Raju also tried to placate his employees and restore their confidence after the aborted Maytas deal. 'We have always worked tirelessly to ensure that a high level of integrity is the cornerstone of all our practices,' he said.[36]

Meanwhile, to make matters worse, *Fox News* reported that the World Bank had banned Satyam as a service provider[37] for eight years and the ban had been imposed since September. The World Bank had paid hundreds of millions of dollars to the company to write and maintain all the software it used throughout its global information network, including back-office operations. The World Bank confirmed the news of banning Satyam on December 23. In a statement, the bank said: 'Satyam was declared ineligible for contracts for providing improper benefits to Bank staff and for failing to maintain documentation to support fees charged for its subcontractors.'[38] On that day, the stock dropped a further 13.6 percent, its lowest in more than four-and-a-half years. On

December 25, when Satyam demanded an apology from the bank for inappropriate statements made by its representatives, the World Bank refused to tender any apology.[39]

By now, some board members were rethinking their relationship with Satyam. The failed acquisition, and the barrage of negative publicity that followed the episode, embarrassed the non-executive directors of the company. Four of them—Mangalam Srinivasan, Vinod K. Dham, Krishna G. Palepu, and M. Rammohan Rao–resigned from the board. Srinivasan was the first to resign. He put in his papers on December 25, following the World Bank's critical statements. Former Cabinet Secretary, T.R. Prasad also eventually resigned from the board.

Another thunderbolt came from Upaid, the US-based mobile and payments specialist, one of Satyam's former clients. In 2007, Upaid had filed a case of forgery, fraud, misrepresentation, and breach of contract against Satyam. After the aborted Matyas deal, Upaid filed a motion in a Texas court seeking testimony from Raju and Satyam CFO Vadlamani Srinivas over the deal. The American company feared that Satyam deigned to deplete its cash reserves with the Matyas acquisitions.[40] If the cash reserves were gone, how would Satyam pay its damages to Upaid—that was their objection.

The tide had clearly turned against Raju. His position as a promoter was threatened.[41] But he would not easily give up. He made a last-ditch attempt to save the situation by announcing on December 27 that the Satyam board would meet on January 10 instead of December 29. The board was to discuss a possible dilution of the promoters' stake.[42] The board, which had come under pressure for poor corporate governance, would also be recast and expanded,[43] Satyam announced.

'Satyam's Board of Directors recognizes the serious nature of certain questions raised by the events of the last two weeks,' said Raju. 'In order to ensure that these questions are properly addressed, and that the interests of stakeholders are fully and carefully considered, Satyam has decided to broaden the scope of its deliberations beyond a possible buy-back of its stock.'

The share buy-back was an apparent attempt to mollify the fuming investors. This meeting would 'allow the board to consider additional options', according to Raju. One of these included conducting a review of the company's strategic options to enhance shareholder value. For this, the services of DSP Merril Lynch had been engaged. All the measures that had to be deliberated upon by the board on January 10 were meant to restore shareholder confidence in Satyam.

Raju's last-ditch attempt to save his position might have worked had Merril Lynch not thrown a spanner in the works by refusing the assignment.

This practically extinguished Raju's last hope of salvaging the situation.

In moments like these, when one can't go on anymore, different people take different routes. Writers like Hemingway and Hunter S. Thompson pull the trigger on themselves. Or throw themselves in death's way, like German billionaire Adolf Merckle did in 2008. After his business empire ran into trouble during the global financial crisis, Merckle threw himself in front of a train near his home.[44]

Raju chose neither of these. He opted for the pen. *The best way to come clean*, he thought, was to do it through a letter—that old fashioned article of communication—to the Satyam board and the government authorities, and not through a televised conference, in front of a hundred hungry journalists and ruthless TV reporters.[45] *That*, he thought, *would be the last thing he would do to save Satyam from total collapse*.[46]

Though Raju decided to resign from Satyam that evening, he had been toying with the idea for a couple of days. The thought of flying off to the US would have proved fruitless. Satyam was listed on the NASDAQ and once he had put in his papers, the American authorities would have gone after him. Americans dealt out harsher sentences to corporate fraudsters. The example of Ken Lay was in front of him. There were many more dreadful examples. India was a better place. At least he had his community to support him and fight for him.

After the failure of the acquisition move, he was so tense that he had asked the community elders (his extended family) to get together. At a community meeting of the Rajus in Satyam Enclave in Medhchal in Greater Hyderabad, he had expressed his fears of getting into legal problems. He told the gathering—all were related to him by blood or marriage[47]—that the company's books were in disarray and there wasn't much cash in the till. The only way to save the company was to quit.

The Rajus were stunned on hearing this. Don't be crazy, don't do this—they pleaded with him. This is like committing suicide, they warned him.

Raju was adamant. Seeing his rigid stance, they told Raju that he could quit any time he wanted to. They assured him that they would support him no matter what. After all, he had done so much for the community. Even the Medhchal settlement owed its existence to Raju's father, Satyanarayana. They pledged to contribute funds to help him fight his legal battle if it came to that.

Now the moment of reckoning had come for him. He contacted his brother Rama Raju, who was also the managing director of Satyam. They both occupied adjacent offices in the Satyam headquarters. Raju didn't need to explain much to him—Rama knew exactly what was going on in the company. The heat on them was so intense that they were avoiding the office and evading talking with the senior executives of Satyam for the last few days. 'We'll have to quit the company tomorrow,' he told Rama. His brother understood.

Before he started drafting his confession, Raju called his son—Teja Raju. He warned him to stay away from home the next day if possible. 'Why?' Teja asked, taken aback. 'There could be some issue with the government agencies. You must be careful, son,' Raju advised him. He hung up without mentioning his letter of confession.

Teja thought it could be an income tax raid, so he did not pry much into the matter.

He did not say anything to his other son, Rama Raju, Jr. *He will come to know about it along with the world the next morning*, he thought.

Now, the letter had to be drafted. He needed his lawyer Bharat Kumar's help. He dialled his mobile phone number. 'Can you please come over to my office right now?' he said. 'I've something urgent to discuss with you.'

'Sure sir,' Bharat replied.

The lawyer was aware of Raju's legal troubles, so he rushed to his office. When Raju told him his plan, he was zapped. 'What's the need to do this, sir?' he said, advising him not to take the plunge. But Raju didn't listen to him. He had made up his mind. With the help of the lawyer, he started working on a rough draft of his confession.

He then told his wife, Nandini Raju, about his decision of writing the letter to admit his wrongdoings. When he told Nandini that coming clean 'now' was the only way to protect his baby, Satyam, she assured him that she would stand by him.[48]

Raju felt cleansed after pouring his heart out in his letter. The chill had left his bones. He was not shaking and shivering any more. And he was ready to face the consequences of his actions and the law of the land.

After drafting the letter, Raju called one of his trusted managers to his office. He was a high-ranking executive and Raju was impressed with his command over English. Raju explained to him why he had been called. 'Please go through the draft and polish it for me,' he said. The stunned executive was motionless for a while but finally, he obeyed his boss.[49]

When the sun set on Hyderabad that day, something had permanently changed. An icon had fallen but the resounding thud of that fall would not be heard until the morning after.

# SHOCK, ANGER, AND BETRAYAL
## The Collapse of Satyam

*Everyone is in shock; no one knows what to do. The stock price is diving. Everyone is scared.*
—Priscilla Nelson, Global Director of People Leadership, Satyam

*January 7, 2009*
*Hyderabad*

It was the day of Vaikunth Ekadasi, one of the holiest days in the year. On this day, it is believed that the gates to Lord Vishnu's inner sanctorum are opened and all the gods descend from heaven to earth. Devotees visit temples and prayers are arranged.

But the mind of tall and debonair Hari T., Satyam's Chief Marketing Officer, was far from any religious thoughts.

He was driving to work for a 10.30 am meeting at the Satyam headquarters. He had been working hard for the last few days and was very kicked about the meeting.

A couple of weeks earlier, the Maytas controversy had erupted, which had created a lot of media interest and caused employee and shareholder anxiety. For sometime, the Raju brothers were not accessible to anyone. They were not coming to office regularly. Some, like Priscilla Cohen and Ed Cohen—who ran the Satyam School of Leadership—linked Raju's recent lack of communication to the ongoing economic crisis that had engulfed the United States and was fast approaching India. When Priscilla tried to speak with him on this matter, he changed the topic and moved off to another meeting. Ed had sent him a note saying that Satyam employees expected some form of communication from him. Raju's silence was clearly a red flag for everyone.[1]

Hari had come to India for his year-end holidays from London, from where he looked after the marketing of Satyam. He lived there with his family, but because of the ongoing brouhaha in the wake of the failed Maytas acquisition, he had extended his stay in Hyderabad.

If the Maytas problem made the Satyam boat sink, he would have no office in London to go back to. Therefore, it was extremely important for him to make things work at Satyam. He wanted to try his best and that's what he was working towards.

After the Maytas acquisition had failed, the media was clamouring to know if the money had already been paid by Satyam. To mollify the media, Hari was trying to get Vadlamani Srinivas, the company's CFO, to talk to the media but Srinivas, too, was not forthcoming. Around the end of December, many board directors were already leaving Satyam and this was making Hari very nervous. Towards the end of December and early January, it came to a state when both Raju and Srinivas were inaccessible to the external world. Things were only getting worse by the day.

To counter this slide, Hari, along with a couple of his colleagues, came up with a proposal to appoint a task force to fix the company's issues. He told his boss (Raju) that while he dealt with all the other issues that he would have to deal with, Raju should announce that there will be a taskforce comprising of five or six people who will run the company.

Hari had drafted a note to this effect and had sent it out to Raju. He met him and other top executives of Satyam between December 26 and January 4 and 5. And the day for his hard work to pay off had arrived. In the meeting that day, the Satyam management was going to conclude that a taskforce would run the company while other issues were being ironed out.

*This will get the media off my back,* Hari thought with a smile as he drove through the concrete jungle that was HITEC City.

Suddenly, his BlackBerry began to ring. *Who could it be*, he thought. It was around 9.45 am and he was only five minutes away from office.

He couldn't recognize the number but he took the call anyway. 'Have you seen the mail that Raju has sent out?' said the guy on the line.

'What mail?' asked Hari.

Hari had not been checking his BlackBerry while driving, so he didn't know that there was an email from his boss.

'Please check your inbox.'

'Okay, I will,' said Hari as he ended the call. For a moment, he thought it was a prank call. But then he decided to check it anyway, thinking, *maybe there is something worth looking in there.*

He immediately logged in and there it was—the email from Raju. The caller was right. When he read the email, it blew his mind; and not in a good way.

He could not believe what Raju was saying in his email. His head reeled. He pulled over the car by the roadside and quickly went through the message.

In his confessional letter, Raju had acknowledged an accounting fraud of mind-boggling magnitude. He said he was tendering his resignation from Satyam while accepting his culpability in inflating the amount of cash on the balance sheet of Satyam by nearly US$1 billion, incurring a liability of US$253 million on funds arranged by him personally, and overstating Satyam's September 2008 quarterly revenues by 76 percent and profits by 97 percent.[2] He said he was the sole perpetrator of this scam and absolved everyone else—members of his family and executives in his company including Satyam's board members, past and present, and senior company officials and executives—of the crime. No one had any idea how he was cooking the books,[3] he admitted in his letter.

He wrote: 'The gap in the balance sheet has arisen purely on account of inflated profits over a period of last several years. What started as a marginal gap between actual operating profit and the one reflected in the books of accounts continued to grow over the years. It has attained unmanageable proportions as the size of company operations grew significantly...The differential in the real profits and the one reflected in the books was further accentuated by the fact that the company had to carry additional resources and assets to justify higher level of operations—thereby significantly increasing the costs.

Every attempt made to eliminate the gap failed. As the promoters held a small percentage of equity, the concern was that poor performance would result in a takeover, thereby exposing the gap. It was like riding a tiger, not knowing how to get off without being eaten'.[4]

It was a very dry letter and there was hardly anything dramatic about it, except that reference to riding the tiger. Raju was a very widely-read man and the usage of metaphors was commonplace in his conversations. Even in reviews and meetings, he would often bring in very unlikely references to a given issue. So using the tiger metaphor was very typical of him—he had effectively conjured up the vision of what he was dealing with.

Nevertheless, it was unbelievable stuff and the more Hari thought about it, the more confused he became. *In some form,* his mind argued, it seemed possible—*Raju was capable of pulling off something like that.* Suddenly the major events of the past three weeks flashed through his mind. Now he could connect the dots: the way Raju was avoiding the media, how he wasn't giving any straightforward answers, and the way he was keeping his distance from everyone in office. All these clues culminated in this final deceit.

But his heart said maybe it was not true, maybe it was something else. When you love someone, you hesitate to associate any malice or bad traits with them; and Hari loved and respected Raju a great deal. He considered Raju an outstanding gentleman, exceptionally humble, and imbued with farsightedness. His humility and modesty made Raju an endearing personality. The one thing that Hari was flummoxed about was how he managed to do something like this and keep it hidden the way he did. *It was almost like a second side to him that nobody in this world,* Hari thought, *would have ever been able to decipher if he had not come out with it or something had not gone wrong.* Even after the confession though, his warmth for Raju as a person, his love for him, remained untouched, unchanged.

Five minutes later he was in office. What he witnessed on people's faces was shock, anger, and betrayal—all at once.

There were many top executives in the Satyam office who were distraught and traumatized by Raju's sudden resignation and admission of fraud. One of those anxious leaders was A.S. Murthy, Satyam's Chief Delivery Officer. A tall, soft-spoken person with a ready smile, Murthy was on the fourth floor of the Satyam headquarters that morning.

Just like Hari, when he opened his email box, he was stunned by one of the emails. It was from his boss, Raju.

Saying that he was disappointed would be an understatement. Working so closely with Raju, Murthy was shocked that he wasn't aware of such deceit taking place.

The shock came without a cushion for Murthy. He was practically wedded to Satyam—he had joined Satyam way back in 1994, when there were less than fifty employees in the company. Prior to Satyam, he was with Tata Consultancy Services for thirteen years. In the last thirty-one years, he had changed his job just once.

Raju had already put the email out to the stock exchanges and some of the senior industry leaders. There was no doubting it, no matter how outrageous it seemed.

Hari's meeting didn't take place that morning. Instead a call came from Raju's office that he would like to talk to the senior leaders of Satyam at 10.30 am.

Murthy and Hari were among those who had been called to the meeting by Raju. Eight or nine of Satyam's top leaders were assembled in his office. It was a scene of total confusion, anxiety, anger, and frustration—those were the kinds of emotions that people present in that room were grappling with.

There was one leader who was actually wailing, literally crying out loud in that room. There were two or three people who had tears in their eyes. One even fainted. Then there were some who were very angry and calling names.

It was a very emotionally charged moment for each one of them.

Raju came on the call and the leaders spoke to him and asked him if what he had written in the email was true. He just had a few lines to say in reply. He said that he loved all of them and had enjoyed working with them. 'I am very proud of what we have accomplished,' Raju told his trusted lieutenants. 'But I am sorry that that it had to come to this.'

Raju also briefly explained to his colleagues why he had taken that extreme step. He said that whatever he had done was in the larger interest of the company at that point of time. Finally, he wished them the best in terms of taking the company forward. It wasn't a long call. It lasted less than five minutes.

The first thing that hit Hari as he stood there in that room, listening to all that was being said and not said, was that this was not about the company at all—this was about the industry, this was about India. He had this horrible feeling that this could bring down the whole IT industry in the country. This was a terribly serious matter.

As Hari walked out of the room, he knew what he was going to do next. He went to his office and read the letter properly on his laptop. Then he picked up the phone and called Som Mittal, the president of NASSCOM,[5] in Delhi.

Som was in a meeting that morning and when Hari reached out to him, his assistants were not willing to disturb him. Hari had to force himself onto them and finally he got to Som.

'Som, I've no idea what you're going to do but I have a situation like this,' he said, briefing him about what had just transpired at the Satyam headquarters. Som was stunned to hear about Raju's confession because Raju had been the chairman of NASSCOM a few years back. 'How could he do it?'

'Can you please send me the letter?' Som asked Hari.

Hari emailed him the letter. Som went through it. Hari told him that there was total chaos and panic at Satyam. Som promised him that he would take the next available flight to Hyderabad. This gave Hari a momentary breather.

On his part, Som Mittal immediately called up the SEBI chairman to confirm that this letter was authentic. This was not a prank. 'Up till now, in the past history, frauds have been discovered, detected but never confessed,' he said.[6] 'It wasn't a fraud that was detected. It was confessed because of whatever reasons.'

'Then I called and met various people in the government—in the Ministry of Company Affairs, in Finance and Economic Affairs—I told them that if anything happened to this company, it would have far reaching implications for the whole industry and the country,' said Som.

The government was initially reluctant to come into the picture. 'There was a discussion that if a fraud has been committed, where is the role of the government to intervene?' said Som. 'Why should the government step in? It is the role of the regulator and somebody who has to ensure governance. I think we were able to convince them that there were good reasons (to intervene). Some of the company's services were mission critical. So, it wasn't about a company going down; it was about everybody questioning whether we were very secure. The government said that it was a good point but they needed to know the facts of the situation.'

Meanwhile, the news of Raju's mega fraud was spreading like wildfire beyond the fifth floor of the Satyam headquarters.

Dr Renu Khanna was in the Mashallah Building in Secunderabad that morning. It was one of Satyam's many offices; it does not exist anymore.

Dr Khanna is a social psychologist in her early fifties. She sports shoulder-length hair with a side parting and is usually seen in a salwar kameez. A powerful corporate honcho, she is the global head of leadership development at Mahindra Satyam. Currently, she guides the team at the Mahindra Satyam Learning World (MSLW), which functions as a real-time training centre. MSLW is an enterprise-wide learning ecosystem that captures and delivers the learning and development needs of Satyam's associates through a single platform. The Mahindra Satyam Learning Centre (MSLC) and

Mahindra Satyam School of Leadership (MSSL) are two pillars of this ecosystem.[7]

Satyam's office in the Mashallah Building was a very small one and Dr Khanna was in a meeting room, huddled with some of her colleagues. There was a knock on the door and someone came in with the news that Raju had put in his papers.

For a minute, Dr Khanna and her colleagues felt they were experiencing an earthquake. The walls seemed to shake, the furniture seemed to rattle. It was truly shocking for them because none of them had seen it coming. Along with it was a little anger as to why it had happened at Satyam after so many years of success and growth and what was the reason behind it.

Dr Khanna's outrage and anger was justified. She had seen Satyam grow from a company with a handful of employees to a behemoth with almost 53,000 people. She had seen this organization grow from just being a simple mainframe player[8] to being a major force in many verticals and domains. She had seen it come up from being a Hyderabad-based entity to an organization that had spread itself right across the globe. She had seen Satyam's business grow in revenue year by year and become one of India's top five IT services company. And she had been a part of it all, making her own contribution to Satyam's success. For almost fifteen years, she had been dedicated to building the culture of Satyam.[9]

That's why when she first heard of Raju's resignation and his confession of perpetrating a mind-boggling fraud, she stood speechlessly for once in that meeting room in the Mashallah Building.

Equally shocked were Dr Khanna's colleagues, Priscilla Nelson and Ed Cohen. Priscilla was global director of people leadership and her husband, Ed, was chief learning officer at the Satyam School of Leadership.

Priscilla's morning had started like any other. She had dropped off her daughter at the international school and had headed for office. Her husband, Ed, was in San Diego on an extended holiday.

Around 11 am, Priscilla was in her office in the Satyam School of Leadership when the news of Raju's resignation broke out on TV. 'We all looked on in disbelief as the news emerged. Those of us who were shareholders saw our investments disappear like a tsunami into a pool of financial destruction.'[10]

She sat in front of a TV along with fifty of her colleagues in a small conference room. 'The screen displayed a photo of Raju on the right and a graph depicting the falling stock price on the left. The value of our stock had plummeted in less than five seconds, drained like an hourglass. I immediately grabbed my phone and called Ed. He did not answer. It rang and rang.'

The soft-spoken, charismatic Raju had sold a dream to the American couple in 2005 so convincingly that they had sold off everything in the US and moved to India. Raju wanted them to work for his leadership school. It was a 240,000 square-foot state-of-the-art facility. The school, launched in November 2005, was 'built on the philosophy of expanding the entrepreneurial energy at Satyam to help keep pace with the ever-changing global business context.'

For three years, they worked hard on the school, taking it to greater heights, giving their best to this once-in-a-lifetime opportunity to build a world-class training institution. The school focused on grooming leaders. Every year, more than 7,000 associates were passing through a fifteen-week entry-level technology programme. Satyam was ranked number one at the American Society for Training and Development (ASTD) BEST Awards in 2007. This recognition made the company the first non-US organization, and the first in Asia to make it to the number one slot at ASTD BEST.[11] During its time, Satyam had been able to tie up with some of the best institutions in the learning universe such as Harvard Business School, U21Global, McKinsey & Company, and Duke University, among others.

But all this hard work by Priscilla, Ed, and their teammates came under siege as Satyam's ship began to sink.

Raju's admission of fraud demolished everything for Priscilla and Ed in one blow. 'Everything we had created at Satyam—our Taj Mahal of learning—was starting to crack and crumble.'[12]

Back in the US, Ed had taken the night off. He was not even taking phone calls. After missing thirty-two calls, he broke down and picked up the phone. It was Priscilla on the line. 'It's all over the news,' she said. 'Everyone is in shock; no one knows what to do. The stock price is diving. Everyone is scared.'[13]

Everyone was indeed scared, and they were to remain scared for weeks and months. Some worried if Satyam as a company would survive or whether their jobs would remain. Some worried about their next pay cheque as they had to put food on the table or pay their mortgages. Life is often unforgiving in its demands.

As the employees were switching on TV sets to catch the world's reaction to the Satyam fraud, news-hungry TV crews and journalists were assembling outside the Satyam building to record the tamasha. Some channels even reported speculatively that Vadlamani Srinivas, Satyam's CFO, had committed suicide. 'They are trying to kill me,' Srinivas feebly joked to one of his colleagues, Sridhar M.V.[14]

---

At 2.05 pm that day, Satyam's interim CEO, Ram Mynampati sent an open letter to all the employees of Satyam.[15] Its subject line said 'Open communication: Today's developments' and it was labelled 'Importance: High'. It read as under:

Dear colleagues,

I write this mail to update you on some critical board and leadership level changes in our company, effective immediately. A series of extremely unfortunate events led to this, which I am sure you have seen covered in the media over the past few hours.

A SWAT team consisting of senior leaders has been formed. Many of them are Satyam veterans with a minimum of ten years experience in our company and more than twenty years in the industry. I have been requested to play the role of an interim CEO and this team will support me, as we steer Satyam through this challenging phase. These are the leaders on the ground and have always had the final call on most customer and associate related matters in the company, so far. This team has committed to work together, to make it happen. The SWAT team represents all customer-facing units, key horizontal-competency units, and critical support units.

Over the past twenty-one years, with your passion and commitment, we have built significant customer assets, formidable service offerings, excellent delivery processes, and scalable support systems. Satyam has been consistently acknowledged for its leadership bandwidth and has a demonstrated reputation for collaborative functioning. Our renowned Full Life Cycle (FLC) model encouraged 'Distributed and Empowered' leadership and prepared us for all situations. This is the time when we have to apply it in real life. What we have been trained for, we will now put to work. Let us continue to handle our respective areas with total autonomy, freedom, and control. This is as good a time as any to remind ourselves that we have been acknowledged as being among the top three Best Employers in India by Hewitt and Mercer in independent surveys in 2007 and American Society of Training & Development (ASTD) named us as the best globally, for our learning practices—the first company outside USA to be awarded this honour ever. Satyam continues to have everything that is fundamentally required for its success—a strong customer base and a committed universe of approximately 53,000 associates.

What we are confronted with is the challenge of continuing our business operations, seamlessly. We will need your involvement and ideas to make it happen. This might involve even more effort at every level, in the near term. This is the time to prove to the world that we are united and will succeed in overcoming the challenges.

This quarter will be tumultuous for us. Rumors will abound and it would be fair to assume that competition will try and leverage it to their advantage. As a proactive measure, we have formed fully empowered Cross Functional Teams, headed by seasoned leaders in the respective areas, to address pan-organizational issues like delivery excellence, customer & associate retention, pipeline management, cost controls, collections, etc. You have helped to build Satyam to be what it is today—and we believe that this cannot be allowed to fail, at any cost. I am confident that I can count on your continued support as I commit to our customers that we will ensure deliverables and commitments are serviced.

On behalf of our new leadership team, I apologize to you for the uncertainty and inconvenience that this incident has caused you and your families. I assure you that we will emerge stronger because of this. Increased focus on transparency at all levels, integrity, and ethical functioning will be ensured. I want you to stand confidently in front of your families and friends and say that we will now be a better company and that we shall soon be a successful case study of how organizations have turned over a new leaf.

We will be conducting 'U Speak' (our Meet-the-Leadership sessions) in each city in India starting next week and will have numerous webinars to address associates in various countries. We will be meeting many of our customers in person over the next two weeks and will meet those of you onsite, at that time. In these sessions, we will explain to you what happened and articulate

> the actions that are being taken to retain your confidence in our company.
>
> Let us fight this battle together. I am confident that we will emerge stronger, TOGETHER.
>
> Ram Mynampati

Later that day, Satyam confirmed that it had received a letter from its Chairman and Founder, B. Ramalinga Raju. Ram Mynampati, who was also a board member, acted as the interim CEO (pending ratification by the board). He was mandated by the board to steer the company through this crisis.

'We are obviously shocked by the contents of the letter,' Ram Mynampati said in a media statement. 'The senior leaders of Satyam stand united in their commitment to customers, associates, suppliers, and all shareholders. We have gathered together at Hyderabad to strategize the way forward in light of this startling revelation.'[16]

Satyam confirmed that its immediate priorities were to protect the interests of its shareholders, protect the careers and security of its approximately 53,000 associates, and meet all its commitments to its customers and suppliers. 'We recognize that our associates have committed a significant part of their careers to build Satyam. We will pursue all avenues to secure their future in the company,' added Mynampati in his message to the media.

At the Satyam headquarters, the guards had shut the gates and only a side gate was kept open to allow women employees to go home. The female employees who were donning salwar suits covered their faces with their scarves and left the building.[17] By 3 pm, most employees had left for home.[18]

It was a moment of shock and shame for every Satyamite.

Fearing public backlash, the local police beefed up security at the Satyam headquarters as well as at Raju's residence in Jubilee Hills.[19] There were rumours that Raju and his brother had fled the country.

# A BOMB EXPLODES IN NEW DELHI

## The Darkest Day for India Inc

*I think this is unbelievable. It is like* Ripley's Believe it or Not.
—T.V. Mohandas Pai, former board member, Infosys

*January 7, 2009*
*New Delhi*

At 10.53 am,[1] B. Ramalinga Raju's faxed letter reached the Satyam Board of Directors, the chairman of the Securities and Exchange Board of India (SEBI), and the stock exchanges.[2]

Those who read the fax immediately understood that it was not an ordinary letter. It was 'like a multi-megaton bomb exploding in the face of corporate India.'[3]

The then Secretary of the Ministry of Corporate Affairs, Anurag Goel, a 1972-batch Uttar Pradesh cadre officer—a portly bureaucrat with a benign, round face—was in his office in Shastri Bhawan when he received a phone call and an email from C.V. Bhave, the then Chairman, SEBI, at 11.32 am[4]

He nearly fell off the chair when he learnt about Raju's confession of masterminding the largest accounting fraud in Indian history.

In his letter, Raju had disclosed mind-boggling numbers. According to him, the company's balance sheet carried inflated cash and bank balances of Rs 5,040 crore and non-existent interest income of Rs 376 crore as on September 30, 2008. Raju also admitted that there was an understated liability of Rs 1,230 crore on account of money that he himself had arranged.[5]

Anurag was flabbergasted to learn of Raju's incredible fraud. How could Raju, a charismatic leader, revered by many and respected by all, deceive his own company? Anurag knew that Satyam was no ordinary company. It was India's fourth-largest IT company with worldwide operations. Raju himself understood the importance of his company, and in his letter, he had tried to soften the blow of the scandal by reminding everyone of his services for bringing Satyam to its big-ticket status: 'I have promoted and have been associated with Satyam for well over twenty years now. I have seen it grow from a company of few people to a company of 53,000 people, with 185 Fortune 500 companies as customers and operations in 66 countries. Satyam has established an excellent leadership and competency base at all levels. I sincerely apologize to all Satyamites and stakeholders, who have made Satyam a special organization, for the current situation. I am confident they will stand by the company in this hour of crisis.'

The problem was that the damage caused by this confession of crime went beyond Raju. It had far-reaching consequences for his company as well as for India Inc.

Like everyone else who had heard the news, Anurag too was in a state of shock.

However, even in that state he was aware of his responsibilities. He realized that the government machinery needed to respond very quickly and effectively to the situation. He immediately informed his minister, Prem Chand Gupta, about the new developments at Satyam and went over to him.

That Wednesday morning, Gupta was also in his office in Shastri Bhawan. He had caught the news of Raju's resignation on the LCD TV that was playing the news non stop.[6]

Satyam had been on the ministry's scanner for the last few weeks. Gupta was aware of the all-round criticism of the Satyam board's decision to approve the Maytas (Maytas Infra and Maytas Properties) acquisition proposal. He had asked the Registrar of Companies, Hyderabad, to collect all relevant material on the proposed acquisition and send it to his office in Delhi at the earliest. In Hyderabad, all the three companies had sought reprieve until January 12.

But now, Raju's resignation had upped the ante. There wasn't any time to waste as the news was taking its toll at the Bombay Stock Exchange (BSE). Satyam shares had crashed over 80 percent.

When Anurag and Gupta discussed the matter, they immediately grasped that the Satyam scam had the potential to adversely impact

India Inc in general and the Indian IT industry in particular. Not that it could have been calculated that way but the timing of the breaking out of the scandal was inconvenient.

It was the start of a new year and India Inc was gearing up to face it with caution. The times were fraught with economic uncertainties triggered by the bankruptcy of the Lehman Brothers in the US in September 2008. The outsourcing industry expected a lean business phase and the busting of a 53,000-strong employee company at this time could have spelt disaster for the Indian IT-sector workers. Top IT companies were already rationalizing their workforce and no one could afford to absorb such a large number of IT workers if all Satyamites were to be laid off. Both Anurag and Gupta were concerned about the families of the 53,000 Satyam employees.

The timing was bad for the political climate too. General elections were only four months away and a disaster like Satyam would create an image of mismanagement among the electorate, especially the corporate sector and the vocal middle class. Assembly elections in Andhra Pradesh were also at hand. The Satyam debacle—imagine the loss of jobs for more than 50,000 people—could become a major poll issue in the state elections. The matter, therefore, could not be allowed to get out of hand.

Anurag realized that the hit on Satyam was serious because it could have an impact on the company's worldwide operations which would be disastrous because other international governments, including Singapore's, were also involved. He knew that there were mission critical things being done by Satyam for many companies and governments. Because of this reason, one of the first things that Gupta and Anurag decided in the course of the day was to salvage the company. They agreed that apart from ordering an investigation into Raju's fraud, they would have to save the company as well.

Looking at the gravity of the situation, Gupta called a meeting with Anurag, his personal secretary R.K. Yadav, officer on special duty Sunil Gupta, and joint secretary Jitesh Khosla.[7]

In the meeting, it was suggested that field officers in Hyderabad be asked to submit a full report within fifteen days. Gupta disagreed—a lot of damage could be done to the company in two weeks. The company might even collapse by then.[8] His fears were not unfounded.

As they were discussing the course of action, media began descending on the minister's office. Since the government had no detailed information at that point of time, Anurag geared up to gather more information and got cracking on starting the investigation and enquiry into the scam. Not only was the task to collect more information from all over, the ministry also needed to look at the available options. There was no precedent for a fraud case of this magnitude, so all the dimensions had to be figured out before the government could take substantial action. On that very day, the ministry asked the the Institute of Cost Accountants of India (ICAI) and the Institute of Company Secretaries of India (ICSI) to enquire into the role of auditors and company secretaries for swift regulatory action.[9]

'Whoever is found guilty in this particular case, action according to law would be taken against him,' Gupta, the company affairs minister, told the agitated media.

## END OF DAYS FOR THE INDIAN IT INDUSTRY?

After Raju's shameful confession, a pall of gloom fell over the entire outsourcing sector in India. It was feared that Satyam's fall would affect the fortunes of other Indian outsourcing giants.[10]

The media quickly dubbed Raju's scam as India's Enron and went to town about it. 'I, in my memory, haven't seen a corporate scam from any large cap index stock of this magnitude,' said one news commentator. 'Ramalinga Raju's big admission has shaken India's corporate world,' said Rajdeep Sardesai, prominent journalist and the chief of the news channel, CNN IBN, in a broadcast on his channel titled *India's Enron*.[11] He called the scam India's biggest case of corporate fraud. 'Once a poster boy of the IT world, today Raju has become the culprit,' he announced.

The reverberations of shockwaves created by Raju's letter were heard in boardrooms across India and the world. 'I think this is unbelievable. It is like *Ripley's Believe it or Not*,' said T.V. Mohandas Pai, Head HR, Admin, Infosys, in a television broadcast. 'I am surprised, I am shocked,' said Deepak Parekh, Chairman, HDFC, to IBN Live. 'It is a scandal. A fraud of this proportion...I don't think anyone expected this out of Satyam Computers.'

The thought that a financial scandal of this enormity had gone unnoticed in one of India's top IT services companies for years unnerved many. They were afraid that a scam like this could seriously dent the image of brand India for the world and for potential investors in Indian businesses. This realization made Raju's malarkey everyone's problem—from the industry and the government to the common man who believed in an India on the move. Hidden in the shock was the apprehension that Raju's failed tiger ride could unseat India Inc's global dreams from the howdah of the elephant that is India. For the outside world, India Inc had supposedly jettisoned the taint and air of the corruption and scandal-mongering when the License Raj was given a burial almost a decade ago by Manmohan Singh's new economic policy of liberalization. The new India knew that the bad smell of scams was anathema for business in a globalized world.

Inconveniently enough, the scandal had surfaced weeks before the World Economic Forum's meet at Davos, Switzerland. This is where the world's top business leaders, international political leaders, intellectuals, and journalists gather every year to discuss the most urgent issues of the world, shaping up world opinion and influencing future investments. For the 2009 meet, some 2,500 guests, including senior executives from some of the world's biggest banks, as well as forty heads of state and government, were to join discussions on the economic crisis, poverty, energy, climate change, and free trade. The Satyam scandal bothered India's industry leaders such as Anand Mahindra, VC and MD, Mahindra & Mahindra; and Nandan Nilekani, Co-Chairman, Infosys board. How would they face the world as representatives of India Inc?

'In the upcoming Davos Conference, I have been nominated as one of the co-chairs and the first thing that struck me was, you know, you go in almost defensively,' said Anand Mahindra, reacting to Raju's confession. 'Clearly you are not going in to project India Shining.'

'This incident is like a black eye because we have been promoting Indian entrepreneurs, Indian corporates as the flagships of brand India globally and when one of this lot really has such deplorable behaviour, then obviously it is not a good thing,' said Nandan Nilekani in a TV broadcast with Rajdeep Sardesai.[12] 'It is a setback to what we have been trying to accomplish. But I do believe that people will look at individual companies, they will look at the track record... I don't think people will operate with a wide brush. Certainly, they will demand more accountability from Indian companies and that is a fair thing.'

'Clearly, there has been a massive failure of oversight in the ecosystem of the company, whether it is the management, the board, the audit committee, the auditors,' Nilekani went on to add. 'For example, one thing that we do at Infosys is that bank statements are directly sent to the auditors so that nobody can intercept that. So, I think it is important to have those kinds of checks and balances to ensure that information flows are not compromised.'

'The Satyam episode is a good warning signal for all managements,' said N.R. Narayana Murthy, Non-Executive Chairman, Infosys and one of most prominent voices in India. In a statement to a newspaper, he said: 'I am shocked and painfully dismayed at what has happened at an important software company in India. It is a total failure of governance. I only hope that relevant authorities get to the bottom of this and take appropriate action.'[13]

'It is important to remember that one Satyam does not make the entire Indian software industry. I believe it is an isolated case. I want foreign investors to realize that there are many honest managements and good companies in this country. While what has happened at Satyam is totally regrettable, I believe that it does not represent India. It just represents one individual and one company. In the short term, investors will start looking deeper into all companies they want to invest in, and rightly so. Once they realize that things are not all that bad and that most companies are decent and managements honest, they will regain their faith. This too will pass. Investors will consider this as an extreme case. Right now, all of us must conduct ourselves in the most legal and ethical manner. It is a good warning signal for all managements.'

As expected, the entire world took note of the Satyam scam. Raju's admission of perpetrating a monstrous fraud raised many questions in the heads of the international investors: What does this scam mean in terms of corporate governance and disclosure in India Inc? Will more skeletons tumble out of the closet and take the shine away from brand India? Does the Indian system of governance have the ability to deal with a disclosure of fraud of this magnitude?

The scam, according to a TV news report, deeply dented the image of India in the global market and eroded the credibility of the Indian IT industry, which sells on corporate governance. 'The question is not just how and when Ramalinga Raju will be prosecuted but how India Inc will repair the damage to its credibility,' concluded a reporter on IBN Live.

## WHY DID HE DO IT?

Raju's voluntary admission of his financial crime baffled the world. But more puzzling was why would he do something like this? What was his motive? The crime he had committed totally went against his image—Raju was known for his qualities of 'humility, helpfulness, care, and social commitment'. 'Unlike the standard crime story, in this case the perpetrators were known at the outset, thanks to Ramalinga Raju's letter,' writes Kiran Karnik in his introduction to the book, *The Satyam Saga*. 'Yet in a deeper sense, the whodunit mystery remains: what kind of person would commit—in an apparently well-planned, pre-meditated manner and for many years—a crime against his own creation? Who was this person?'

Karnik further argues that if money was the motive behind Raju's economic crime, it is not borne out by his action. According to his confession, he took no money out of the company. He rather brought money in. 'Even the disastrous attempt to acquire the two Maytas companies (the real estate and infrastructure companies promoted by him and his family) was not, as many first surmised, an attempt to move Satyam funds to the family-owned Maytas, but vice versa,' he says.

'Raju's actions remain an enigma,' reckons Kiran Karnik. 'Is it a matter of split personality, schizophrenia, or was the goodness only a façade?... The motive may have been greed, ego, or competitive compulsions: at this stage one can only speculate.'

In contrast to what Karnik theorizes, the *Times of India* on January 8, 2009, reported that Raju's letter on shareholding was misleading. Raju's claim that 'neither myself, nor the managing director (including our spouses) sold any shares in the last eight years—excepting for a small proportion declared and sold for philanthropic purposes' was not entirely true. Raju had further claimed that 'Neither me, nor the managing director took even one rupee/dollar from the company and have not benefited in financial terms on account of the inflated results.'

'The idea clearly was to suggest that the promoters of Satyam have not sold the company's shares for several years and hence have not benefited from artificially inflating the share price by overstating performance.'[14]

The newspaper, however, said that the promoters (that is the Raju family) sold roughly 1.5 crore shares between 2001 and 2006 as the family's shares slid down from 25.6 percent of the total shares of the company (7.2 crore shares) to 8.2 percent of the total equity (from 4.5 crore shares to 3 crore shares). 'During that period, the average share price of the company was in the range of Rs 700. That means the family would have realized something of the order of Rs 1,000 crore from the sale of its shares.'[15]

A similar opinion was voiced by C.P. Chandrasekhar in *Frontline*. 'To start with, it now does appear that Ramalinga Raju's "confession" was aimed at concealing more than it revealed,' he wrote. 'In particular, two of his claims are now suspect. One is that the process that led up to the claimed Rs 7,000 crore-plus hole in the company's balance sheet was the result of an unmanageable cumulative process that was triggered by a small (even if unwarranted) manipulation of the accounts many years back. This, according to the chairman, put him in a position where he was "riding a tiger". However, if the information being yielded by the ongoing investigations is true, it was not a small error but a planned, audacious, and outrageous scam which was expanded in scale over time and eventually led to the company's near collapse.'[16]

Chandrasekhar further wrote: 'The other claim that is obviously untrue is that neither he "nor the managing director (including our spouses) sold any shares in the last eight years—excepting for a small proportion declared and sold for philanthropic purposes". The truth is that the stake of the promoters has fallen sharply after 2001 when they reportedly held 25.60 percent of equity in the company. This fell to 22.26 percent by the end of March 2002, 20.74 percent in 2003, 17.35 percent in 2004, 15.67 percent in 2005, 14.02 percent in 2006, 8.79 percent in 2007, 8.65 percent at the end of September 2008, and 5.13 percent in January 2009.'

'While the last of these declines was due to sales by lenders with whom the promoters' shares were pledged, earlier declines were partly the result of the sale of shares by promoters', wrote Chandrasekhar. 'The promoters are estimated to have sold around four-and-a-half crore shares in the company over a seven-year period starting September 2001.'

'The suspicion from day one has been that Raju probably owned up to inflating accounts as the punishment for this is significantly less than that for siphoning funds,' said a report in the *Outlook*.

The report claimed that perhaps it was the sub-prime crisis and its indirect impact on the Indian real estate market that forced Raju to get off the tiger. Raju must have been rotating funds from Satyam to his construction firm (Maytas) hoping that he would plow them back after he had earned the profits from the real estate boom. When the boom turned into a bust, the game was over for Raju. ('Rotation of funds refers to the practice of illegally moving funds from, say, Business A and investing it in Business B. Once the investment in Business B turns profitable, the original money is quietly put back in Business A', the *Outlook* recorded.)

These were still early days and no one really knew why or how Raju perpetrated the fraud. Every journalist and commentator was speculating over Raju's motivations and the modus operandi of the scam. All kinds of rationale and insights were being attributed to Raju's actions.

'Media reports and investigations into his past revealed that Raju wanted immense success and respect. With Satyam's success, Ramalinga Raju started taking his status as an icon seriously, but was very unhappy that he wasn't spoken of in the same breath as Narayana Murthy (of Infosys) and Azim Premji (of Wipro),' wrote Sugata Srinivasaraju in a piece titled 'Andhra's Very Own' in the *Outlook*. 'He also made a serious effort to intellectually elevate himself to the level of the big boys of the IT industry,' said Sugata.

Writing of Raju's nature after talking to his friends and relatives, Sugata concluded: '...However seemingly modern and multinational Satyam became since the 1990s, some primitive qualities never left him and his company. They say he was somewhat clannish, feudal, and also dynastic. Qualities that one usually identifies with agrarian Andhra Pradesh. They point out that he was an inveterate gambler of sorts with a deep sense of destiny. They also describe him as an 'aimless entrepreneur' who dabbled in different, disparate ventures before he chanced upon fame through the IT industry in the 1990s.

Since there was no central vision to his entrepreneurial journey, they believe, Ramalinga Raju mixed his old economy, license raj habits with the spirit of the new to create a heady cocktail that ultimately brought him down.'

While some outsiders saw Raju's work of charity through the Byrraju Foundation in his ancestral village as clannish and feaudal, people in his native place saw him as a man doing good work for the poor. According to a report in the *Hindustan Times*, most residents of Garagaparru and other coastal villages in the Bhimavaram block, about 400 kilometres southeast of Hyderabad, did not understand Raju's crime. Nor did they want to. 'We're supporting him because he's a nice man,' said Prasad Raju, a 26-year-old electrician who works in Hyderabad and was in his native village for Sankranti. 'He has done a lot for us. Because of him we now have safe drinking water. We don't have walk to Bhimavaram for medicines. Ambulances are a call away.'

Unlike the grateful villagers of Andhra, the media in India and abroad were relentless in the analysis of the scandal. The Raju scam had opened a can worms—and the debate veered towards the larger question of ethics and morality in the Indian corporate sector.

'It's really a miracle that it (the fraud) lasted so long', said Shardul Shroff, a corporate lawyer in a TV programme, *Face the Nation*. 'It should have been bust long ago. I think there are three, four layers which failed here—it flows from the duties of an independent director, the duties of the audit committee under section 292 A of the Companies Act, the code of corporate governance as is there in Clause 49 of the Listing Agreement, and issues in relation to how the statutory auditors, internal auditors are looking at these kind of questions. Take a simple event like closing cash balance and bank balance. Now, he (Raju) has admitted that there is a difference of Rs 321 crore just on the cash and bank balance. I cannot understand how anybody could not have verified the closing cash and the closing bank because there are bank statements… It's really serious.'

'I am surprised that we are discussing this because Ramalinga Raju just came out in the open and confessed,' said a vociferous

Suhel Seth, a well-known public relations expert and Managing Partner, Counselage. 'If you think corporate corruption does not happen in India, you have another thing coming. I think you need demonstrable action. It is a slur on brand India... With what face do you talk about cutting edge corporate governance in India? And I think there are a whole host of reasons. Reason one: You created a situation in India where you have more and more rich lists coming out every day. So, all these guys who don't give a damn about their shareholders, don't give a damn about values and ethics, are interested in jumping on to these rich lists and staying there based on valuation. The stakes are high. It's in the glare of publicity. It is in the glare of media. I think demonstrable action needs to be taken against the PricewaterhouseCoopers of the world. You can't let these people walk away because it is not the damage that they have caused to the stock market which should worry everyone, which seems to be the case in any case in our country. You should talk about the collateral damage that this has caused brand India. So you have a situation where Ramalinga Raju is the poster boy of criminality in India. He is not the only person...you know about the nexus between corporate India and politics. So, when these things come to the fore, we then suddenly say, 'Oh my God, we didn't know it existed.' Of course, it existed. All this while you didn't have a Ramalinga Raju who wrote this nice little "ode of melancholy", almost Keats-like, about his company. The tragedy is—are stakes in corporate India too high? Are we making gods out of people who have feet of clay? Are we creating the wrong role models in our society? And most importantly, is the stock market the value barometer or is ethics going to be our ethics architecture? These are the principal questions that need to be asked if you want a long term, enduring solution where values replace valuation.'[17]

Talking about Raju's letter of confession, Pranjoy Guha Thakurta, economic analyst, draped in a blue suit and a red scarf, advanced his own Freudian analysis in the same TV programme: 'This letter is truly amazing. It is like a little boy going up to the mother and saying, yes, I spilled the milk, but don't punish me too hard. I am confessing after all, I spilled the milk. Be a little soft when you punish me. That is the kind of tone which is coming through. Second point, what I find truly amazing is towards the end of his letter Mr B. Ramalinga Raju has said, "Mr T.R. Prasad is well-placed to mobilize support from the government at this crucial time". Who is Mr T.R. Prasad? He is a former cabinet secretary. Suhel talked about the unholy nexus between big business and politics. It is there in black and white.'[18]

'Pathetic levels of probity in public life, absence of an ounce of corporate transparency, and widespread bureaucratic malfeasance are components of much that is Indian society today,' said columnist and business editor Dilip Cherian in *Tehelka*. 'Yet, to point out that we are today largely venal verges on the unpatriotic, and is sacrilegious. But just last year, India was ranked a lowly 74 among 180 countries of the world on the worldwide Corruption Perceptions Index. Enough said.'

Veteran Indian journalist and commentator M.J. Akbar mourned the lack of character (ethics) in today's business leaders. 'Character was a moral asset that combined honesty and loyalty to a fellow citizen or comrade-soldier,' he commented. 'It is a reflection of contemporary morality that we have changed the meaning of the word. Today, a character is either a chap with a tic in his metabolism, or a role in fiction, film, or television. From a truth, character has changed to artifice.'

Akbar said that the fraud at Satyam is not a mere economic offence. It is also a political offence, he stated on his blog. 'Satyam is a Hyderabad story. Crooks who steal shareholders blind cannot do so without political patronage. Bankers—some of whose hypocrisy is matched only by their pomposity—hand out huge amounts in the full knowledge that the money is going to be stolen by promoters they cozy up to. The kickbacks are substantial, because the first principle of dacoity is that there has to be equitable (if not equal) distribution of the spoils. The slicing order of the stolen cake is this: company promoter takes the biggest chunk, politician gets the second bite, and banker nibbles at the third.' Akbar goes on to give examples of many businesses in Andhra Pradesh where thuggery is rife.

'Satyam is India's sub-prime crisis, and the effects will be long and painful as the corruption in the system is unraveled,' remarked chartered accountant-turned filmmaker Shekhar Kapur (of *Bandit Queen* and *Elizabeth* fame) cynically on his blog. 'It will reach the highest echelons of our corporate world, for Raju could not have perpetrated this fraud at this level and for so long, alone. It needed the collusion of the banks, the accountants, and the government. And I would bet that he knows that he will be let off lightly as the investigations will somehow be stopped before it engulfs the whole system.'

The cynicism over the Satyam episode couldn't be missed. Though many pieces of the puzzle were still missing, by and large, there was agreement on the scam being yet another manifestation of India's corruption-infested system.

## THE MODUS OPERANDI OF RAJU'S CON GAME

Raju and his accomplices forged fictitious order receipts. They were electronically created.

They gave forged letters from banks to its external auditors, PricewaterhouseCoopers, certifying that the money was there with the banks.

Income tax was paid on these fictitious deposits. Tax deducted at source on the interest income on these deposits was Rs 61.04 crore in 2007–08 alone.

According to his letter of confession, Raju had been inflating both income and operating profits of Satyam since 2001. The company's profits were parked with banks in fixed deposits. That's what he showed to the world in quarterly reports.

This forgery and fraud was possible because only a few people at the top knew the secret workings of Raju's plan. For example, there were 1,500 team leaders in Satyam across sixty countries but only as few as twenty were reporting to Ram Mynampati, President and Director, Satyam. No single leader had a complete picture of the company's performance at the operational level.

## BLOODBATH ON THE STOCK EXCHANGE

Once the scandal hit the headlines, Satyam's shares drastically went down.[19] The benchmark Sensex stock index dropped 7.3 percent and Satyam shares fell nearly 78 percent on the day as investors fled in droves. 'By the end of trading hours at 3 pm, the BSE Sensex had lost 749 points and wiped off US$23 billion worth of investors' wealth. Satyam's stock, which had closed at Rs 179 (for an equity share of par value of Rs 2), fell off the cliff and ended at Rs 40.'[20]

Many lost their savings in this bloodbath, including pensioners and institutional investors. The Life Insurance Corporation of India lost Rs 949 crore. A school teacher in Phagwara committed suicide after losing around Rs 14–15 lakh in the stock market.[21] The bourse managers at the New York Stock Exchange suspended trade indefinitely on the Satyam ADR (American Depository Receipt).[22]

The day the scam broke out, the Andhra Pradesh government ordered its investigation. However, Raju was not arrested by the police. 'The Hyderabad Police Commissioner, when quizzed by eager media persons, said that he could not arrest Raju for the simple reason that there was no complaint against him. "On what basis do we take him into custody?" the Commissioner asked, hinting that a confession was no proof of Raju's wrongdoing.'[23]

In contrast to this, SEBI sprung into action. 'This is an event of horrifying magnitude and it is the first of this kind, so I am sure we will have to learn a few lessons from this as we get to the facts,' said C.V. Bhave, Chairman, SEBI. 'We are also in touch with other stock exchanges to see what will be the appropriate action.'

From the government, the Department of Corporate Affairs said it would probe Satyam as well as its auditors, PwC. 'The role of independent directors and auditors of Satyam is now under the scanner,' said a TV news reporter. 'The fear is this could be the first of many more skeletons inside corporate cupboards.'[24]

The Andhra politicians didn't know how to react to this episode. 'Most of them had lionized Raju and many of them were beneficiaries of largesse and donations from him. They could not berate a man who had been their benefactor. By the end of the day, the beleaguered politicians found a way: they began to express concern for the 50,000-plus employees of Satyam and asserted that jobs would not be lost.'[25]

In the afternoon, Raju made his way to a private guesthouse in the Jubilee Hills area—where he had his residence—and had a meeting with an important leader. He calmed Raju down. 'Don't worry, all the clouds would soon dispel,' he told him.[26]

## SLEEPLESS IN DELHI

While the media was going berserk over Raju's scam, baying for his blood for cheating Satyam's shareholders and for bringing shame to India, Anurag Goel could barely sleep that night.

The day had been hectic for him and he had to help the government find a way to save Satyam—the company's survival was tied up with many things, such as the impact on the IT industry, India Inc, and on India's image abroad as an investment destination. It was only at midnight that he got the time to sit down quietly by himself and think it through.

The government at the highest level decided to distinguish the fraud from the fact that Satyam was a high-quality company. The concern was for the shareholders, the over 50,000 employees, and the clients—many of them Fortune 500 firms who depended on Satyam for mission-critical support. *These people have not done any wrong*, Anurag thought. To him, the clients of Satyam, several of whom were overseas, were as much victims of the fraud as the company's non-promoter shareholders.[27]

It was also clear to him that a strong message needed to be sent out that India should not been seen as a country where this kind of fraud could take place and lead to a comprehensive shut down of the company.

Anurag and his minister had this task of taking punitive action against Raju but at the same time, there had to be corrective action to salvage Satyam. *How do I go about it*, Anurag tried to figure out. The challenge was that he had no precedent to follow. Also, there was very little information available to him at that point of time.

As he kept mulling over the matter, from midnight to 2 am in the morning, the plan of action slowly began to crystallize in his mind. The then board of Satyam had to go. Its members had lost all credibility. The government needed to appoint a board with persons of the highest, unquestionable credibility. And more urgently, something needed to be done quickly to save the company from falling off the rails. *Arranging money for staff salaries, for example, would not be easy*, he thought.

As Anurag retired to bed in the wee hours of the morning, he knew what he was going to do. An emergency inter-ministerial meeting needed to be called the next day even though it was a holiday.[28]

# HYDERABAD BLUES
## Raju Surrenders, Satyam Flounders on

*The admission of fraudulent manipulation of the financial affairs has created an adverse impression in the minds of trade, business, and industry across the world. This has also resulted in serious damage to the reputation of the Indian corporate sector and the regulatory mechanism in the eyes of the world.*
—S. Balasubramaniam, Chairman, Company Law Board

*January 8–10, 2009*
*Hyderabad and New Delhi*

Som Mittal, the president of NASSCOM, had landed in Hyderabad on the night of January 7. His arrival was a big relief for Hari T. and his colleagues.

Som's role was of talking to the Government of India, telling them that there was an issue—he had to review the situation from the IT industry's perspective. Therefore, his presence at the Satyam headquarters was extremely important. The report that he would carry back to New Delhi would have a lot of weight and potentially even decide the future of Satyam.

Hari knew that Som was there to ascertain whether the whole operation was a lie or only part of it was a lie. Four senior accountants of Satyam devoted themselves to examine the company's accounts overnight. They came up with some figures for Som, such as what payments were available, what were the company's outstandings, and what kind of customers Satyam had. Som spent the next day at Satyam headquarters, talking to these accountants and other officials, looking at some of the office documents and records, and concluding that Satyam actually did business and the company actually had fairly large customers.

Som found out about how critical the situation was in terms of finance—the salaries could not be paid, and the insurance premiums could not go. On the other hand, he reckoned that if the authorities came in and sealed off the company and the mission critical processes were shut down, then there would be a problem.

Fifteen hundred kilometres away, in New Delhi, the Minister of Corporate Affairs—Prem Chand Gupta—had ordered an inspection of the records of eight companies that morning (under section 209A of the Companies Act). All these eight companies were associated with Satyam. They were: Maytas Properties, Maytas Infra, Satyam BPO, Nipuna Services, Knowledge Dynamics, Nitor Global Solutions, CA Satyam ASP, and Satyam Venture Engineering Services. Some of these companies were privately held such as Maytas Properties while others like Nipuna and Satyam BPO were subsidiaries of Satyam.[1]

Gupta then had a meeting with Finance Secretary, Arun Ramanathan, Corporate Affairs Secretary, Anurag Goel; and some other bureaucrats. They decided that the best way to deal with the situation from a credibility perspective for the industry would be for the government to not step in and save the company by investing money, while at the same time finding a potential buyer to whom it could hand over the company. A decision was taken to involve the Andhra Pradesh government into the matter.

Goel contacted the Andhra Pradesh government's Chief Secretary, Ramakant Reddy. Reddy committed his assistance to the regional Registrar of Companies (RoC), Henry Richard, and other central agencies.

In the meeting at Shastri Bhawan, it was clear to Gupta and Goel that the existing Satyam board had to go as it had lost the people's trust. They decided to bring in names of creditability, so that trust in the company could be restored. The bureaucrats were entrusted to come up with some names of eminent and respectable people from IT, finance, and legal backgrounds. These mavericks would become part of the new board of Satyam.

At around 11 am, Joint Secretary in the Ministry of Corporate Affairs, Jitesh Khosla, 'instructed Henry Richard to immediately move the local courts to carry out a search and seizure operation at Satyam. It was feared that if the company's books were not seized, they might be tampered with or even destroyed.'[2]

Even though January 8 was a court holiday, Richard managed to obtain a court order for the operation. Armed with the order,

Richard, with his team of twelve, reached Satyam's registered headquarters at Begumpet at about 7 pm and served notice to Satyam Company Secretary, G. Jayaraman. The search went on till 11.30 pm. By then, all statutory records on the premises had been seized. 'The documents, along with the list of "members" and share transfers kept in two pen drives, were sealed in a room.'[3]

Next, the search team arrived at Satyam's Bahadurpally office where the main server for finance and accounts was also located. There, the search and seizure continued until 4 am the next morning. Richard and his team members were tired but the operation was still not over.

The seizure operation was resumed seven hours later at the Satyam office in HITEC City. This was the company's treasury hub. Simultaneously, another team reached Satyam's Raj Bhavan Road office where the IT records were kept. 'Satyam Vice President (Finance), G. Ramakrishna, was asked to show all records and files at the HITEC City office. These were found arranged neatly in racks. Since going through the whole lot would have taken his team a long time, Richard asked employees working in Satyam's finance department to catalogue the documents and hand over the list to his team. All documents were then sealed, and the old data related to accounts in 2002 was copied onto a pen drive. By 6.30 pm on January 9, Richard and his team were done at these premises, though the search and seizure operations continued, on and off, for several days.'[4]

Meanwhile, all kinds of rumours were floating around about Raju and his brother. One rumour was that they had escaped to a foreign land. Another was that they had gone traceless. Interestingly, even the Ministry of Corporate Affairs was not aware of Raju and his brother's whereabouts—that's what they said in a written statement to the Company Law Board (CLB).[5]

The public anger against Raju was at its height, whipped up by the media frenzy. On January 8, the *Indian Express* ran a story with the headline: 'Raju may face 10 yr jail, Rs 25 cr fine.' According to the report, Raju could face up to ten years imprisonment along with a fine which could extend to Rs 25 crore.[6]

Newspapers, TV portals, and websites buzzed with people's comments against Raju. One of the readers reacted to the story like this: 'These are the terrorists. These are the real ones. I am scared more of these sophisticated terrorists than the one who shows a gun to me. Imagine how many people he has murdered. How many families has he destroyed for good? How many babies and toddlers are crying? The world is suffering from capitalism terrorism [sic]. Why are people not shouting? Why are people now mum? How come police has not arrested him in terrorism charges? What is the bigger crime than this? Tell me.'

There was anger as well as pessimism because Raju had been such a high-profile entrepreneur. 'If such people who are supposed to be visionary leaders who set path for others to follow, commit such fraudulent acts in the name of corporate governance, then its hard to predict the future of our country and its people,' wrote another reader.

Bad news continued to pour in. Some of the clients of Satyam also started openly talking about moving to other IT services providers. For example, Tesco said that it could move Satyam projects to rivals.[7] 'Trust is a critical factor in all our outsourcing decisions, and all I can say is that there is tremendous competition among companies such as Infosys, Wipro, TCS, and Satyam,' said Mike McNamara, Director, Operations and Information Technology, Tesco Global.

On top of it all, reports came in that 'two US-based law firms—Izard Nobel LLP and Vianale & Vianale LLP—have filed class action lawsuits against Satyam on behalf of shareholders of the software services firm's American Depository Receipts'.[8]

In the face of uncertainty and bad news coming in from all fronts, some senior leaders at Satyam, including Hari, pledged to remain in the company and work together to steer the organization into a situation of stability. Ten of the most senior executives of Satyam, including interim CEO Ram Mynampati, collectively committed not to resign from the company. About forty other top managers from various geographical regions—known as the 'leadership council'—also gave their commitment to remain in the company.

Besides Ram Mynampati and Hari T., the ten top managers in the leadership included Subu D. Subramanian, Head, Manufacturing & Automotive; T.R. Anand, Head of Telecommunications, Infrastructure, Media and Entertainment, and Semiconductors; Keshab Panda, Head, Europe, Energy & Utilities; Virender Aggarwal, Head of Asia Pacific, India, Middle East, Africa; Manish Mehta, Head, SAP & Testing Practices; A.S. Murthy, Head, Global Delivery and Global Leadership Development; Murali Venkataramani, Head, Commercial; and S.V. Krishnan, Head of Human Resources.[9]

'The pledges of commitment from these leaders, coming hours after disclosures and the resignation of Mr Raju, underscore the unity and determination of the Satyam leadership to steer the company through this crisis,' the leaders said in a joint statement.

The leaders decided that they would hold a press conference at 5 pm IST in Hyderabad to outline an action plan to address key concerns of various stakeholders including customers, investors, employees, and business partners.

Som went back to New Delhi on January 8 and reported to the government what he thought of the issue. He relayed a lot of information of the criticality of the situation to the government and what would happen to the image of the company, the country, the business, and the clients if the company was shut down. The government sprung into action. He suggested some names for the new board of governors.

'We were running two risks (at that point of time),' he said. 'The company could explode because of two reasons: either the customers migrate or the employees migrate. We had no other assets other than employees.'

On January 9, the Ministry of Corporate Affairs moved the CLB to remove the Satya, directors and auditors. It requested for appointing ten new directors to take charge of the company.[10]

On Sunday, NASSCOM had a conference call with the past chairman of the body and the entire executive council was on conference call. They agreed that government intervention was good because they needed to protect the image of the industry. They also made a commitment not to poach the assets of the company. 'If everybody went poaching both the employees and customers, then there would be no company left anyway,' said Som. 'Unanimously people said that they will not "wilfully" poach customers or employees. We made public this particular decision. It was comforting for both customers and employees.'

While all this was happening, the third big stakeholder was the stock market. All companies are expected to have a substantial amount of cash on their balance sheets. The press, media, and analysts started asking questions about how one could know if the same wasn't happening in other companies. 'This happened in early January and our annual results were to come out in the next two weeks,' recalled Som. 'We also took a decision that we will have very specific audit done of the cash balances that we have and give out the statement from our auditors that those cash balances are genuine. This was for the entire IT industry.'

On the same day (January 9), CLB chairman, S. Balasubramaniam passed an ex-parte order. 'The admissions of Shri Raju straightaway impacted the stock market by which on a single day share price crashed from Rs 188 to Rs 38.40,' he said. 'The company has a very huge international presence through a large number of international subsidiaries and they service many important clients across the globe. The admission of fraudulent manipulation of the financial affairs has created an adverse impression in the minds of trade, business, and industry across the world. This has also resulted in serious damage to the reputation of Indian corporate sector and the regulatory mechanism in the eyes of the world. Therefore, the Central government has formed the opinion that the interests of the company will not be safe in the hands of the present board of directors and as such they should be restrained from discharging any function as directors and that the Central government should be authorized to appoint ten directors.'[11]

In its order, the chairman mainly ordered as follows:

- The present Board of Directors stands suspended with immediate effect. None of the present directors shall represent himself to be a director of the company and shall also not exercise any powers as a director
- The Central government shall immediately constitute a fresh board of the company with not more than ten persons of eminence as directors. The Central government may also designate one of them as the chairman of the board. This board shall be entitled to exercise and discharge all powers vested in it by the Articles and the Act. The said board will continue till further orders
- The newly-constituted board shall meet within seven days of its constitution and take necessary immediate action to put the company back on the road
- It shall submit periodical reports to the central government, with a copy to this board on the state of affairs to the company

Now the stage was set to appoint new members to the board of Satyam.

## THE RAJU BROTHERS SURRENDER TO POLICE

Meanwhile, the noose was tightening around Ramalinga Raju and his brother. A team of officials from the Serious Fraud Investigation Office (SFIO) had arrived at Hyderabad on Friday morning (January 9). They visited the RoC and went through the records already seized by Henry Richard and his team.

On Thursday (January 8) itself, the SEBI-appointed, Chennai-based General Manager, A. Sunil Kumar, had summoned Ramalinga Raju and his brother Rama Raju to appear before him at 4 pm the following day (on January 9) along with the necessary legal documents. Raju deputed his advocate, S. Bharat Kumar, to represent him before the three-member SEBI team. The advocate said that he was not able to furnish the numerous documents sought by SEBI, as the summons was served at short notice. He sought three days' time to answer the queries.[12]

The SEBI team, however, asked him to ensure Ramalinga Raju was present on Saturday, January 10.

Raju and others drove to the office of the director-general of police in Lakdikapaul around 10 pm on Saturday night. They were taken into custody and sent to the Chanchalguda prison. 'Police refused to divulge details, though DGP S.S.P. Yadav claimed that Raju was arrested and had not given himself up voluntarily.'[13]

'Climaxing three weeks of high corporate drama, the former Chairman of Satyam Computer Services, B. Ramalinga Raju, and his brother and former Managing Director, B. Rama Raju, accompanied by three close relatives, surrendered to the police on Friday night,' announced the *Hindu* next morning (January 10).

'The arrests did little to deflect criticism that the Rajasekhara Reddy government was going slow on the investigations into Mr Raju's misdeeds, coming as they did more than sixty hours after he resigned from the company's Board of Directors and admitted to cooking up the account books,' the report added. 'Opposition leaders alleged that Mr Reddy was shielding Mr Raju because Satyam and Maytas Infra had projects worth over Rs 30,000 crore under way the State. Police failed to locate Chief Financial Officer Srinivas Vadlamani who was not given a clean chit in Mr Raju's confession.'

After Raju's arrest in the night of January 9, the hunt was on for Vadlamani Srinivas. On January 10, that hunt too culminated: Officials of Crime Investigation Department (CID) first interrogated Vadlamani at the Hyderabad CID office for a couple of hours and later arrested him. Inspector General of Police, CID (Economic Offences Wing), V.S.K. Kaumudi confirmed the arrest.[14] He said that Vadlamani was being held on charges of criminal conspiracy, forging accounts, and cheating.

The following day, the Andhra Pradesh CID conducted raids on the residences of Ramalinga Raju, his brother Rama Raju and former CFO Vadlamani Srinivas. The search was over by 9 pm.

While the arrests of Ramalinga Raju, B. Rama Raju, Vadlamani Srinivas were a curtain call for act one of the Satyam saga, the fate of Satyam's 50,000-plus employees was still in limbo. Exactly how the government was going to save Satyam—that was the primary question on everyone's mind.

# THE LEAGUE OF EXTRAORDINARY GENTLEMEN

## Government Appoints Six New Members to the Satyam Board

*Our job was like a bomb disposal squad and we were sent there and you knew that this was ticking.*
—Kiran Karnik, member of the new Satyam board

*January 11–15, 2009*
*Hyderabad and New Delhi*

It was 11 am on Sunday, January 11. Former NASSCOM President Kiran Karnik was at home in Delhi. He was looking forward to a quiet weekend after days of being on the road.[1]

His phone buzzed. The caller was Anurag Goel, Secretary of Ministry of Corporate Affairs, Government of India. Without beating about the bush, Anurag requested him to be part of Satyam's new board.

Karnik had been following the Satyam story ever since it broke on January 7. Being an industry veteran, he knew the implications of Satyam going down. It was a crisis for both India and India Inc. But he also saw it as an opportunity. What if India could fix Satyam? It would make India the only country in the world to have done that. The shame of India could be turned into the pride of India. It was a difficult proposition but not an impossible one.

Karnik could feel a palpable sense of urgency in Goel's voice. Being a representative of the government, Goel seemed determined to save the situation at Satyam. Karnik gave in and said yes, accepting the 'responsibility' in principle.

As soon as he acquiesced to Goel's request, the bureaucrat asked him if he could fly to Hyderabad the same day.

'What? Today, itself?' *Things were going too fast*, Karnik thought.

Karnik said he would check the flight availability and get back to him. In the next few hours, the ministry not only booked a flight for him but also arranged for his accommodation in Hyderabad. 'Karnik was impressed. The government worked on Sundays.'[2]

Just like Karnik was brought on board, the ministry of corporate affairs roped in Deepak Parekh and C. Achuthan in the same manner to be part of the new board.

Was it easy to get all of them on board? Not really. The biggest of these miracle workers' concern was 'the possibility of them becoming a party to the litigation, especially the class action suits in the US. They were, however, convinced that the government would move a petition with the CLB to indemnify them from any legal angle.'[3]

Back in Hyderabad, even though January 11 was a Sunday—a day of rest and recreation for most people—there was immense restlessness and anxiety among the Satyam employees. The last two days, January 9 and 10 had seen the high drama of arrests of the two Raju brothers and CFO Vadlamani. But the future of Satyam as a company was still uncertain. Arresting the Rajus was all fine and good but what was uppermost on the minds of people both inside and outside Satyam was whether the Government of India would step in and bail the company out, and if yes, then in what form?

The government had dissolved the old Satyam board that very Friday. All eyes were now on Prem Chand Gupta, the Minister of Corporate Affairs, to replenish the board with fresh faces.

This anxiety was laid to rest on Sunday when the Indian government announced a new board for Satyam. Once the three distinguished personalities had given a nod to be on the board, Gupta held a press conference in New Delhi. 'Having considered all aspects of the current situation, the government has decided to constitute a board of eminent persons having expertise in different fields like finance, information technology, law, and administration. Such a board will provide the necessary vision along with a responsible and accountable leadership to the company in this hour of crisis,' said Gupta.[4]

He then announced that the government had selected three 'eminent persons' to serve on Satyam's board: Deepak Parekh, Chairman, HDFC Bank; Kiran Karnik, a former head of NASSCOM, and C. Achuthan, a lawyer and former presiding officer of the Securities Appellate Tribunal (SAT).[5]

In his press conference, Gupta said that the board would meet within the next twenty-four hours and decide who would serve as Satyam's new chairman. He also said that the new board could select other directors as required.

Gupta said that the government would consider requests from Satyam's large shareholders for seats on the board, but that it was up to the new board to decide who would be invited to join. 'All options are open,' Gupta said. 'It is important to ensure the continuity of the company in the interest of its shareholders, employees, customers, and other stakeholders—both in India and abroad,' he added.

Satyam welcomed the ministry of corporate affairs' appointments. 'Satyam welcomes this key development, which will ensure the company's continued operations, help maintain customer confidence and associate morale, and restore investor trust. The new members are eminent and accomplished leaders, recognized in India and around the world for their expertise in finance, law, administration, and the IT services industry. Satyam's leadership team has complete confidence in them, and pledges to work closely and in full cooperation with the new board', the company said.

'This is a vital stabilizing development for Satyam, and it marks the beginning of a new chapter in the company's history. It is the best news we've received in the past four weeks,' a company spokesperson added.

## THE BOMB DISPOSAL SQUAD ARRIVES IN HYDERABAD

When the government-appointed league of extraordinary gentlemen landed at the Satyam headquarters in Hyderabad, they felt like members of a bomb disposal squad.

'Our job was like a bomb disposal squad's and we were sent there and you knew that it was ticking,' said Kiran Karnik remembering when he was sent on the assignment to Hyderabad. 'We didn't know which wire to cut. And yet we had to act quickly. If not it would blow up more than your face and do damage all around.'[6]

The newly appointed board members held their first meeting on January 12, in the same board room on the fifth floor of Satyam headquarters where Raju used to lead the board meetings. The core team that had looked into the financial position made a presentation to the new board. In the presentation, these members showed that the company had marquee customers, there were real collections, the position of receivables which were to be collected over the next two months, the backlog of payments, the unencumbered assets in terms of land and buildings—so there was real money in the pipeline and a real chance of survival. At that time, it was estimated that the the company needed nearly Rs 1,000 crore for meeting the cash flow requirements (this included payments against borrowings and payments to creditors). In the meeting, the new board members concluded that their top priority was to restore confidence in the customers, employees, suppliers, and investors by ensuring business continuity. The members also understood that for the immediate survival, the company urgently needed cash infusion.

In a press conference held on the same day, they said the government was going to appoint a few more board members soon, immediately after which the full board would then decide on the appointment of the chairman.

'Given the enormity of the issue and the urgent attention required, the board will have to meet frequently for the next few months,' the board said. The board was to meet fifteen times between 12 January and 27 March, 2009.

They pointed out a few concrete steps that they were going to take. One was appointment of an independent accounting firm within the next forty-eight hours to restate the financial accounts and announce the Q3 results. Deepak Parekh said restating the accounts would be critical, as 'people do not have faith in the numbers at this stage'.[7]

The other concern was to ensure that the company had sufficient funds to continue operations. 'Working capital issues require immediate attention and we will work with the team to tide over this situation,' said the board.

'Our immediate priority is to ensure sustainability of services with minimum disruption,' said Deepak Parekh. 'We will provide strategic direction to Satyam, not run it on a daily basis. We are looking to induct fresh blood like the chief executive and chief financial officer into the company, but it will take time.'

As they enunciated their next steps, they made it a point to show appreciation for the commitment of Satyam's leaders. 'In the past few hours that we have been here, we have been impressed by the commitment of the officers that we have met,' the board stated. 'Many Satyamites have reached out reaffirming their commitment to the company and their desire to see Satyam reach greater heights. The associates are definitely of high quality and they have shown tremendous resilience and commitment, amidst all the adversity that they have been subjected to. We are told that they have united and rallied to get Satyam out of this crisis. We feel assured that they will show the same determination to deliver high-quality work as per SLAs (Service Level Agreement), and help restore the glory for this organization.'

They also commented on the list of customers that Satyam had on its plate: 'We are also impressed with all the marquee customers that Satyam has, which reads like the who's who of global corporations. We would like to assure Satyam's customers that our immediate priority is to ensure sustainability of services with minimal disruption. The government is keen to do everything possible to quickly get the organization on its feet and conduct business as usual.'

These statements by Satyam's new board members raised hopes for Satyam's future. It injected confidence in the employees.

One immediate effect of the board's statements after their first meeting was that they sparked life in the beleaguered company's moribund share price. 'Satyam's battered shares rebounded nearly 45 percent to close at Rs 34.4 as investor confidence was boosted by the government-installed board.'[8]

At the same time, the Bombay Stock Exchange removed the company from its benchmark 30-share Sensex index in reaction to the accounting scandal.[9] That was inevitable anyway, so nobody was surprised.

Two days later (January 14), the board of directors announced the appointment of Deloitte and KPMG to assist the board in the restatement of accounts.[10]

The board also announced that it had launched a search to identify candidates for the positions of chief executive officer and chief financial officer of Satyam.

After the first board meeting, Karnik started calling key customers of Satyam. The aim was to convince them not to cancel their orders. He assured them that Satyam would fulfil all commitments and highlighted the fact that the government would not allow the company to implode.

## THREE NEW BOARD MEMBERS ADDED

On January 15, the Ministry of Corporate Affairs bolstered the Satyam board with three more eminent names. They were T.N. Manoharan, former president of the Institute of Chartered Accountants of India (ICAI); Tarun Das of the Confederation of Indian Industry (CII), a leading business association; and S. Balakrishna Mainak of the Life Insurance Corporation (LIC) of India.

The company welcomed these new additions: 'Satyam welcomes the addition of these distinguished board members, who were selected for their leadership and expertise in industry matters, investments, and accounting. As the reorganization of the board of directors proceeds, the company is better positioned to focus solely on ensuring continued service to customers and restoring stakeholder confidence.'

With these three new appointments, the number of board members named by the Ministry of Corporate Affairs totalled to six.

'The addition of these new members to the Board of Directors signals the beginning of a strong new foundation for Satyam. We embrace the new board members and look forward to working closely with them,' a Satyam spokesperson added.

Most importantly, Satyam announced on the same day (January 15) that it had completed the disbursement of the first of the two cycles of salary payments of its workforce in the US for the month of January 2009.

Even though the salaries were paid, concerns remained about the financial viability of the company. Deepak Parekh said the IT firm could raise funds by mortgaging assets—dispensing with the need for central assistance. 'Until we know the real position, how can we speak of bailout…The company has receivables of Rs 1,700 crore,' said Parekh. He added, 'financial assistance can be generated by hypothecating some of the assets of the company.'[11]

The speculation about the bailout package bubbled up after Economic Affairs Secretary, Ashok Chawla, said that the government had received a mail or two from former acting CEO Ram Mynampati. Apparently Mynampati had indicated that Satyam needed about Rs 150 crore to stay afloat. Chawla, however, did not explain where these emails were coming from. This was a little mysterious as Mynampati, who was no longer a board member, was in the US meeting clients.[12]

However, the government's stand was categorical. There was no question of the government bailing out Satyam with taxpayers' money. This was evident from a statement that Gupta made at a press conference. 'I am confident that NASSCOM and major companies in the IT sector in the country would support the efforts of the present management of Satyam in sailing through the present crisis,' said Gupta.[13]

Besides Gupta, Parekh also met the Planning Commission Deputy Chairman, Montek Singh Ahluwalia. He reiterated that Satyam had large receivables and assets that could be hypothecated after getting a report from the accountants, who could take eight-twelve months. 'The collections are coming every day... As Satyam is a running company, lots of collections are planned... We are trying our best to salvage the company,' said Parekh. Earlier in the day, Gupta said that the company could raise funds from banks, if needed.[14]

To start with, there were many challenging moments for the new team. Their biggest fear was that they would fall flat on their faces. For Manoharan, too, it was a challenging moment when he got the call to join the board. But a bigger challenge awaited him after he accepted the government's invitation. 'The most challenging moment was restoring financial responsibility and being a finance professional myself, the board wanted me to monitor it on a day-to-day basis. We did restore financial stability and did not default on any occasion from the point of view of any statutory dues and more particularly the salary payments.'[15]

These were men put together in a boardroom who had never worked together before, due to which, initially, there were some disagreements on issues and approaches. But eventually, they all got ironed out. They became so involved that they continued working and discussing the issues at hand until midnight every single day.

The second big challenge for them was reaching out to employees and customers and keeping everybody together.[16] The third was in the form of other government agencies that were investigating the fraud, and would often come in the way of the board members who were trying to get the business going. The board was trying to raise money by mortgaging off or selling off the superfluous land that Satyam had, whereas the investigating agencies would not think twice before attaching Satyam's properties. Therefore, lack of coordination between the agencies was a major stumbling block.

And in all this was another worry for the board—raising the Rs 600 crore needed to pay the January salaries to the company employees. Raising money of this kind was an uphill chore. They could not go to the government begging for a bailout. So they identified land that could be used as collateral for raising funds at commercial rates from a bank. 'But a large tract of land given to the company by the Andhra Pradesh government had a clause stating Satyam had to provide employment to 6,000 people by 2012. The bank, taking abundant precaution, asked the board to get a no objection certificate from the state.'[17] 'Andhra Pradesh either got jittery or was deliberately dragging its feet...so some crucial days were lost. But, finally, it gave the NOC,' said a board member.

In order to get the funding, one of the conditions was to get the no objection certificate from a state infrastructure nodal agency. Considering the chaotic situation, no official was willing to take a decision and hence the matter had gone to several departments in the Andhra Pradesh government. Finally, it landed on the table of the then Chief Minister, Mr YS Rajasekhar Reddy. 'That approval from the Chief Minister was very crucial,' said a former senior Satyam official who was closley associated with Satyam's fluctuating fortunes. 'I know that every department the file went through was not very favourable with several questions raised, but the late Chief Minister went with his own mind and approved the release of the no objection certificate. It was a big relief for us. Without that, we wouldn't have got the necessary loan from the banks.'

The government's proactive stance, in large parts, helped save Satyam. 'It was none other than a distressed Prime Minister Manmohan Singh who made the first call to get a private sector high-profile board in. Even after he went in for his heart surgery, he asked External Affairs Minister Pranab Mukherjee to extend all help.'[18]

'Mr Mukherjee actually ensured senior government secretaries called up some key clients who did not want to work with a tainted company. Except for one client, all others stuck on to Satyam and a large part of the credit goes to Mr Mukherjee's deft handling of the situation,' said Tarun Das.

Similarly, when there was a cash crunch at Satyam, the cabinet secretary helped in the arrangement of the first loan of Rs 600 crore from IDBI Bank and Bank of Baroda. 'In my forty-five years of working with the government for the industry, I have not seen such close involvement of the government,' said Das.[19]

'Some of the foreign banks that used to handle Satyam's foreign accounts became very nervous and were the first ones to land in our office,' said a former Satyam official who wishes to remain anonymous. 'We found that they had given some unsecured loans and when the scandal broke, they sent us recall notices / notice to freeze facilities. They said that without security, they would not let us use a single dollar from our own accounts with them. This was a big crisis in itself because this meant that we could not pay salaries to our staff working overseas. If that continued even for a forthnight, our customers and employees would have lost all confidence, and that would have been disastrous. Also, in the US, for health insurance, companies started asking for advance and threatened to cancel the insurance facilities offered to our employees. I remember a senior Satyam employee crying on the phone saying that one associate's wife was not getting admitted when she was due for delivery and the insurance facility was getting denied and few of the associates pooled their personal money to meet any emergency. This was heart-rending. In those days, all of us were working for days and nights together. Some of the directors were also staying back in the office and advising us from time to time. We would put out one fire and another fire would come up. The first week was terrible with fires all around and most of us hardly went back home.'

'So, we were stuck at home and abroad,' he further added. 'It was a double whammy. At home, the Income Tax department had frozen our accounts. Abroad, the foreign banks had done the same. It was only through the intervention of the government and the board members that we got out of the sticky situation. Mr Deepak Parekh and other members of the board talked to the bankers and convinced them that they should support a falling company and help it find its feet. The whole affair was an example of great team work. Mr T.N. Manoharan, and Mr Partho S. Datta played a very critical role in arranging the oxygen, that is money, for Satyam. Mr Manoharan used to stay put in Satyam's office and help us deal with every critical situation. He was hands on and accompanied us to the banks, IT department etc. and made himself available for execution as well. Mr Manoharan and Mr Datta visited several of the banks personally and pleaded for support. The Rs 600 crore that was finally sanctioned to Satyam was the lifeline that turned the tide.' The board had appointed Homi Khusrokhan, former Managing Director, Tata Chemicals, and Partho Datta, former Finance Director, Murugappa Group, as special advisers on May 5, 2009. Homi played a significant role in bringing the business team together.

'There is no problem insurmountable if there is a team and the team works in tandem,' said Parekh. And it was the team spirit, imbued with a common goal to achieve for Satyam's survival, which kept the board going.

---

### THE SAVIOURS OF SATYAM

Kiran Karnik, the former president of NASSCOM (The National Association of Software and Services Companies), is a prominent public figure in India. Prior to joining NASSCOM, Karnik was the Managing Director at Discovery Networks in India from 1995–2001. He spearheaded the launch of Discovery Channel and Animal Planet in South Asia. For over twenty years, he worked in the Indian Space Research Organization (ISRO). He also worked briefly with the United Nations in New York and Vienna. He has been a consultant to UNESCO in Afghanistan, the World Health Organization, the World Bank, UN Institute for Disarmament Research, and the Ford Foundation. He holds a first degree in physics from Mumbai University and a second degree from the Indian Institute of Management, Ahmedabad.[20]

Deepak Parekh is a well-known name in India's finance sector and is credited with pioneering mortgage financing in

India. He is known for his straightforwardness and honesty. 'Trustworthiness has taken 65-year-old Parekh from being one of the most successful mangers to a corporate leader whose counsel is valued by his peers and the government alike. The Indian financial services industry would have lost Parekh to some multinational bank if it was not for his uncle, the legendary H.T. Parekh, who founded HDFC in 1977 and convinced him to join.' Parekh is a qualified chartered accountant from England and had worked at Ernst & Young, Precision Fastners, ANZ Grindlays, and Chase Manhattan Bank, Mumbai, prior to joining HDFC. 'He turned a fledgling HDFC into a financial services conglomerate with assets of US$28 billion and a one third share of India's mortgage finance market. Parekh's reputation as a problem solver with a flair for leadership grew and the government often asked him for advice.'[21]

C. Achuthan was a legal expert, and a former presiding officer of the Securities Appellate Tribunal (SAT). He also chaired the new Takeover Regulations Advisory Committee of the capital markets watchdog, SEBI. After retirement from the SAT, he was working as partner with a Mumbai-based law firm Corporate Law Chambers. Achuthan was born and initially educated in Atavan, a small village in Mallapuram district of Kerala. With a Masters in Economics and a degree in law from Mumbai University, Achuthan started off with the Indian Legal Services and served as a legal advisor to the Central government, and also served on the Company Law Board, before being promoted as the SAT's sole presiding officer from 1997 to 2003. He passed away on September 19, 2011, following a massive cardiac arrest. He was 70.[22]

When he joined the Satyam board, Tarun Das was the Chief Mentor of the Confederation of Indian Industry (CII). He had served with the Confederation of Indian Industry for a long period and was its Chief Executive from 1974 to 2004 and also served as its Director General. He had been closely involved with major policy-making groups concerned with Indian industry and in promoting business cooperation internationally. He graduated in Economics/Commerce from Calcutta University, India and Manchester University, UK and was awarded an Honorary Doctorate in Science from the University of Warwick, UK.[23]

T.N. Manoharan has the distinction of being the first accountancy professional from Tamil Nadu to be conferred with the Padma Shri award. He is a distinguished professional and was president of the Institute of Chartered Accountants of India (ICAI). Son of T.L. Narayana Chowdhry, a 93-year-old freedom fighter, Manoharan, is a partner in Manoharan Chowdhry Associates.

Suryakanth Balakrishnan Mainak, a chartered accountant, joined the Life Insurance Corporation of India in 1983. Later on, he became the head of the equity research cell of the insurance giant. Mainak serves as Director of National Stock Exchange of India Ltd. He holds a Bachelor's Degree in Commerce from the University of Mumbai (earlier known as University of Bombay).[24]

January 11, 2009 to March 31, 2009

| Name | Category | Designation | No. of meetings[1] | | No of Directorships in other companis[2] | No of committee positions in other companies[3] | | Attendance at last Annual General Meeting[4] |
|---|---|---|---|---|---|---|---|---|
| | | | Held | Attended | | Member | Chairperson | |
| Mr. Deepak S. Parekh | Independent Director | Government Nominee Director | 13 | 12 | 12 | 2 | 5 | NA |
| Mr. Kiran Karnik | Independent Director | Government Nominee Director | 13 | 13 | 2 | 1 | – | NA |
| Mr. C. Achuthan | Independent Director | Government Nominee Director | 13 | 13 | 2 | – | – | NA |
| Mr. Tarun Das | Independent Director | Government Nominee Director | 13 | 10 | 1 | – | – | NA |
| Mr. T. N. Manoharan | Independent Director | Government Nominee Director | 13 | 11 | 2 | – | 1 | NA |
| Mr. S. B. Mainak | Independent Director | Government Nominee Director | 13 | 12 | 1 | – | – | NA |

[1] Meetings were held on January 12, January 17, January 22 & 23, January 27, February 4&5, February 12, February 21, February 26, March 05, March 13, March 20, March 21 and March 27, 2009.
[2] Excludes private companies, foreign companies and companies registered under Sec 25 of the Companies Act 1956 and alternate Directorships.
[3] Represents Audit committee and Investor Grievances committee in public limited companies.
[4] NA—Not applicable as the appointment of Government nominee Directors was post Annual General Meeting.

# THE HEALING BEGINS
## *Unlocking the Spirit of Satyam*

*It all began with a communication. At 9.32 in the morning of Wednesday, January 7, two neatly type-written pages rolled off a fax machine at Satyam Computer Services headquarters in Hyderabad. The fax machine hummed softly, but what those two pages contained was to shake the organization to its foundations... That the company didn't shake apart into pieces...is also due to communications.*
—From 'Getting the word out', a paper brought out by Satyam Computer Services, 2009

For the first three days, nobody knew how to exactly go about handling the frenzy at Satyam, remembers A.S. Murthy, the then Chief Delivery Officer at Satyam. After Raju's resignation, the company was like a headless chicken.

Satyam had over 50,000 employees and the company's worldwide operations—it counted 185 Fortune 500 firms as customers and had operations in 66 countries[1]—were organized in five regions: North America, Europe, Asia Pacific, India, and the rest of the world. Within a region, the operations were organized in terms of verticals such as manufacturing, banking, and financial services. Even regionally, it was a large organization with thousands of employees at various levels. Also, there was a hierarchy among employees. There were project managers and business unit heads, and so on. How to communicate with them all—that was the challenge before Satyam's leaders.

Luckily, many in the Satyam's senior rung of leadership had more than ten years of experience in the organization. So, they knew their customers intimately, their associates very well, and took a lot of pride in what they did. As the crisis unfolded, within a matter of few hours, they formed small teams to keep the operations going.

'We thought we ought to focus on the two entities—the customer community and the associate community,' says Murthy. 'So, we started taking the ownership of addressing the associates, sending emails (to them), because even those three to four days between January 7 to 11—11 is the date when I think the government appointed directors—were very long.'

There was total uncertainty and confusion at Satyam for those three to four days. 'People started taking control of the respective geographies, and tried to reach out to their customers,' he says. For example, Ram Maynampati, who handled the US market, reached out to Satyam's customers in that market. Virendra Agarwal was in charge of the Asia Pacific market and he made an effort to allay the fears and concerns of customers in that region. 'We also had a couple of open houses in those three-four days in Hyderabad. We were also not very sure what the way forward was, and what was likely to happen. The board itself was not there. So, until the government actually appointed the board, there was thorough confusion. Even if a customer asked us, we did not know exactly what to tell what the way forward was. This was a company without a board, without a CEO and a CFO.'

Despite that confusion, nothing actually came to a standstill. And that worked in Satyam's favour. Satyam was such a well-oiled organization that the operations at the company never stopped. The ball kept rolling.

## TOUCHING PEOPLE

As the saga unfolded, both Ed Cohen and Priscilla Cohen at the Satyam School of Leadership were overwhelmed by the 'heart' Satyamites showed. 'Everyone saw Satyam as Raju and Raju as Satyam and so when failure happened at the top, the immediate reaction was—it's all over!' he said in an interview. 'A minute later though, everyone came around saying, 'How can we save this? How can we pull this together? We have a responsibility to our customers, employees, investors, even to society.'[2]

In view of the crisis, Priscilla and Ed's roles changed overnight. 'Immediately, we were asked to take significant responsibility for creating and managing new strategies to heal the deep wounds in the organization,' she said.[3]

'Fortunately, the leaders who remained at Satyam were determined to produce the best outcome they could. Although saving the company would be difficult, they developed a rigorous plan to help leaders deal with employee fears, concerns, and disruptions so that productivity would remain as high as possible while the company explored its post-crisis options,' she says. 'As part of this process, Satyam turned to a pool of professionally trained coaches to work with the company's managers to make sure that these executives did not allow a single employee to withdraw or lose hope without having tried hard to engage him or her.'[4]

'We didn't want to create shockwaves right cross,' Dr Khanna said, remembering the developments on January 7. 'We huddled all our people into a little room and we told them—don't worry, this has happened; there are lots of other people within the organization who can carry the flag on; you don't have to panic in any way. That's something that we did immediately. That was a Band-Aid kind of an approach, not convincingly knowing ourselves what the future had in store for us.'

That time while everybody was talking, murmuring, gossiping—the phones were abuzz. 'There were lots of calls from media,' Dr Khanna says. '"Please talk to us for five minutes", the media people would request. And then we were told that don't talk to anybody right now because we didn't have complete data about anything. As far as I'm concerned, I didn't answer any of the media calls at that time and I just said I'll get back to you.'

One thing the company did right, according to Cohen, was that as the crisis hit, and its magnitude was felt, people started doing scenario planning. They started planning for scenarios such as what if the company is sold in pieces? What if the company was to be bought by the employees? What if the company was to be picked up by IBM?[5] 'They followed a start-stop-continue plan—what should they start/stop/continue doing over time—for the next 30/60/90 days,' Cohen said in an interview.

Three of the principal things that the Learning World team did during the crisis were—communicating broadly, admitting ignorance, and responding to raw emotions.[6]

## THE FIRST FORTY-EIGHT HOURS

While American lawyers were filing lawsuits, back in Hyderabad the company's leadership team had huddled together in a cramped conference room on the fifth floor of the company's headquarters. They identified ten major-issue areas—customer retention, associate retention, finance, sources of funds, etc—and formed four task forces, dedicated to customer, associate, financial, and legal concerns.

The Associate Task Force (ATF) comprised twelve members from human resources, marketing & communications, and Satyam Learning World. Charged with keeping Satyam's 50,000-plus associates intact, the ATF faced both familiar and uncharted territory. Associates were going through a well-understood sequence of emotions:

**Denial**   ranging from conspiracy theories to false information
**Shock**   resulting in a sense of numbness and disbelief
**Shame**   leading to withdrawal from co-workers, family, social groups
**Anger**   a sense of betrayal and frustration

To address these, the ATF quickly established some basic communications principles:
1. Inform Associates
    a. First, before other sources, especially the media
    b. With factual information—as and when events unfolded
    c. Via a dialogue, not a monologue

2. Influence Associates
    a. With suitable metaphors and examples to maintain positive morale

> b. To act as their own 'brand ambassadors' to encourage each other and avoid rumours and speculation
> 3. Go Beyond Associates
>    a. Acknowledge and speak to spouses and families as well
>
> However, the ATF faced practical challenges: Satyam's workforce is highly dispersed—not just across countries and time zones, but at both Satyam and customer facilities. Reaching them all, at the same time, and in a uniform manner is difficult under the best circumstances. Furthermore, sensitivities surrounding governance, disclosure, accuracy, timeliness, etc, means that every communiqué has to be scrutinized and validated by management, legal, and other consultants.
>
> Thus, the ATF and HR teams collaborated with other units in the organization around the clock—literally 24x7—to enable the rapid dissemination of credible facts, each day, every day. A twenty-four hour help desk was set up for associates to ask questions, express concerns, or make suggestions. Floor meetings, department conference calls, emails—even YouTube postings—were swiftly used to reach as many people as possible.
>
> At the end of the first week, the team gathered initial reactions and devised a more structured communication programme.

## OPEN YOUR HEARTS AND SHARE THE PAIN

The first thing the Learning World did was to open the communication channels within the organization—it was like cutting open the veins to let the blood flow, to get past the clots that had formed due to shock and anger. 'We've got something which is called Planet Satyam here,' says Dr Khanna. 'It is a radio and TV station, the first of its kind which was ready at that point of time.'

Planet Satyam consists of two rooms. When you enter it, you see a room with three work stations. This room leads you to a black box, which is actually a TV studio with two sofas facing a teleprompter and a camera (a Sony HDV). It is a three light set up and there is a corporate backdrop behind the sofas.

'We said let people express their feelings the way they are,' Dr Khanna recollects. 'Let's not hide it, let's not camouflage it. So, we, some of the members of the Learning World, just went there and started talking very, very honestly as to what we were going through. That was broadcasted right cross the globe, to the centres where the connectivity was present. We said this is what's going on, this is what's happening to our families, this is what our spouses said, this is what our children said, this is what I read in the morning, and so on. So, very honestly people started sharing (their stories). That was the first thing that we did. It started three to four days after Raju's resignation.'

'Then people started saying yeah, yeah, we can also connect with you. My parents also said why did this happen. So, there were conversations that started building. That was the starting point; people then started huddling together and saying similar things, sharing, expressing.'

---

### WALKING INTO A CRASH SITE

For the first few days after Raju's resignation, Satyam appeared like a crash site to Hari T., the company's Chief Marketing Officer. Every day that he went to office—it seemed as though he was walking into a place where there was a big pile up and what he and other Satyam leaders found themselves doing was, in some cases, pulling out people from broken-down vehicles. There were local leaders who were standing by and trying to restore a semblance of order. There were people who were actually helping people, without anyone thinking who the boss was. They were all busy figuring out how to stabilize the scene.

While the government-appointed board had a set of challenges such as generating cash, Hari and others were struggling to reach out to different customers of the company, briefing them on the developments in the company and assuring them of uninterrupted service. Then, there were some leaders who were dealing with how to communicate with the associates, and kill all the rumours which abounded. The rumour mill was working overtime then.

The rumours were emerging from the markets. Every day, new ones reared their heads, adding to the already charged atmosphere at Satyam. So quashing the lies became the number one priority for Hari and his team.

He established a programme by which, irrespective of which part of the world he was in (and that meant sometimes two or three o'clock in the morning), every day at 6 am or 6.15 am IST, he would have a call with his communication team at the Satyam headquarters. This was a two-member team which would collect all the newspapers, scan for all the news items, categorize them into truths, half truths, and lies. By 7 am when he would finish the call, he would have conceptualized and articulated Satyam's response to every news item that appeared. He would then, before people came to the office at 8.30 or 9 am that day, have this note go out on to the website called *Rumour Squashed*.

The communications team would start with *Rumour Squashed*—the website would clearly categorize which was the news item, which was the rumour, and then state the reality. That became like a huge reference document for everyone. Satyamites would come in, look at it, and use that to counter allegations from their customers, their families, etc.

Indraneel Ganguli (known as IG) from the marketing and communications department was part of this team. There was J.P. Sahu from the same department who was Hari's programme manager in this whole exercise. He had a three-member team. They would collect all the data and make sure that everything was in order.

There were two major elements to the communication plan:
- The strategy on what needs to be done
- The platform through which Hari's team communicated

Planet Satyam provided the Satyam leaders an opportunity to communicate. Through Planet Satyam, they would reach out to all the associates, in India and abroad. For example, it was at Planet Satyam where they established the news reading practice at 6 pm and 9 pm every day. They had a guy who would read the news, which was nothing but a summary of that day's events. Interviews of leaders were also broadcast. It was run like a typical news channel. And people could see the broadcasts on their desktops. This continued for a few weeks.

The Satyam leaders also made Learning World responsible for having focus-group discussions. These discussions were necessary because Satyamites were going through this traumatic and complex experience, and it was affecting their personal lives. Roles and stability of their jobs were the main issues. To effectively deal with these, they arranged for focus-group discussions.

The Satyam leaders also did floor walks in every office. Every business leader, HR leader, and Learning World leader, was involved in floor walks—talking to different parts of the organization about what to do and how to deal with it.

However, before these groups fanned out and communicated, they would consult with the Leadership Council which consisted of about forty of Satyam's leaders, including Hari. They would get on a conference call every day and discuss the day's developments—issues, key messages to be transmitted, etc.

> Clearly, the Learning World had a big role to play in terms of enabling these focus group discussions, in comforting people, and in counselling them.
>
> Planet Satyam belonged to the Learning World but people from the marketing and HR departments were involved in running it. So, irrespective of roles and departments, all Satyamites came together and nobody had any idea where the lines blurred and where they connected. Everybody did everything that was required to make the reconstruction progress seamlessly. [7]

## THE SARAH MODEL

The second action the Learning World took was implementing the Sarah model. 'Each alphabet stands for something,' says Dr Khanna of the model. 'First, there is shock, then there is anger, then there is a lot of resentment—how could this happen to me, my people, and my orgnanization. 'A' stands for action—that is, what's the action that we are going to take, and 'H' stands for hope. So we said what's the action that we could take and we still saw hope in this organization. Can we all come together and take this organization a little further? This is the time for us to be together. So we really promoted this model (SARAH) through lots of conversations—virtual and real conversations, floor walks right across. It was not structured, but there were a couple of leaders doing this and the Learning World played a big role in this.'

| | | |
|---|---|---|
| S | = | Shock |
| A | = | Anger |
| R | = | Resentment |
| A | = | Action |
| H | = | Hope |

## RESTORE

The third thing that the Satyam Learning World did to render a healing touch to the organization was more hands on—it was called Restore.

Restore was a kind of activity-based campaign. 'We put charts right across the rooms, and we said tell us what you are going through,' remembers Dr Khanna. 'What would you like to see this organization doing? What is the kind of message that you would like to give to the CEO of this company? We just put charts and gave post-its to people and everybody put some post-its right across. And then we collated and we said, well, people are going through very similar kind of emotions right now—the fear of who is going to take us over, which organization is going to buy us, are we going to survive on our own, will our own leaders come together and build this organization again.'

Besides these organization and leadership-related questions, the question that was at the forefront of every employee's mind was that of job security. 'People who had lots of EMIs (Equated Monthly Installments with banks) in their kitty—how were they going to survive,' says Dr Khanna. 'The first thought was security. Will my job remain or will my job go? I think that was the fundamental question on everybody's minds. For the junior guys, it was okay as they all started applying elsewhere. *Monster.com* and *Naukri.com*—all got flooded with resumes. At a given point of time, there were almost 30,000 resumes floating in the market.'

---

**REACH OF SATYAM'S COMMUNICATION PROGRAMMES**

'About 60 percent of the company's associates received communication instantly, in real time, during the first two weeks; the balance received them after some delay. Through the innovative use of internal broadcast and print media, however,

> we achieved 90 percent real-time reach within an additional two weeks.
>
> The company was able to reach some 4,500 associates, housed at subsidiaries, customer locations, or certain development centres by using their team leaders as a channel.
>
> Each communication trigger was forwarded or chain mailed using web-based networks as well as informal meetings.
>
> To enable reach from home-office computers, Satyam developed a password-enabled Extranet which could host on-demand rich content.'

## THE RISE OF THE PHOENIX

The fourth thing the Learning World did to inspire its staff was to run a motivational campaign called the Rise of the Phoenix. 'It was a series which was talking about how organizations had undergone crises like this, how did they evolve, how did they reset themselves,' explains Dr Khanna. 'What did they do? Like Johnson & Johnson and Arthur Anderson—we gave a lot of stories like these. We did a lot of research; we pulled out literature; we started talking about it, telling people that our organization is not the only one that has gone through (a crisis), there are many organizations that have gone through it and they have survived. So, in the SARAH model, hope—why can't we survive if we work together—was what the Learning World gave people. We travelled right across, we told people that this will pass. The dark clouds are there, but there is a silver lining. Anything that comes also goes, and anything that goes down definitely has to come up. These were some of the fundamental messages that we started giving. We said we will reboot ourselves after sometime. And then every day, we read the newspapers, hoping somebody would buy us, and we hoped for the opportunities to grow and rebuild ourselves. Satyam had always been known for resilience—the ability to bounce back.

We did that when there was recession around 2001—people were pessimistic and they said they were not sure if they would be able to move beyond the Y2K phase of the company.[8] I think that's the role the Learning World played of a good counsellor at that point of time. It held people together. It didn't let people drift apart.'

'We looked at some positive people who could work as change agents, who would be the messengers of positivity even when there was a deep crisis; that's something we did.'

All of this happened during the first three to four month period—between January 9 and April 30. This was the story of the first ninety days, after the crisis hit. 'This period was truly critical for all of us,' Dr. Khanna recalls. 'I think we worked the maximum during that time. When people said there was no work, the Learning World was actually working 24/7. There were phone calls coming even late in the night. People were asking what's going to happen. The second question was: I am holding so many stocks, what's going to happen to my stocks? Some had bought accounts, some had stocks in their DMAT account, some had exercised it, and some of them had not. Just days ago, people felt they had a lot of money, and after the crisis, suddenly they felt like paupers. There were lots of questions; there was a financial crisis and an emotional crisis; people starting falling ill; some of them started complaining of blood pressure, chest pains, and all that. So, there was also a lot of medical help that was provided.'

While all this was happening, Planet Satyam was working round the clock, too. It was operational right across the organization. Every member of the Learning World's team was active—in Chennai, Pune, Bengaluru, and through Satyam's HR representatives all over the world. 'We were having weekly and fortnightly calls,' says Dr Khanna. 'People were allowed to ask any questions that they had. And the questions were about survival and jobs, how much time we have, the customers were going away, the projects were not there, will you remove people and so on.'

## WEEK-WISE PROGRAMS DATELINE

| Dateline | Program | Frequency | Lead |
|---|---|---|---|
| Week 1 | Floor Walks | Daily | Human Resources |
| | Mailer from Head HR | Daily | Human Resources |
| | Help Desk | 24x7 | Human Resources |
| | Mailer from Head, Marketing | Daily | Marketing & Communications |
| | Conference calls within teams | Daily | All Units |
| | AIC Communication | Regular | Unit Heads |
| Week 2 | 'SURF THE BOARD'—Board Member broadcasts | 24x7 | Associate Task Force (ATF) |
| | 'BREAKING NEWS'—Associate communication on appointments updates | Regular | ATF |
| | 'NEWSTODAY'—e-paper to all associates on daily updates and rumour quashing; extended to the WEEKLYNEWS | Daily & Weekly | Marketing & Communications |
| | 'NEWSTODAYLIVE'—10 minute news bulletin on Planet Satyam on daily updates and rumour quashing | Daily | ATF & Satyam Learning World |
| Week 3 | 'VOICE OF THE LEADERSHIP'—a series of mailers and embedded video bytes carrying messages from Satyam's Leaders | Daily | ATF |
| | 'DIRECT FROM THE MEDIA'—embedded video bytes carrying interviews of Satyam's Leaders & Associates | Regular | ATF |
| | 'FROM THE CEO'—a three part series from the new CEO | Once | ATF |
| Week 4 | 'FROM THE CHAIRMAN'—a three part series from the new Chairman | Once | ATF |

Source: Getting the word Out, Satyam Computer Services.

Besides the anxieties arising out of Satyam's uncertain future, there was something else that was affecting the Satyam associates. It was the changed attitude of the public at large.

People had started disowning Satyam employees. The same Satyamites who were welcomed everywhere (shops gave them special discounts), became recipients of pity and ridicule. Some even pooh-poohed them for the dire straits they were in. 'It was not a good sign,' says Dr Khanna. 'We used to walk with a lot of pride, with our badges, that we are Satyamites.' But the scandal changed that and it affected the proud Satyam associates. 'Suddenly, you started seeing people talking about the organization and the people like "oh, this person works with Satyam?" The police ceased to charge poor Satyamites. I remember lots of guys coming and telling us, "Ma'am, when I said I am a Satyam employee, the policeman said, 'Poor Satyam fellow, let him go, I don't know whether he is going to get his salary or not'." There was sympathy, there was compassion from some quarters, and there was rejection from others. Everybody went through this combination of feelings. So while people said things like why did this happen, this shouldn't have happened, there were others who said they are responsible, so probably they all deserved it.'

Another repercussion of the crisis that affected employees was that the banks stopped giving them credit. Once the Satyam scandal broke, banks reduced the credit limits of the tainted company's employees. 'Suddenly, you got a message saying that your credit limit had become zero,' says Dr Khanna. 'Overnight, thousands and thousands of employees got that message. That was shocking. They thought, "I have nothing to do with the scandal, why am I being penalized? I am a simple employee".'

In mid January, news came that a week before, Satyam employees in the US received a letter from Northwest Federal Credit Union that their credit card accounts had been terminated. This was, of course, denied by a Satyam spokesperson.[9]

Similarly, Satyam employees in the US reportedly found that they were ineligible for insurance. They were provided health insurance by Great-West Healthcare (now acquired by insurer Cigna). A New York-based employee alleged that the management had failed to inform staff that they were no longer eligible for health insurance. Again, Satyam clarified that it was not the case. The company spokesperson said that health insurance for US employees had not been cancelled and that the insurer was just conducting a brief re-verification process.

It was only after some time that the credit limits of Satyam associates in India were restored, says Dr Khanna.

## LOWEST EMOTIONAL POINT

As a consequence of the scandal, Satyam's employees went through financial crisis and emotional trauma. Many Satyam employees had taken EMI-based loans for their houses and cars. Some had taken study loans and were worried about repaying them. How were they going to do it? Their worries were well founded. Even if they got a job, they would be absorbed either at the same salary or at a much lower salary. This would affect their capacity to repay the loans. Many people just wanted to get out—they turned suicidal. 'The lowest was, "Oh my God, how am I going to survive?"' remembers Dr Khanna. '"I have ageing parents at home. And if I don't have a job for a month or two, how am I going to survive?" That was a very difficult time for people.'

According to Dr Khanna, the scandal had driven some people to the point of suicide. 'That was the lowest point,' she says. 'People said I don't know (what to do), I have loans. Mostly it was about EMIs.'

The *Times of India* published the grim news of the suicide of a Satyam employee on January 15:

**'Satyam employee commits suicide fearing job loss'**

'Apparently fearing that he may lose his job, a 23-year-old employee of scam-ravaged Satyam Computers allegedly committed suicide here, police said. Vishwa Venkatesan, hailing from Salem, yesterday consumed poison.

He was referred to the General Hospital where he died, they said.

Fear of losing his job drove him to take the extreme step, they said. Venkatesan had earlier also made similar attempts after the scam broke out early this month but was saved due to the timely action, police added.'[10]

When he heard the news of Raju's fall, Rahul Andrews, a leader with the Satyam School of Leadership, felt 'the rug was pulled out from underneath us all'. Being in the leadership school, he was forced to heal rapidly so that he could help others to heal. But the crisis got the better of him. 'I broke down and wept; not once, but several times. Sometimes these were not confined to a private space.'[11]

'A senior executive broke down in tears during a session with his leadership coach, devastated that he had given more than ten years of his life to a company whose CEO had been caught in massive fraud,' remembers Priscilla. 'With just a year to go until reaching mandatory retirement, he had invested most of his savings in the company's stock, which was now worth next to nothing. Another of the company's managers, fifty years of age, received a call from his father urging him to leave the company before his own reputation was further tarnished. A young supervisor realized his impending wedding was at risk when it appeared he might lose his job because of the scandal.'[12] There are thousands of stories like these that are emblazoned on the hearts and minds of those who were there at Satyam when the crisis struck.

'I am a counsellor by profession,' says Dr Khanna. 'My phone never stopped ringing. I couldn't sleep in the night. I was taking tranquillizers to sleep at night.'

At that point of time, most Satyam employees thought their salaries would not be paid. But that never was the case. 'We never suffered from our salaries not being paid even one day late,' says

Dr Khanna. 'The nation was worried about whether we would get our salaries on January 31. All of us were worried. The government came in. They ensured that people got their salaries.'

But even that was not enough to assure people that this trend would continue. 'I think that (not getting salaries) was a very disturbing thought for people. Loss of sleep, acidity, emotional trauma, going to psychiatrists, counsellors, taking pills—all this happened,' recalls Dr Khanna.

'We also started an out-placement cell,' she says. 'For those people who really wanted to look for jobs, we started talking to companies wanting to absorb them. So we trained people on resume writing and on how to face interviews. While there was a lot of intellectual stuff happening, there was lots of emotional stuff happening too.'

## NEVER SAY DIE

If one had to pinpoint one thing—one objective, goal, or motivating factor that kept them going—what would it be? Was it hope?

'It was never say die,' says Dr Khanna. 'When the going gets tough, the tough get going. I think there were some people in the organization who had this hope, who had this fire, who kept kindling it right through and saying, "Yes, it is a tough time but in the tough time, we are all together, and we will wade through these waters together".'

---

### LESSON WELL LEARNT

'The role communications has played in Satyam's survival and turnaround is strikingly clear and vital. We have learnt—again—that, to be effective, communications must encompass the emotional as well as the rational; that credibility requires transparency and directness; that timeliness and consistency are key; and that nature abhors a vacuum—and will fill it with rumour and wild speculation if you don't fill it with fact.'

# AN UNLIKELY CEO
## From Chief Delivery Officer to Chief Executive Officer

*I was never ever groomed as a likely CEO or a successor.*
—A.S. Murthy, interim CEO, Satyam

*January 17–February 5, 2009*
*Hyderabad*

If Raju's sudden departure was a shock for the soft-spoken A.S. Murthy (known as ASM), he was to receive another jolt on February 5. But this time it was a different kind of shock.

Murthy, who was then the chief delivery officer at Satyam, suddenly found himself elevated to the position of interim CEO. 'Extensive board discussions over the past few weeks made it clear that the new CEO should come from within,' said Satyam board member, Deepak Parekh. 'ASM, an extraordinary executive with widespread support among all stakeholders—internal and external—will do an exceptional job leading Satyam at this critical juncture.'

ASM has a deep understanding of the organization and proven management expertise; he has led a business unit, overseen global delivery, nurtured customer relationships, and spearheaded the entire human resources function. Moreover, he is extremely well respected for his ability to integrate teams and foster collective decision making—critical skills as Satyam continues to revive.'[1]

Since Satyam's new board had decided it, Murthy accepted the job with his trademark modesty. 'This is a unique opportunity to provide direction and guidance and I accept it with all humility,' he said. 'I have no misgivings about the enormity of the task in front of us, but I am confident Satyam can accomplish great things—now and well into the future. I look forward to working very closely with the board, our advisors, and all Satyamites, to restore Satyam to its well-deserved glory. Our immediate priority is to chart precise and practical thirty, sixty, and ninety-day plans that encompass and address the interests of all stakeholders.'

Even though he had accepted this enormous challenge, he was, in his own words, an unlikely, even a reluctant, CEO.

'All my background was in technology, in technical leadership,' says Murthy. 'I was never ever groomed as a likely CEO or a successor. For me it came all of a sudden. With a few minutes' notice, they just told me that we want you to lead it (Satyam).'

Murthy had joined Satyam in 1994 as head of delivery and led the company's largest business unit. At the time of his promotion, he was head of Satyam's Leadership Development Group. In that role, he developed strategies and programmes to enhance 'associate delight'—in Satyam's parlance, associate delight refers to measures related to employees' happiness and welfare. The Real Time Leadership Centre, the Satyam School of Leadership, the Satyam Learning Centre, and Business Facilitation Group were under his purview. He was also responsible for Satyam's global delivery and information security; he oversaw human resources and was a member of the apex committee.

His reluctance to become a CEO arose out of two concerns: he was not comfortable with finances and he had no training in dealing with the media. 'I frankly admitted that I had no finance background because as a CEO of a company, you need to have a comfort level with finances, especially with this kind of a state of affairs (was prevalent at Satyam), and we needed to interpret various data elements and then talk about it to the media.'

At the time when the Raju episode happened, media interest in Satyam was at its peak. 'So I was not expected to know more about finance or media management—because media has a lot of interest in trying to know every hour what's happening in this company.'

The board understood his dilemma. They assured him that he only needed to concentrate on customers and employees. The board said that they would handle finance and investor relations. 'So at the Board of Directors level, they had told me that you just make sure that customers are protected, customers are retained, and good associates don't leave you,' he recalls. 'Projects should continue—that was a major expectation of me. As long as I talk to the customers and I make sure that delivery is fine, that was good enough. That's where my strength lies too. My strength is with people. I was the HR head of this company for seven years. Hari T.[2] was working for me. I have no HR credentials either but it's your interest in human resources and things like that (that matter).'

Murthy's HR background also helped him in running the company as an interim CEO. He was involved in the recruitment of all the senior people in the last fifteen years or so. Among his many accomplishments at Satyam was how he had led efforts to align the company's HR organization more closely with the company's business goals. Before becoming CEO, he was transforming Satyam's approach to leadership development and talent management.[3]

As an interim CEO, his job was to talk to the customers, and present to them the actual position of the company. 'I tried to plead with them that give us a chance and give us some time and we will be all right,' he says. The other major component of his job was to participate in the board meetings and try to understand the big picture.

Maintaining delivery excellence levels was not unusual for Murthy. Perhaps what was unusual was attending the board meetings that were held at least once a week. 'These were day long meetings,' he remembers. 'Various issues were discussed. I used to go and tell them about the projects, the customers, any new customers who wanted to leave, whether we were bringing in any new business, and whether we were able to retain the employees. From these two dimensions, I was giving them up-to-date reports. To the credit of our associates, they were delivering everything. So, I always had positive things to report to the board.'

As an interim CEO, it was important that Murthy make some efforts to meet his customers. 'I went to Australia, Singapore, the US—because seeing is believing,' he says. 'When a new CEO goes and talks to them (Satyam's customers), they also know what is the way forward and what are you (Satyam) going to do. By that time, by the end of February, it was more or less decided that this company will be sold off because there was no way it was going to run on its own. This was inevitable because of the kind of balance sheet we had. I used to share with our customers very openly that it was a matter of time that a suitor was found for this company. Also, at any point of time when I was meeting our customers, I had only positive things to report to them in terms of their projects. They themselves used to acknowledge that our people were coming to office, and that they had no problems on the delivery escalation, and they used to say that we should continue to do that to stay in the game.'

'They wanted to know only one thing—one or two months down the line, what was likely to happen and what kind of companies were bidding (for Satyam). What was the whole procedure? How long was it going to take?'

## THE LIGHTS-ON APPROACH

'The good thing was that people at the ground level, people who were involved in projects, people who were on the billable jobs, both in India as well as elsewhere in the world, almost in sixty, seventy countries, were actually operating,' says Murthy. 'Almost all the people were working on the projects. That was a very positive thing. At the end of the day, if you recall and recollect, they carried on with the projects without exactly knowing what was likely to happen. Maybe they were discussing the issues with their fellow workers but the actual operations never stopped. The satellite communications links were working, people were going to their clients' premises onsite, and people here in India were also working.'

'Because of this lights-on approach (uninterrupted service to customers), customers did not see anything affecting their day-to-day work. This kind of uninterrupted service to customers continued for several days, and even for several weeks. Ultimately, the delivery excellence which was demonstrated by Satyam was the one factor which put us back on the rail actually,' concludes Murthy. 'That is the single most important thing, because if the customers started seeing people leaving, not finding the people in office, then there was no way they would have continued (with us). Even the customers who left us, I am 100 percent sure they have not experienced any delivery problems.'

---

**DELIVERY WAS ALL THAT MATTERED!**

It was in January 2009. Incidentally, just before the Raju scandal broke out, Raju had visited the US. At the time B.K. Mishra was managing a strategic customer engagement—one of the largest oil and gas customers. 'I was the account executive, so I was managing the P&L for that account,' he says. 'It was a large account, US$45–50 million, in the Bay area. Raju visited me almost two-three months back to meet the chief information officer (CIO) because whenever he used to visit the US, we arranged those CIO meetings. That was the time when the CIO appreciated Satyam and its management, all the things we had done, corporate social responsibility, and so on. After that we came back to India and the Maytas episode happened.'

'I was in the US at that time and managing a customer business,' he recalls. 'Somebody called me and then I saw it (news about Raju's fraud) in the *Economic Times*. We were terribly shocked. That was when I felt we needed to do something to sustain the business. In that moment, the idea was that what we can do to keep the business going because there were around 700 people working with me in that customer engagement. What could I do to keep these 700 jobs? Guess what, some of the employees were onsite—they were working in the premises of the customers. We were not sure if some of them would get their next pay cheque. We were very worried that the customer will pull the plug. When this (the Raju episode on January 7)

> happened, in the next one or two days, my customer's entire leadership, including the CIO, were sitting in the room. They had to decide whether they should continue with Satyam. Should they look for alternatives? How long can they wait? Two days, fifteen days, one month, two months? They wanted to hear it from me: what did I think of the situation. I told them that I had served as an account executive of Satyam in this business for the last five years. I reassured them that if the boat was going to sink, I would be the last person to jump. I'd ensure that their business was not impacted. If Satyam collapsed, I would ensure that their business was transferred to the right partners and only after that happened I would leave that place.'
>
> Mishra's confidence and words of assurance did the trick. 'Not only did we keep the business, but we managed to grow it another 20 percent. And it was because of the resolve, the passion, the spirit...,' he says.
>
> 'That was a real test of leadership. And I am very glad, very proud that I lived up to that crisis and managed that crisis very well. Today, when I look back, the customer business that I was managing, that is still part of my business.'

How did this miracle of autonomous action happen? Was it conveyed to the employees that they had to continue the delivery excellence or was it something they did on their own? Were they, the associates, working in a default mode?

According to Murthy, it happened because of two reasons: one was the way Satyam was organized in terms of teams and operations, and the other was the economic climate of that time. In hindsight, perhaps the global recession was a good thing for Satyam's survival.

For the people at the lowest level, their job was important to them. 'At that point of time, luckily, there were not enough jobs in the country (India) for the first time,' Murthy says. 'If you look at the last twenty years, that was the worst period for employment opportunities in this country. There were no jobs and recession was going on. So people wanted to cling onto their jobs. People must would have started applying for jobs but they did not want to take the risk of leaving abruptly. There was no reason for them to leave without something else in hand actually. So, for them to continue, they needed to contribute. That in a way was a silver lining. The recession and not having job opportunities for almost six months helped us to retain them especially at the junior-most levels.'

In fact, there was a third factor too, according to Murthy—the media's negative campaign against Satyam. The media's stance acted as a galvanizing force for the Satyamites. They wanted to prove that they were untouched by any corruption and could excel in performance, despite the stigma brought to the company's name by Raju's accounting fraud.

The media's provocative stance against the company also became a push factor for the Satyam employees, and affected their performance, believe it or not, positively.

'People wanted to prove the point that as far as we are concerned and the projects are concerned, we are absolutely good,' says Murthy. 'Because a lot of provocation happened in the media and the media said things like Satyam is not a good company; that Satyamites are fraudsters, that kind of stuff—it affected people. So they took in the rubbing and they took it personally and ensured that at the level of each project, things were fantastic.'

In fact, for the first three months, there was hardly any attrition at Satyam and productivity levels actually went up. There was zero attrition at onsite locations, especially in the US. 'Customers were really seeing all the people coming to office and their contribution,' says Murthy. 'As far as they were concerned, they had absolutely no knowledge about the fraud or whatever it was. They knew the technology, they knew who to go to, and how to get the work completed. So customers used to tell us, we don't know what happened but the productivity levels had started going up in those two-three months.'

The results were quite pleasing for the Satyam management. They started getting appreciation emails from the customers.

The customers said everything was going fine with their projects. 'If at all some customers left,' he says, 'the decision that was taken was that of their boards. Because for a financial services company or an insurance company, the board must have decided not to work with a company which was fraud hit, and not because a project was going wrong.'

The customers who decided to leave Satyam's fold were dealt with delicately.

'Then too, we did everything that was possible to ensure that a customer was not getting affected,' he says. 'When a decision was taken and communicated to us—saying that we had to hand over a project to XYZ company, an IBM, an Accenture, an Infosys, or a Wipro—we were extremely professional about it. We told our associates that we would also try to make sure that when a project is transferred to some other company, most people would also get transferred along with the project. Because if the people stayed on and the projects had gone, who would pay their salaries? At that time, we were not very sure about our bank accounts. So our interest was that customers should not be affected and at the same time, to some extent at least, the employees also should go smoothly (over to the other side) so that they are also having the jobs.'

Cooperating with the customers was a priority for Satyam. 'First we tried to request the customers to stay with us,' says Murthy. 'When they have taken a decision that they have to leave, then we cooperated to make sure that their projects are not getting affected in the transition period. And to the extent possible, the people were also transferred along the projects. So whoever has inherited this project are not without people. They have the same people actually. That is the reason that in the three-four month period, nowhere has anybody complained that the transition wasn't proper or because of the Satyam problem, a customer started suffering. Not even a single customer out of our six hundred-plus customers have aired the view that there is a problem.'

That is no mean achievement for a company working in the IT services market. 'Even today, after three years, if you go back and talk to any of the customers who left us, I am sure they will have positive things to say about us. The way we have conducted ourselves, the way we helped them in the transition, and till the last minute how the delivery excellence was protected, those were the kind of things that we are very proud of. Our customers have recognized that and they have shared that with us.'

> Between January 17 and February 5, when ASM was appointed the CEO of Satyam, the board took many important decisions. It created an audit committee comprising Mr T.N. Manoharan (Chairman), Mr C. Achuthan, and Mr. S.B. Mainak. It also appointed Brahmayya & Co., a Chennai-based accounting firm, as internal auditors. Brahmayya & Co. was engaged to review day-to-day internal operations while Deloitte and KPMG focused on helping the board restate Satyam's accounts. Also, Amarchand & Mangaldas & Suresh A. Shroff & Co., one of India's premier law firms, was appointed as legal advisors to the board.
>
> The board directors met again on January 22 and 23 in meetings chaired by Tarun Das, and focused on ensuring Satyam's business continuity. The board said that Satyam was in the final stages of arranging additional funding to help cover operational expenses, including salaries and vendor payments, through March. The board said it expected to secure funding soon. The directors also said that collections from receivables had been robust.
>
> Additionally, the board announced that it had narrowed its list of candidates for chief executive officer and chief financial

officer to three each, and would be announcing appointments to these positions in the following week.

In the interim, board members had spoken to almost two dozen key customers and were sending personalized, direct communication to all key customers, articulating recent positive developments, to restore their confidence in Satyam.

'There is a pronounced shift in customer attitudes—from alarm in the initial days to a sense of cautious optimism,' said board member Kiran Karnik. 'Actions we have taken, and those we plan, are having a distinct impact on customer confidence.'

Furthermore, the board said it was closely monitoring customer attrition; no material impact has been seen thus far. On the employee front, Satyam leaders increased and enhanced interactions with associates at all levels to understand their concerns and update them about developments. Associate attrition also remained well under control. 'Associates continue to show great resilience and exceptional commitment towards Satyam and its customers during these challenging times, in spite of the sustained media onslaught,' Das said.

The board members met again on January 26 and announced the appointment of Goldman Sachs and Avendus as the company's investment bankers. The board also appointed the Boston Consulting Group (BCG) as management advisors. Three senior BCG representatives were to work closely with Satyam's board and leadership team to spearhead the organization's revival. 'It is important to note that BCG will not charge a fee for their services. This reflects their commitment to the task on hand,' said Satyam board member, Deepak Parekh.

The board also said that the company's immediate operational expenses would be managed and January salaries would be paid as scheduled from internal accruals and receivables. They also validated Satyam's headcount. Sufficient data now proved that that numbers reported earlier were accurate.

The board also revealed that outsiders were showing interest in Satyam. 'The board has received several proposals from corporate entities and from private equity firms,' said board member T.N. Manoharan. 'Some are interested in evaluating Satyam as an integrated entity, while others have expressed interest in portions of Satyam's business. However, selling "parts" of Satyam would be contrary to the Indian government's mandate regulating the company's affairs as a going concern. Therefore, we are not currently considering that option.'

Larson & Toubro had bought 12 percent in the company from the market. Manoharan was circumspect about this move by L&T. 'The reasons for that move would be best explained by the buyer,' he said. 'At this stage, it should not be taken as an indication of support by the government-nominated board for a change of control at Satyam. The board has received an adequate number of bidding interests. As such, in consultation with SEBI and the Indian Government, it will devise appropriate, fair, and transparent measures to enable open bids. It is important to remember that Satyam is a government-administered company, reporting to the Company Law Board and the ministry of corporate affairs.'

In the meanwhile, Satyam leaders and the board continued to reach out to customers to ensure business continuity. 'I speak with quite a few customers and partners every day, and it is heartening to note that they continue to engage with us, confidently,' said board member Kiran Karnik. 'While a few are discussing risk-mitigation plans, most are monitoring our performance closely and want to see Satyam return to long-term sustainability.'

Interestingly, several key customers had sent strong messages to other service providers asking them to refrain from poaching

Satyam's associates or business. A steady improvement in statement of work extensions was also revealed.

Manoharan said these actions reflected Satyam's determination to restore stakeholder confidence, ensure stability and growth, and 'bring back the glory Satyamites truly deserve'.

On February 5, along with the announcement of appointing A.S. Murthy as Satyam's CEO, the board made two more appointments: Homi Khusrokhan, the former managing director of Tata Chemicals, and Partho Datta, the former finance director of the Murugappa Group, as special advisors. These experienced executives were to lend their expertise to Satyam's management and finance areas, respectively. The special advisors, along with Boston Consulting Group, were to work pro bono and help Murthy and the board define and executive key strategies.

The board also confirmed that it had secured approximately US$130 million in financing, which would be directed toward working capital requirements.[4]

# A MARRIAGE MADE IN HEAVEN
## Tech Mahindra Acquires Satyam

*The takeover by Tech Mahindra, a much smaller company, did not come about without its share of anxieties. But this is a classic case of a public-private partnership that worked well. Not just in India, but anywhere in the world. The proactive role played by the government was really amazing.*
—Kiran Karnik, chairman of the government-appointed board of Satyam

*April 13–June 24, 2009*
*Mumbai and Hyderabad*

Early morning on April 13, Kiran Karnik, the Chairman of the government-appointed board of Satyam, walked into the Taj President Hotel in South Mumbai. A hall had been booked there for the entire day. Today, Satyam was going to be auctioned off.

As Karnik entered the premises of the hotel, two Indian television reporters accosted him. They wanted a sound bite. However, the establishment's security guards were quick to turn them out of the hotel.[1]

This was one of the most important days in the Satyam saga when the beleaguered company was going to change hands. Who would get Satyam? No one knew.

The company's board members hoped that the sale would be completed by the afternoon. Karnik had to take a flight back to Delhi the same day and Tarun Das was to board a flight for the US that night. However, they were ready to stay put for as long as it was necessary.[2]

Kiran and his fellow board members had been looking forward to this day. They had been working hard for the last three months preparing for it.

In the last three months, the board had essentially achieved success on two major fronts: one, board members had convinced Satyam's clients to stay with the company, and two, they had been able to instill confidence in the company's employees. Staff salaries were being paid on time and some clients were, on the board's request, talking to the Satyamites to boost their self belief. A.S. Murthy's appointment as the interim CEO had also gone down well with both

Satyamites and the company's clients.[3] A dipstick survey conducted by the company revealed that employees' anxiety had dropped after eight weeks.[4] All these were remarkable achievements and proof of the board's hard work and grit of the Satyamites.

The cherry on the cake was the extra income of US$250 million that Satyam had brought in during this period. 'The indomitable spirit of Satyamites has helped us to win new purchase orders (POs) and work extensions totalling over US$250 million since January 7, 2009,' said A.S. Murthy, CEO, on February 21, 2009. 'The recent successes include a single order of US$50 million and multiple orders from across industry verticals, technologies, and geographies, reflecting an all-round positive trend. More than half of this value comes from new POs, which reinforces the confidence that customers have been sharing with us in our discussions.' As Satyam's delivery and service standards went up, customer attrition stayed within the 5 percent range.[5] Under the guidance of the board, the condition of the patient was certainly improving. Commenting on this development (income of US$250 million), Kiran Karnik, Chairman of the board said, 'The board is satisfied with the progress of the company's stabilization programme and appreciates the sustained efforts of Satyamites that has helped the company's revival on a fast track mode.'[6]

Good deeds speak for themselves. The news of Satyam's steadfast recovery was reaching the ears of the high and mighty in Delhi. Progress in Satyam was being monitored at the highest level. Prime Minister Manmohan Singh was keeping a personal watch on it with the help of Cabinet Secretary, K.M. Chandrasekhar. When Satyam faced doom after Raju's resignation, Singh had publicly stated that Satyam was too big to fail and that its rescue must not get embroiled in inquiries being undertaken by various government agencies.[7]

The Ministry of Corporate Affairs was happy with the new board's work and they wanted the board members to continue working for at least six to twelve months. The board, however, had a different course of action in mind. They wanted a permanent solution to the problem and that meant allowing another player to own and manage Satyam.

A section of the government, no matter how well meaning, was not ready for Satyam's quick takeover or merger with another company. The giants on the Satyam board—Deepak Parekh, Tarun Das, and Kiran Karnik—pulled up their socks to charm the government with their convincing chops. 'Unlike the old days, when most companies were in the manufacturing sector with tangible assets such as land and building which would only appreciate in value, Satyam was an IT company, its assets were its human resources and intellectual property. The best analogy I could give the government was that of fruits and vegetables—how with time and little care and nurturing, they perish and carry no value,' said a board member who did not wish to be quoted. The ministry finally came around the board's viewpoint.[8]

Before Satyam could be palmed off to a new buyer, the board had to clear some legal hurdles to ensure a smooth takeover of the company. The capital market regulator SEBI, the Company Law Board (CLB), and the Corporate Affairs Ministry—all came together to level the process of bidding. The CLB allowed the government and the board to identify a buyer. Similarly, SEBI, led by Chairman C.B. Bhave, changed the tough rules governing takeovers. 'It took just a day to do it. Significantly, the amended rules disallow open offers from rival bidders if an acquirer has already made an open offer. It allowed the Satyam board to work out a plan which provides for transparent, open, and competitive process for the continued operation of the company in the interest of all stakeholders and does not favour a particular acquirer. All this happened in eight weeks. The Satyam board made it clear that the acquirer will not be permitted to sell any equity shares for three years from the date of the acquisition.'[9]

By early March, the board had agreed on the sale process of Satyam: it was to be a global bid and investors were expected to have total net assets in excess of US$150 million. Satyam would issue

31 percent shares to the winner; for the remaining 20 percent, the winner would have to make an open offer for another 20 percent. Bidders had to register online by 5 pm on March 12.[10]

Indian businessmen started jockeying and lobbying to acquire Satyam. Amongst the most interested parties were Anil Manibhai Naik, the Chairman and Managing Director of L&T. One of his companies' subsidiaries is L&T Infotech, an IT services provider. With 10,000 employees, this company ranked tenth among India's IT companies.

When Satyam was doing well, Naik wanted to strike an alliance with Ramalinga Raju. That's why he had bought a stake of 4.48 percent in Satyam in 2008. L&T's quantum of shares matched that of Raju's stake in Satyam. Naik wanted to 'co-own and co-manage' Satyam along with Raju.[11]

However, all his plans went awry with Raju's confession of fraud. On January 20, Naik met Anurag Goel, Secretary of the Ministry of Corporate Affairs, and expressed his interest in 'acquiring management control' of Satyam. On January 23, L&T bought 51 million shares of Satyam in two lots, thus increasing its stake in Satyam to 12 percent.

The other interested party was Singapore-based Indian businessman B.K. Modi of MCorp Global Communication. He floated a special entity called Spice Innovation just to acquire Satyam. However, Modi chose to steer clear of the bidding process, citing lack of transparency in the process.[12]

The third contender was Tech Mahindra, from the Mahindra & Mahindra Group. With 23,000 employees, it was India's sixth-largest software exporter. British Telecom was its biggest customer as well as part owner (31 percent stake).

Other noticeable suitors for Satyam were IBM, Cognizant, Wilbur Ross, the Hindujas, and iGate.

Initially, 149 companies registered themselves to acquire Satyam. Out of these, only ten submitted their expressions of interest. The Hindujas and iGate opted out of the race, probably fearing litigation (there were 13 class action lawsuits against Satyam which could have totalled up to claims of US$440 million to US$840 million). The price of Satyam's shares could also have played a role in their decision.

Finally, Monday, April 13 arrived. It was the day when potential suitors of Satyam were to submit their technical and financial bids to acquire the company. The board was to scrutinize the bids and declare a winner.

When the board met in Mumbai on April 13, they were not sure how many companies would actually submit the bids. Finally, three bidders—Larsen & Toubro, Tech Mahindra, and Wilbur Ross—applied to acquire Satyam. Cognizant, which was also in the running, chickened out the night before the meeting (April 13) and did not post a financial bid.

Starting at 9.15 am, the board first went through the technical bids of all bidders—all of them went past the muster. Then Justice S.P. Bharucha opened the financial bids at 11.15 am.[13]

The three bidders had quoted different figures (share prices). Tech Mahindra quoted Rs 58 per share, L&T Rs 45.90,[14] and Wilbur Ross Rs 20. At 11.30 am, Venturbay Consultants Private Limited (Venturbay), a 100 percent subsidiary of Tech Mahindra, was announced the new owner of Satyam.[15]

'Satyam had been driven off course and now it will be reborn with a new investor,' Karnik told the media, sharing the news that Tech Mahindra had emerged as the winner at the auction.[16]

Under the terms of the deal, Tech Mahindra was to acquire a controlling stake of 51 percent in Satyam for Rs 2,889 crore at Rs 58 per share, pegging the total value of the company at Rs 5,665 crore. 'In the first stage, Satyam was to issue 30.27 crore shares to Tech Mahindra, representing 31 percent of the company's share capital. In the second stage, Tech Mahindra will have to mandatorily make an open offer to Satyam's existing shareholders for another 20 percent.'[17]

Between 11.30 am and noon on Monday, Tech Mahindra's winning bid made its way to almost all news channels in India. 'It's official now,' said a TV news reader. 'Tech Mahindra is the winner for Satyam. At the end of a three-month-long process, Tech Mahindra takes the honour.'

Tech Mahindra emerged a dark horse in this process. Most had thought that Cognizant might bid more aggressively but at the last moment, the company had backed out.

That very day, Tech Mahindra's shares went up by 13 percent in reaction to the takeover.

Announcing the winning bid, Kiran Karnik said: 'Today, we have reached a final culmination stage, and though there are a few steps more to go, what it marks is the end of uncertainty.'[18]

'It is a good development. It was an uphill task which we took up. We have been able to bring it to a logical conclusion. We have maintained complete transparency in the process,' said Corporate Affairs Minister, Prem Chand Gupta after the takeover announcement.

However, not everyone was happy with the Tech Mahindra bid. Some IT analysts called it 'disastrous'. In defense, Tech Mahindra Chairman Anand Mahindra said, 'When you are running in a race, you don't look behind who's chasing you. We believe our bid is rightly priced.'

Mahindra knew that Satyam's liabilities could be as high as US$1 billion. However, he bid aggressively for Satyam because, according to Tech Mahindra Director Bharat Doshi, the bid price was determined by the company after taking into account Satyam's liabilities.

Talking of Mahindra's approach, Falguni Nayar, the MD of Kotak Investment Bank (KIB and UBS were Tech Mahindra's advisor on the bid) said, 'They went ahead with their own conviction.' Clearly, it worked in their favour.

The media also applauded the role of the government-appointed board. 'The board needs to be commended for pulling it off,' said a television anchor. 'In just three months they got it out at a reasonably good price. Deepak Parekh and Kiran Karnik can hold their heads high.'

Reacting to the news, Som Mittal of NASSCOM told a TV channel that 'the deal was synergistic for both companies. All three bidders were worthy.'[19]

J.R. Varma, former member of Securities and Exchange Board of India (SEBI), told the media that Tech Mahindra's 'winning the Satyam race was not a surprise. The bid price [at Rs 58 per share] has come within the expected range. There will have to be some realignments of common clients.'[20]

Legal expert Akil Hirani of Majmudar & Co said that 'a potential merger of Tech Mahindra and Satyam may be possible though a merger', and that 'if it does take place, it would happen only after a year'.[21]

'Tech Mahindra has a broader plan for expansion', and the company is seeing an 'opportunity, rather than just taking over Satyam's clients', said Sudin Apte, an analyst with Forrester Research in Pune. He also said that some Satyam clients, however, might be concerned about Tech Mahindra's lack of experience in industries outside of telecommunications.[22]

'The main challenge for Tech Mahindra is to maintain value proposition to Satyam clients,' Apte said. 'Tech Mahindra will get US$800 million to US$1 billion revenues over six-eight months,' he added. 'But it would be difficult for Tech Mahindra to revive Satyam completely.'[23]

## BACK ON ITS FEET

'We will work to restore the reputation of Satyam', said Anand Mahindra, Chairman of Tech Mahindra, after winning the bid.

'I will personally talk to Cisco's Chief Executive Officer John Chambers and Citigroup's CEO Vikram Pandit,' Mahindra told reporters, referring to Satyam's major clients.[24]

'We are happy that Satyam is back on its feet with a new buyer and confident that Tech Mahindra will take it forward. We are also thankful to the government for the tremendous support it has shown in saving Satyam,' said Kiran Karnik after the takeover announcement.[25]

Once the bidding process was over, the board had the challenging task of ensuring a smooth transition. It was not a marriage of equals. 'Tech Mahindra has just 23,000 employees and revenues of about US$1 billion. Six clients account for 85 percent of its turnover. It has taken over a company with 50,000 employees that till yesterday was the country's fourth-largest IT company.' It was a mismatch in terms of numbers.

Obviously, the board members were concerned about these pain points.

Back in Hyderabad, when the merger was announced, the atmosphere at Satyam was that of jubilation. 'It was as if India had won the world cup,' remembers Hari. The announcement was shown on TV in the office cafeteria and people clapped on it, cheering the decision. People were so happy with the takeover that they distributed sweets. Anybody who was associated with Mahindra and Satyam expressed himself or herself on social media. There were lots of comments on how happy they felt.

'The takeover was a good sign,' remembers Hari Babu. 'When Tech Mahindra bought Satyam, there was a lot of positivity around it. At least there was positivity in the sense that Mahindra was a good technology company. The minimum feeling was that at least we were going to get our salaries. So confidence levels went up.'

Like Hari, all Satyamites took a collective sigh of relief. 'It was like (being on) the Titanic,' Renu Khanna remembers. 'Was it going to sink or will someone bring it up? Enter Tech Mahindra. They buy us over and all of us, every day, we were glued onto the TV—who are the new directors who are coming in, what new action is happening, what's going to happen. Finally, Tech M did come in and there was a sigh of relief.'

'The takeover by Tech Mahindra, a much smaller company, did not come about without its share of anxieties. But this is a classic case of a public-private partnership that worked well. Not just in India, but anywhere in the world. The proactive role played by the government was really amazing,' said Karnik.

However, even within Satyam, the news was surprising for some. 'Frankly speaking, till that point of time, many of us, including myself, were not aware of a company called Tech Mahindra,' says A.S. Murthy. 'Really speaking, if you talk about the top few companies in these things, TCS, Wipro, Infosys, and HCL are the kind of names that come to your mind. Because Tech Mahindra is a company which focused primarily on the telecom market. More than 92 percent of their revenues come from that vertical. In my opinion, they had also not widely marketed themselves at that point of time. When we went back and talked among our fellow Satyam colleagues, they were also very surprised. What is this Tech Mahindra company? How big is it? And they were very surprised to know it was already a billion-dollar company at that point of time.'

Still, more than Mahindra or Tech Mahindra or whatever company it was, Murthy says the very fact that some company had acquired Satyam was a huge positive. 'Because till that point of time we were never sure whether somebody would really come for the bidding,' he says. 'All said and done, there were so many complications, legal complications, fraud of unimaginable magnitude, it was a risky thing for any company to come and put a stake. Because as early as April 2009, when the bidding happened, only three months had passed since the January 7 episode. Not much information had actually leaked out. To the best of their abilities, the data room was set up and they talked about number of customers, and invoices, and various kinds of things, but looking at the magnitude of the legal problems (the Upaid case and all that kind of stuff), nobody had any clue about how things were going to get settled. It was a very bold step by Tech Mahindra. So we were happy.'

## REBOOTING SATYAM

After the takeover, Satyam had to move into a new direction. 'We realized that we needed to continue, we couldn't stop,' says Dr Khanna. 'Now it was a big cultural change—the leadership had changed. A whole set of new people were taking over the organization. Some people were still leaving the organization because they were still not sure of its future—they thought, should we stay on or should we go? So people made their personal decisions to stay on or to go off.'

Now that Tech Mahindra had come into the picture and the initial uncertainty about Satyam's future was gone, the next challenge was to kickstart the process of the organization's revitalization.

'We started something called the Reboot,' says Khanna. 'Can we reboot and revitalize the organization? We did this right across. We almost covered all the people. Maybe about 80–85 percent of people within the organization and the key message was, "Yes, it is a new organization, it's a new structure, and change is inevitable. Can we quickly adapt ourselves to the change? Can we understand who are the key people in the organization? Can we come together once again and build the high-performing team because this is the time for us to show that yes, we are together?" This was a simple three-hour module that we created. And it was a physical activity—we put in some quizzes, got the leaders to speak to these guys, and the Learning World did a phenomenal job in connecting people. This went on for almost about six to seven months till the whole reboot started. In the meantime, while finance was recounting and re-auditing all the account, stating the accounts from the people front, the Learning World reached out and did a lot of floor walks, created new material for people, and tried to promote all the new leaders within the organization.'

'We had lost lots of accounts by then, so people were worried whether their job would still remain or not. We said we will build a pipeline (of projects) and make sure that people get something (accounts to work on). All that happened simultaneously. The first three months were much more critical.'

'After the takeover, we felt hope was there. We added 'AD' to the 'SARAH' model. We moved from SARAH to SARAHAD—for aspiration and destination. There is a destination for us. Can we aspire to reach the destination together?'

| | | |
|---|---|---|
| S | = | Shock |
| A | = | Anger |
| R | = | Resentment |
| A | = | Action |
| H | = | Hope |
| A | = | Aspiration |
| D | = | Destination |

Though Vineet Nayyar, Vice Chairman, MD, and CEO of Tech Mahindra (and post-acquisition, the new chairman of Satyam), called the acquisition a marriage made in heaven, the honeymoon for Satyam was yet to commence. A lot of hard work was to be done before anyone could jump into the conjugal bed for some good fun.

While Tech Mahindra set about fixing Satyam after acquiring it, some very top-level executives left Satyam, including Ram Mynampati, the former interim CEO of Satyam. Others who left the company were Deepak Nangia (head of Satyam's Australia unit), Naresh Jhangiani (Satyam BPO Global Head, Human Resources), V. Satyanandam (Head of Corporate Services), and Kulwinder Singh (Head of Marketing, Asia Pacific).

Satyam's Senior Vice Presidents Virender Aggarwal (Regional Business Unit Head for Asia Pacific and Middle East) and Gary Teelucksingh (Senior Vice President for Satyam Americas that includes Canada, Latin America, and the Caribbean region) put in their papers too. Satyam had one of the strongest SAP practices among the Indian IT services companies. It got hit with the departure of key executives such as Krish Kumaraswamy, SAP Technology practice head, and Ramesh Babu, the second-in-command for the SAP business unit.

On May 22, four nominee directors of Tech Mahindra, including its CEO Vineet Nayyar, joined the Satyam board. The other three nominees were C.P. Gurnani, Sanjay Kalra, and Ulhas N. Yargop. With their induction, the Satyam board now had ten members, including the six government-appointed directors.

Along with a new owner, Satyam also needed an image makeover. According to Santosh Desai, CEO of Future Brands, there was a need to rebuild the brand in a real sense—inside out and outside in. After the takeover by Tech Mahindra, the rebranding exercise of the embattled company started. Finally, Satyam was rebranded as Mahindra Satyam.

However, the company clarified that Mahindra Satyam will only be a go-to-market brand, and the company's name would stay the same. 'This rebranding exercise symbolizes an amalgamation of the Mahindra Group's values with Satyam's fabled expertise, even as it retains that part of Satyam's identity which signifies commitment, purpose, and proficiency of the organization and its people,' said Anand Mahindra, Vice Chairman and Managing Director, Mahindra Group, in a statement on June 21, 2009.

On June 24, a very important announcement was made: C.P. Gurnani, who headed Tech Mahindra's global operations, was inducted as the new CEO of Mahindra Satyam and S. Durgashankar as the new CFO. This marked the end of term for A.S. Murthy as the CEO of Satyam. Durgashankar, who was a senior vice president at a Mahindra Group company, filled the shoes of the previous CFO Vadlamani Srinivas, who was now counting his days in prison.

With these appointments in place, Satyam was being ushered into a new phase—a new dawn was waiting to break on this company and its employees. However, doubts still remained about Satyam's resurgence as an IT giant in the Indian IT sector.

Satyam had survived the crash, had found sanctuary in the arms of the Mahindra Group, but the question was: will it regain its place of pride in an industry where trust and reputation are everything?

# THE CAMEL RIDER
## Mahindra Satyam Gets a Chief Happiness Officer

*My biggest concern, to be very honest, was that I didn't know whether I was doing the job right.*
—C.P. Gurnani, CEO, Mahindra Satyam

*June 23, 2009–10*
*Mumbai and Hyderabad*

As the head of global operations in Tech Mahindra, C.P. Gurnani had played a key role in expanding the organization's non-British telecom business. In the last one year or two, he and his boss, Anand Mahindra, had been eyeing to buy a stake in Ramalinga Raju's Mahindra Satyam.

For him, the motivation stemmed from a desire to make Tech Mahindra successful. And the key to achieving that was to not enter telecom services but be in the business of enterprises—providing enterprise solutions and IT services in supply-chain management, client-relationship management, business intelligence, business-process quality, engineering and product lifecycle management, and infrastructure services, among other key capabilities—and the reason was very simple. Some of its large clients served two parts—consumer and enterprise, and Tech Mahindra did not have enough solutions for enterprise.

The second reason was the need to reinvent. 'I am a strong believer that every company needs to reinvent itself every few years,' Gurnani says.[1] 'You know what was good yesterday was only good yesterday.'

He cites his father's example. 'I often say that I am confused whether the life my father led was a better life or the life that I lead is a better life because my father had a 10 am to 6 pm job. For him, travelling was like one day, I mean, it wasn't like fifteen days away in international waters.'

Clearly, Gurnani is a pragmatic person, and nostalgia, no matter how sweet and sepia tinted, is still nostalgia for him. As a major company's global leader, he understands the demands of the present to stay relevant in the future.

That is why he and Anand Mahindra were eyeing Satyam. Mahindra wanted to globalize his firm and for him IT was the first lever to make the company global. They had been in conversation with Satyam, and Raju had given them meeting dates twice but had cancelled them each time.

Raju's attitude had puzzled Gurnani but slowly he began to grasp what was going on beneath the surface of the successful mirage of Satyam.

Around the time when Satyam announced the Maytas merger, Gurnani was flying home from an overseas trip for his annual, end-of-the-year holiday ritual with his family in Delhi. Bloomberg Television called him asking him if he could drop by into their studio. They wanted to talk to him about Satyam. He went over and during the interview, he told them that 'there is everything there but not truth' (in whatever Satyam's chairman was divulging then, defending his decision to merge Maytas with Satyam). Gurnani had smelled a rat in Satyam's closet exactly at that point of time. He clearly knew that there was something there which was not right. 'One tried to piece things together by talking to friends and people in the industry,' he remembers. 'Everybody was a little taken aback with the overall news.'

How did he know what was going on inside Satyam? 'This industry is so well connected that you could constantly poll in data about each other,' he says. 'The reality is people talk about seven levels of separation. In the Indian IT industry, there are one or two levels of separation. We all know each other. So from that perspective, we knew what the company was and what it would do.'

When he got out of the studio that day, he felt lucky. 'The thought flashed through my mind that we had decided to buy Satyam and how lucky we were that we had not bought Satyam three months ago. How lucky we were that Raju cancelled two meetings after initially finalizing them,' he says.

After Raju confessed his crime and resigned from Satyam, both Gurnani and Mahindra knew that buying Satyam was a risk, but they were also very clear (that) without risk there are no gains. Second, Satyam was a great asset. There was no doubt about it. So they kept trying to buy Satyam even after the crisis unfolded.

Months later, when Tech Mahindra finally won the bid for Satyam and Gurnani was named the CEO, it didn't come to the 50-year-old top executive as a surprise. He knew that he will always have the responsibility of leading the company whether he led it as a CEO, a board member, or a supervisor. The board of Mahindra & Mahindra and the board of Tech Mahindra had faith in him because of his past track record.

Gurnani was born in 1958 in Neemuch, Madhya Pradesh, India. His father was an officer in the narcotics bureau. He did his schooling in Chittorgarh, Kota, Rajasthan and received a chemical engineering degree from the National Institute of Technology, Rourkela. In a career spanning over 26 years, Gurnani has held several leading positions with Hewlett Packard Limited, Perot Systems (India) Limited, and HCL. Prior to joining Tech Mahindra, Gurnani was the chief operating officer and a co-founder of Perot Systems (India) Limited, initially set up as HCL Perot Systems. Gurnani has extensive experience in building international business, start-ups, turnarounds, joint ventures, and mergers and acquisitions.

This is quite an illustrious career for an engineer who has had no formal training in management. Interestingly, in his early career, when he got an admission offer from the Faculty of Management Studies in Delhi, he decided not to take it because he was having so much fun in his career.[2]

At 50, Gurnani was heading Tech Mahindra's global operations, sales and marketing functions, and also leading the development of Tech Mahindra's competency and solution units.

When he got the responsibility of leading Satyam, telling his wife to pack their bags for Hyderabad had proved to be the most difficult part of the new assignment. He personally always loved Hyderabad because he had his maternal uncles living there and had been going there for visits since his childhood.

## WALKING INTO A TEMPLE OF LEGACY

On June 23, Mahindra Satyam announced its new CEO. It was C.P. Gurnani.

'Walking into Satyam was like walking into a temple of legacy and I knew that I had to protect the legacy,' he says. 'Ultimately there was so much work to be done. Frankly, I don't think that anyone of us believed or understood this to be a walk in the park. We always knew that this is going to be a good challenging assignment so I did the first address to the leadership. People expected that I would come up and say something like about fixing things as of yesterday and I said it is going to take us three years. A lot of people were disappointed that I gave a three-year time frame. In the IT industry, nobody understands three years.'

'The good news is that as we went along, the number of naysayers reduced because ultimately the culture is still very open, it is still (such that) we challenge each other, but the number of naysayers definitely reduced.'

In his first media interaction, Gurnani said he had four immediate priorities: to strengthen corporate governance, enhance customer delight, regain market share, and build the brand.

'I am delighted to have the opportunity to lead the organization toward those objectives, and I am confident we will succeed,' he said. 'We have a clear vision, world-class leadership, the industry's most talented professionals, ample resources, and an unswerving drive to succeed.'

With his becoming the CEO, Gurnani started a three-part programme to revive Satyam. The first phase of integration, starting in 2009–10, 'went into stabilizing the combined entity— arresting client attrition, ensuring governance in place, right sizing the organization, and steadying the cash flows'. The second phase (2010–11) was focused around investing time and money into 'building confidence among our customers and associates and to clear legal hurdles'.[3]

'Putting right leadership in place and getting the financials back in shape was no mean task. The task was also to rebuild and strengthen legacy core offerings such as enterprise applications and business intelligence and also to invest in areas such as vertical BPO and alternative delivery models such as cloud,'[4] he wrote in an article.

For 2011–12, the company's theme was growth to 'leverage consolidation that we have done so far—profitable growth across portfolios, across verticals and regional focus.'[5]

But going through all these phases was a mammoth task. 'In spite of all the homework, I mean it's like preparing for the Olympics, you still don't know how well you are going be on that day,' he says. 'My biggest concern, to be very honest, was that I didn't know whether I was doing the job right. Internally, I had to question myself many times because morning to evening, from 6 am till about midnight, I would be talking to employees a lot and there were different levels of emotion that I was dealing with through the day. And the level of emotions were sometimes anger, sometimes frustration, somebody saying due to "my lack of promotion I didn't get recognized", somebody saying "I did not get my salary", somebody saying this how far back he is on his house payment, or somebody would talk about dreams and how he was made verbal promises. And then there were games.'

There was also a lot of history that was coming to him. Some brought him complaints, others good advice. Some of his colleagues gave him a list of fifteen things to do. Someone suggested that he should flush out at least 50 percent of the managers, because they would resist the change and right now, change was the first thing he needed to bring into place. 'I am just telling you that there are some guys who are so much brighter and more helpful than their suggestions,' he says. 'I still remember one of the guys Sharad, who…came with a presentation and which basically said that use this opportunity for change management. So the reason why I felt inadequate is that many times I thought I have not been trained as a psychoanalyst… Basically, my strength was coming in from all those guys who came in with good suggestions. I mean fundamentally, I am an optimistic guy and it helps that people like Vineet (Nayyar) are very good sounding boards.'

---

### THE CAMEL RIDER

'One day, there was this group of people who were challenging everything that I was saying. I mean, you call it insecurity, you call it whatever. Then I went through the seven-eight points that they were making and I went to Vineet (Nayyar) to generally have a Saturday morning coffee with him. I put on all the eight points and I said that listen, "I am getting very frustrated and I think we should take such and such steps and so on". He looked at me and said "C.P., do you realize the position you are in? It's like riding a camel. When you ride a camel you are so much high above that you shouldn't bother about dogs barking". You know the folklore, the wisdom that he brought in. He said, "You will take decisions, some will be right, some will be wrong, and people will have a comment. Your job is to make your decisions work. Your job is not to keep looking back and looking at people who are barking". In Hindi, he said, "Chaudhry oont pe chadhiyohe, kuttey to bhaunkenge hi". (When the village head rides a camel, dogs are bound to bark at him.)'

—C.P. Gurnani

---

In his moments of self-doubt, Gurnani drew a lot of strength from his colleagues A.S. Murthy (now Chief Technology Officer) and Rakesh Soni (Chief Operating Officer). 'I drew a lot of strength from a few of the firefighters like Rohit (Gandhi) stepping in because Vir

(Virendra Aggarwal) had decided to leave immediately.' Atul Kunwar, Global Head of Sales, stepped into take over the US operations because again Ram Maynampati had to leave. They moved Keshav Panda from Europe, but ultimately he had his own desires. He was one of the candidates who wanted to be the CEO. So there were changes, and Atul stepping in, Vikram Nair, Head, MSat Europe stepping into Europe, such people taking over the customer interface part, and Vineet (Nayyar) helping a lot in the finance and legal issues gave me enough time to focus on other burning platforms.'

## THE 100-DAY PLAN

Once he had settled in, Gurnani embarked on a ninety-day, hundred-day plan. The first step was to dismantle the organization. The organization had fifteen to sixteen layers of management; it had to be reduced to seven or eight. 'We did a fair amount of work in that direction,' he says.

The second thing was to constitute different task forces. Mahindra Satyam engaged a high-end consulting company, Bain & Company at that point of time and started taskforces on various initiatives. Gurnani also called in one of his ex-colleagues, Padma Parthsarathy, to head those taskforces. They brought in a fair amount of youngsters (the global leadership cadre youngsters) into the company.

The taskforces were about the power of collective thinking. The power of collective thinking meant that as much as possible, the management made sure that the decision points were being done by multiple people together rather than one individual. So, whether it was organizational redesign or bringing sales and delivery together (two in a box model): that was a fundamental decision change.

At the core of these taskforces, the customer was put at the centre of everything. Taskforces were created to find solutions for issues such as how do we reduce the invoicing and processing time to a customer in the new situation, or how do we take capabilities of

Mahindra Satyam to Tech Mahindra customers and vice versa. So, the taskforces looked at leveraging the existing capabilities of the organization and people and deploying them. There were multiple taskforces on different lines. For example, there was a taskforce only focused on collections because the company needed money and needed to figure out why certain money was not being collected and what could be done to make that happen.

Then there were many fundamental staff-related things that needed Gurnani's attention. They had to be set right. Number one was to get data on people. Number two was to right–size the company. They didn't know how many people were there and how many people were required. Number three was to take stock of all the customers. 'In the first hundred days, I had to meet almost hundred customers,' says Gurnani. 'Not only me. Vineet (Nayyar) came to Australia, Anand (Mahindra) went to US, and a lot of other activities were happening parallely.'

One of the painful parts of the restructuring process was to lay off 10,000 people. It was done through the Virtual Pool Programme (VPP).

The total number of Satyam associates on March 31, 2009 was 41,267 as against 45,969 on March 31, 2008. There was a need to bring in a healthy balance between revenues and expenses while retaining the key talent. For this purpose, an innovative proposition called the VPP was launched. This one-time measure was a humane and sensitive approach aimed to achieve the multiple objectives of cost reduction and resource optimization (from a business perspective) while ensuring job continuity for the affected associates. Close to 7,500 associates were placed on VPP.[6]

Once the company was right–sized, Gurnani began to introduce new concepts to give a fresh lease of life to the company. One of the new concepts he introduced at Satyam was that of the Shadow Board (we will discuss the Shadow Board soon in greater detail).

According to Gurnani, two fundamental concepts were introduced in the company. 'One was a big theme around courageous, connected, and agile,' he says. 'Courageous was fundamentally that we are not a hierarchy, you can talk to anyone anytime. Courageous is that if you have an idea, you want to challenge anything you can challenge it. Connected was connect with your customers, and connect with your fellow employees, because communication makes such a big difference in that environment. And agility—no one is perfect. You will make right or wrong decisions but make it at your level.'

The other concept was that of encouraging youth leadership. 'The youngsters of our organization are the game changers, and we must encourage them,' he once told his employees. One of Gurnani's Seven Commandments of Delivery was to 'balance 'experience' with 'experimentation', 'for it is this healthy mix of experienced leaders and young energetic minds (such as the Shadow Board and global leadership councils), that will act as a lever to our success'. 'The need of the hour is an energetic organization, with infinite passion and zeal to make a difference,' he further added. 'This can only come from the young, energetic, enthused and 'raring-to-go' lot and I am quite sure with the guidance of the experienced leaders in this organization, these youngsters will take Mahindra Satyam to the next level.'

### THE STORY BEHIND THE SHADOW BOARD

'Where did I get the idea of Shadow Board from? I don't want to name the person but a senior guy said (that) in the US, he gets up at 5 am and calls up India to understand what's going on. And then he plants a few of his requests and over the period of the day, he monitors them and gets an approval.

'What the shit is this? If you want to do something, you can directly request for a conference call. There are five people involved in a decision because that's the culture we have at Tech Mahindra.'

> 'We don't go around being managed by a few people. We don't have a coterie to manage us. You know that is the way it was—that we call up x guy, y guy and then he gets it. I said this is not going to happen. I mean this is first thing that I need to change.'
>
> 'The biggest part for me was that make the leadership available and accessible. The Shadow Board was just one way of trying to turn around the organization upside down, and basically saying that no manager whether in the US or in Australia, can skip levels. And it is not about me, it is about creating an organization which is not head-office centric and not hierarchical.'
>
> —C.P. Gurnani

Both the concepts, of encouraging openness and giving opportunities to young talents, was part of a cultural change at Mahindra Satyam. That cultural change was a necessity.

Personally, Gurnani tried to change the organization's culture by taking small steps such as penning a blog every fortnight. In his July 16, 2009 blog, he wrote: 'As I step into my new role in the physical world as CEO of Mahindra Satyam, and in the virtual world as a first-time blogger, I am filled with a sense of purpose. A purpose to reach out and connect with each one of you; a purpose to turn Mahindra Satyam around; a purpose to welcome change and be the change agent.'

In his blog posts, he often provided a big-picture view of the company, how the company was being perceived outside, how well it was doing—all meant to enthuse the employees. The employees also reacted passionately to his blogs and many of his posts attracted hundreds of comments on the company's official intranet.

For example, in one of his early blogs, he said he takes himself more as a chief happiness officer than a chief executive officer.

'Over the last few weeks, I have been formally introducing myself as the CEO of Mahindra Satyam,' he wrote in his blog on July 28,

2009. 'And every time I do it, I have been introspecting as to whether it symbolizes what I stand for and what I am trying to do.'

'I have been toying with the idea of calling myself a CHO—the CHO that I am referring to stands for chief happiness officer.'

'In today's stressful age, with all of us multi-tasking and juggling our personal and professional lives, it is all the more important for us to be happy and positive, in order to maintain our sanity. However, just being sane does not get us ahead of the game. In order to be successful today, one needs to have the drive, zeal, and enthusiasm, and all this is possible only when one is happy. As elusive as it may appear, my definition of happiness is being excited about what we have to do—whatever it may be. At Mahindra Satyam, my appeal to our leaders has been to look after the interests of all our stakeholders—in particular, our associates, because together, we represent this happy entity called Mahindra Satyam. At the end of the day, every associate wants to grow, be recognized, have an enriched learning environment, an adequate salary and most importantly, have time for "fun and family". Several of us spend more than ten hours per day at work—probably much more. At the end of it all, we need to have our personal time—for family, friends, and fun.'

In the first ninety days, he had many sleepless nights. There were always those moments of self-doubt but ninety days later, once the team was communicating and talking, he had no doubt in his mind that he had walked out of the darkness. 'The first ninety days were tough because once I had 80 percent of leadership—this is a people business, we have no other product—in place, once I started having weekly calls with them, I knew we would be out of the woods,' he says. 'Frankly, I started sleeping well after those ninety days.'

Within those three months, Gurnani also had to make some personal sacrifices. His son was going to college in the US. He had just finished his high school and his daughter had just finished her undergrad in the US. So he had made plans that they would all go for the graduation ceremony and then they would take a big holiday.

The big holiday obviously didn't happen and he could actually go just for his daughter's graduation for one day.

He thinks his wife made a lot of sacrifices. She had to move houses and 'she had to live with a husband who was never around, either mentally or physically'.

During the turnaround, there were many low points for him. One of the low points was when one of the key employees who had spent endless hours with him on fixing the future state of the world came back and said he was going to leave the corporate world because he didn't want to go through the stress of corporate life. 'You make plans around people, you expect they will shoulder responsibility, and you spend endless hours, you know, planning, convincing, strategizing, and then the guy says, oh, thank you, this is not a life,' he says. 'And why is that the lowest point? Because that was exactly the time when you were having these questions in your mind and this guy said he has analyzed it for money or for anything and that this job is not worth it.'

But there were high points too. 'I think the first quarterly results when we went up and declared restated financial accounts, was a high,' he says. 'Playing sixty-four matches in FIFA and playing them flawlessly was a high. Again you have to take into introspection the point that day. They were more like middle of the journey. Around the same time, the largest chemical company in Europe agreeing to do business with you (that was a high). There are many highs. Then similarly, when some of the ex-employees came back and those who were critical and had left in a huff returned or wanted to join and some of them joined—they were ultimate compliments and they were the highs.'

During the turnaround, there were a few things that Gurnani thinks he could have done differently.

Referring to the layoffs, he says, 'My personal feeling is that on people issues we could have been a lot more decisive. The reason is that we would do a VPP[7] in the best interests of the employees, in the best interest of everything but the problem was these 10,000 people were talking to other 40,000 people and telling them how bad we were. And this went on for six months. The extraordinary efforts it took to counter the 10,000 people, wishing you bad luck, I won't say all 10,000 of them but some of them.'

Second, he thinks he was too paranoid about the stickiness with employees and customers. 'They wanted us to succeed,' he says. 'So the amount of time that I spent on the road during those days trying to communicate the same message, when I look back, out of those 365 nights, I was out for 250 nights. When I look back I think I was over paranoid, overcharged, over energized. I didn't have to. I could have been equally effective sitting and communicating from my office. I didn't have to burn myself out at that stage. That is the second lesson for me, which is basically that like in golf, they say putting too much of energy does not carry your ball. It is actually the smoothness and the way you swing carries that the ball. There is enough strength in your club and shoulders, you don't have to worry about putting so much of pressure. I think we pushed ourselves a little too hard.'

Three, he always felt that he should have never settled with Upaid and carried forward. 'Not because I am questioning that judgement,' he says. 'I am only saying that I felt that the claim was wrong. At that moment, negative publicity was hurting us so much, they took advantage of it.'

Sometimes, he also felt very agitated with the media, because the media in India is in a unique situation: for every news item, there are a few more reporters than necessary. 'Somebody will have some relationship somewhere and somebody will be disgruntled,' he says. 'So when people used to say how effective your whistleblower policy is, I said my whistleblower policy is run by the media. You know who does what right, what wrong.' He says that and laughs. But he also sees a positive side to the media. 'They obviously helped a lot because if you notice, overall the news has been reasonably good, positive, and responsible,' he says.

On September 29, 2010, Satyam Computer Services (now Mahindra Satyam) announced the audited financial results for the financial year 2009 (year ended March 31, 2009) and financial year 2010 (year ended March 31, 2010). This was a major milestone for the new management.

Below are the key financial numbers:
- Revenue was Rs 88126 million and Rs 54810 million in FY '09 and FY '10 respectively
- Loss after tax was Rs 81768 million and Rs 1246 million in FY '09 and FY '10 respectively
- Due to the restatement efforts and the extent of the fraud, there were certain exceptional items in the financial statements
- Exceptional items were Rs 79920 million and Rs 4169 million in FY '09 and FY '10 respectively
- Loss after tax adjusted for exceptional items was Rs 1,848 million for FY '09 and Profit after Tax was Rs 2923 million in FY '10
- Cash and bank balances were Rs 21768 million as on 31st March 2010.
- The loan balance as of 31st March 2010 was Rs 42 crore

'This is one of the most significant milestones for Mahindra Satyam and I must commend Vineet, C.P., and his team for leading the company through challenging times,' said Anand Mahindra, Vice Chairman and Managing Director, Mahindra Group. 'However, our true heroes are the Mahindra Satyam associates across the world, who demonstrated a high degree of passion and commitment to meet global customer requirements. I am certain that tomorrow holds a renewed promise for all Mahindra Satyam stakeholders.'

'With this announcement today, we have fulfilled an important commitment and kept to our promise of transparency and agility,' said Vineet Nayyar, Chairman, Mahindra Satyam. 'It also marks the beginning of a more significant journey of growth and the future. We will inculcate the highest values of corporate governance, for which the Mahindra Group is renowned for, in shaping the future of this organization.'

'With this milestone behind us, we are in a position to commit ourselves with renewed energy to the tasks at hand,' said C.P. Gurnani, CEO, Mahindra Satyam.

## C.P. GURNANI'S BLOG: SOME EXCERPTS

**July 16, 2009: 2.55.39 pm**
**Survival of the Agile**

I have noticed that many things happen to me rather simultaneously—in waves—all at one time, some anticipated, some sudden and eventually, they seem to fall into place. I remember the saying that 'Life is what happens to you while you are busy making other plans'. Very true indeed, considering what all happened to me in the past weeks, particularly over the last fortnight!

I met customers. I met colleagues. I met analysts. I met the media. I met friends, well wishers, and advisers. Across cities—Chennai, Delhi, Mumbai and Geneva, London…and here I am, in the US now, penning a few thoughts…

As I come out of another 'happening' week, one thing is becoming clearer than ever—India surely is recovering faster than many other economies. There is a sense of purpose and strong-hearted leaders are emerging. Grandiose plans are being drawn up—even when many developed countries across the globe are struggling to keep themselves afloat. Large Government plans, projects and opportunities are on the anvil, and quite a bit pertains to our Industry. The National Identity project is just a case in point.

My interface with Mahindra Satyam leaders across technologies, solutions, and domains (SAP, Auto, BI, Futurus) were 'eye openers' and left me inspired. We would however need to remember that while the company has assets, we need customers to sustain and use them. Therefore my overloaded focus on 'customer first' prevails.

As I step into my new role in the physical world as CEO of Mahindra Satyam, and in the virtual world as a first-time blogger, I am filled with a sense of purpose. A purpose to reach out and connect with each one of you; a purpose to turn Mahindra Satyam around; a purpose to welcome change and be the change agent.

Charles Darwin coined the phrase 'Survival of the fittest'. No doubt, this had stood the test of time, and continues to do so. Many people swear by this adage and that probably prompts my unswerving determination to be on the treadmill every day! While this is very relevant, adapting to the changes around us at a great pace is probably more important—I have therefore been talking to all those around me about my new concept—'Survival of the agile'!

I am convinced that in today's day and age, accelerated change and seamless adaptability is the key to success. They are intertwined. Adaptability rests on a strong foundation of change. Examples of change are all around us—the rise and fall of global markets, the change from Satyam to Mahindra Satyam, the positive change in the attitude of customers towards Mahindra Satyam, and the change in the market perception towards Mahindra Satyam—the steady holding of the stock price being a clear indicator ! In a manner of speaking, all of us have changed in some form or the other over the last few months. If anything, these few months have made us even more courageous, connected, and agile. The combination of expertise and leadership within Mahindra Satyam, Tech Mahindra, M&M

and British Telecom, should bolster our resolve to take on the world (storms included!).

While on the topic of storms, today, I see ourselves as the central focal point, within the eye of a storm. Within this vortex, I see us managing multiple stakeholder demands, changing market and customer perceptions, bringing about new realities within our company, and taking difficult decisions that will transform us. None of this would be possible without the three things that I mentioned earlier—courage, agility, and the ability to connect. It is imperative that each of us imbibe these three characteristics, especially in today's day and age.

A telling example of this change was when the distinguished television anchor from CNBC Europe asked me for my opinion (I try to quote verbatim here)—'Mr Gurnani, what would your advice be to the entrepreneurs in Europe to help fight the recession?'. As I answered the question, it struck me that till not so long ago, we were being barraged with a totally different set of questions around our survival. And today, the media slant has shifted from there to us being recognized as a serious player, back in the game. I felt happy. I felt energized.

Let us also not forget that this is possible only with the active support of the people around us—partners, vendors, colleagues, friends, and family. Today, the reason Mahindra Satyam has prevailed is because of the active support of each of its associates and their families. I would like to sincerely thank each and every associate and members of their family, for providing the much-needed rock solid support during uncertain times without which we would not have been able to change and adapt at this pace.

In conclusion, I would like to state that while these are but small steps that we are starting out with—let us all embrace change—after all, it is not just a state of mind. It is a question of survival, isn't it?

Our go forward plan should be that 'Size is not our strategy. Speed is'. And therefore 'survival of the agile' has a whole new meaning now.

CP

PS—I will attempt to blog as often as I can and shall earnestly attempt to respond to your feedback always. I realize that the pressures of work and my travel schedule may make this a challenge, but then, I have always loved challenges!

## July 28, 2009: 3.08.48 pm
## Chief Happiness Officer

Over the last few weeks, I have been formally introducing myself as the CEO of Mahindra Satyam. And every time I do it, I have been introspecting as to whether it symbolizes what I stand for and what I am trying to do.

I have been toying with the idea of calling myself a CHO—the CHO that I am referring to stands for Chief Happiness Officer.

In today's stressful age, with all of us multi-tasking and juggling our personal and professional lives, it is all the more important for us to be happy and positive in order to maintain our sanity. However, just being sane does not get us ahead of the game. In order to be successful today, one needs to have the drive, zeal, and enthusiasm, and all this is possible only when one is happy. As elusive as it may appear, my definition of happiness is being excited about what we have to do—whatever it may be. At Mahindra Satyam, my appeal to our leaders has been to look after the interests of all our stakeholders—in particular, our associates, because together, we represent this happy entity called Mahindra Satyam. At the end of the day, every associate wants to grow, be recognized, have an enriched learning environment, an adequate salary and most importantly, have time for 'fun and family.' Several of us spend more than ten hours per day at work—probably much more. At the end of it all, we need to have our personal time—for family, friends and fun.

All these are geared towards ensuring not just our happiness but that of our stakeholders too. It is this very happiness that is reflected in our 'Customer First' attitude and drives our positive energy—an attitude that ensures that we stand tall in the face of extreme adversity, an attitude that is ingrained in our organizational and individual DNA and an attitude that is now openly being admired and respected by our peers, influencers, and competitors.

On July 14, I was in Houston for a customer roadshow. The weather was holding at about 105°F in the shade (reminded me of Hyderabad, a city I have started to enjoy!) and the reception was being held at Kiran's, one of the nicest Indian restaurants I've come across outside India. What impressed me most was the passion of Kiran Verma, the proprietor and the principal chef. She made it a point to meet with each one of us, explained the cuisine and dishes, and even went to the extent of detailing how they were cooked, the best combinations, etc. It was a great help to understand the nuances of Indian food. Courteous staff, agile to every detail and need, and passionate about their service standards. Within no time, our clients were discussing our services in a happy ambience, some were even committing to provide continued business to Mahindra Satyam! When I told Kiran that I needed to leave early, as I had a fairly long drive back, she asked me to wait and shortly came back with a thermos of hot masala chai for the road. I was stunned! This was her way of going the extra mile, ensuring customer happiness, and adding her flavour of positive energy to the entire experience at the restaurant.

The same week, while visiting the offices of Chevron, I saw—The Chevron Wall. A blank canvas area in almost every section of their office where employees are encouraged to post thoughts, suggestions, invite ideas, and randomly doodle. While this might seem like an innocuous idea, this spoke volumes of the transparency within the organization. I could see employees who had charted out existing business process flows, comments on improvement, brand ideas among other things. All in all, the Wall spoke to me and it spoke of an organization that was connected, was transparent, that thought out-of-the-box. Most of all, an organization where people were courageous and spoke out. Only happens when a company is inherently happy. We should surely attempt this.

I am sure that most of us are individually positive in our outlook. What can we do to ensure that as an organization, as a collective entity—we inject this positive energy to make the entire ecosystem positive? In other words, 'How do we increase the happiness quotient at Mahindra Satyam?' As I understand it, the proliferation of happiness within any system is possible through innovative programs to spread cheer and inspiring leaders who can conduct and run these programs effectively. I believe that today, we have all of these and much more, within Mahindra Satyam, and I am more than willing to do my bit to increase and augment the happiness quotient here.

To further corroborate this fact, over the last few weeks, I have met up with customers in UK and the Americas. Interestingly, while both these are completely different regions and have distinctly different cultures, all of them were unanimous in their answer when asked to name three things that they loved about Mahindra Satyam. Their answers were delivery excellence, positive attitude and quality of people. This alone, speaks volumes for us. This is a clear indicator of our inherent strengths. I see no reason as to why we cannot build on these and enhance our corporate culture to make it a culture that is fun-filled, a culture that encourages happiness, a culture that exudes a sense of belonging—a culture that stands for its own family. The Mahindra Satyam family!

As always, I look forward to your thoughts and comments. Keep posting!

CP

## Happy Diwali!

Wish you all a very Happy Diwali!

Diwali stands for different things to different people, but ultimately signifies the victory of good over evil; of light over darkness; of hope over despair. I feel one should perceive it as an analogy of vanquishing not the demons, but the darkness within—with the light of courage, confidence, commitment, and perseverance.

Spending the Diwali weekend in the US, I missed my large MSat family this festive season. What held and brought this family together and made us stronger was the silent and understanding support from each one of you. We have been through the strangest of times of late, haven't we? I am now more than convinced and proud to say that family is truly everything! They have made us realize that our turnaround and upturn is because of their unflinching support.

I would have loved to be in India to celebrate this festival with all of you. However, duty beckoned, and hence I was in the US, attending the Oracle Open World Conference, held at the legendary Moscone Center in San Francisco. At the event, I was filled with an immense sense of pride on seeing the quality work that our folks delivered. In fact, several customers were very appreciative of our services and clockwork precision with which activities were conducted for them at the event. I would like to personally congratulate Balaji Nagarammoorthy, GV Rao, Karthik Jagannathan, Manish Gupta, Nishad Somalwar, Nitin Shinde, Pankaj Joshi, Rajiv Mathur, Sujoy Hajra, Todd Smith, V Srinivasarao (VSR), and all the others who worked behind the scenes in making this event a success for MSat.

At the event, I also had the opportunity to listen to an address by Larry Ellison, the CEO of Oracle. Sharp, spry, and as combative as ever, the 65-year-old veteran of IT has a unique ability to make waves, speak his mind, tangle with competitors and create excitement in the marketplace, even after thirty-two years in Oracle! His zeal, passion, and chutzpah really had me impressed.

We also had our US West Coast Customer Reception last week, and Arvind Malhotra, Shanmugham Bala, Atul Kunwar, Nishith Mathur, GV Rao, and their sales and marketing teams made this reception a big success.

All in all, a week that was extremely productive and positive.

I'd like to once again wish you and your families a very 'Happy Diwali'. Here's to a year of radiant prosperity, glowing achievements and robust health for all of us.

Cheers!

CP

### February 25, 2010: 6.49.35 pm
### We Are the Champions

Most of you may have seen the communiqué about our very own Shadow Board winning the contest at the M&M Blue Chip

Conference 2009. At the outset, I would like to congratulate the winning team for this remarkable achievement.

History stands testimony to the fact that most 'new' and 'out of the box' thinking comes from the minds of the young and vibrant talent in any organization / country. We are a nation of youngsters, given that the majority of our population is below the age of 28 or so. In this 'Youngistan' (according to a popular advertisement), we need leaders who understand generation 'now'. Leaders such as Sabeer Bhatia who's brainchild Hotmail was one of the world's first free email service providers, and paved the way for a slew of other companies offering similar services including Google; Anupam Mittal, Founder and CEO of People Group who web-enabled the world of matrimony by launching Shaadi.com; and Vardan Kabra who set up the Fountainhead School. These are but some of the leaders, who I believe can contribute to the current generation, carve a strong enterprise and in the process, a stronger India.

In several of my previous posts on my blog, I have cited examples to reiterate that the youngsters of our organization are the game changers, and we must encourage them. In fact, in my last post titled 'Events and more', I had introduced the Seven Commandments of Delivery. One of the core Commandments in that was 'Balance 'experience' with 'experimentation', for it is this healthy mix of experienced leaders and young energetic minds (such as the Shadow Board and GLCs), that will act as a lever to our success.' The need of the hour is an energetic organization, with infinite passion and zeal to make a difference. This can only come from the young, energetic, enthused, and 'raring to go' lot and I am quite sure with the guidance of the experienced leaders in this organization, these youngsters will take Mahindra Satyam to the next level.

Winning the M&M Shadow Board contest is a perfect example of this confluence and balance. This has been possible only through the hard work of both parties—the youngsters and their mentors.

For all the other aspiring young leaders within the organization, who probably aren't aware of how big an achievement this is, allow me to summarize the stringent tests, activities, selections, and protocols that were an integral part of this activity.

Invitations to form a Shadow Board at Mahindra Satyam were sent out all the 2096 Fast Track and MBA associates (Band Bi & below) with an S/M rating. Each associate was asked to prepare a presentation on certain topics in any one of the four areas:
- Leadership
- Positioning
- Domain/Services
- Financials

We received close to 217 nominations and these were then divided into 12 groups for evaluation. The panel of evaluators comprised of one Tech Mahindra GLC and one senior leader from Mahindra Satyam. Each presentation was rated across several parameters including content, value generation, sustainability, and communication skills. In the second round ASM, Rajan Nagarajan & Padma Parthasarathy conducted telephonic interviews with 32 shortlisted associates.

It was from these 32 that the Mahindra Satyam Shadow Board was formed comprising of 8 members. These members were guided and mentored by senior leaders including Hari, Vijay, Padma, Arvind, ASM, Rajan, and Nishith. After exhaustive brainstorming sessions, the team came up with the two innovative ideas of 'Vision 2012' and a 'One-Stop Solution for Scalable & Smart Healthcare'.

Both these ideas were presented to the senior management, and it was decided that the Healthcare idea would be presented to the Group Management Board. The team meticulously worked at detailing the content of their presentation, and supported the same with regular weekly calls and physical meetings whenever possible.

Sripathi Sripada & Sai Saripalli presented to the Group Management Board in November 2009 along with all the other Shadow Board Teams from the other companies under the Mahindra Group. Of these, Shadow Board Teams from four companies—Automotive Sector, Mahindra Satyam, Farm Equipment, and Mahindra Finance—were shortlisted to present at the Blue Chip Conference. Our team then represented MSat at the Conference this week, and walked away with the award for the Best Idea/Presentation. Of course, we missed Swami (the chairman of MSat Shadow Board) at the event, as he was at customer meetings in Australia.

By excelling at the Blue Chip Conference, the team from Mahindra Satyam has truly made a difference, and has set the bar for future Shadow Boards to come. As I pen down my thoughts on this achievement, I am reminded of some of the lines from the IT sector anthem that we created for the conference. This anthem set the stage for entire event, and was one of the most talked about pieces. Here are a few verses from the same:

> We are the Champions
> We see it clear
> We are the Champions
> Our future is here
>
> We let it fly
> Our dreams, hopes, and passion
> We will rule
> With collective emotion.

Let's all make this a part of our being, our mantra if I may, for this is the way to move ahead, to grow and evolve.

Cheers,

CP

### April 6, 2010: 2.41.19 pm
### The Buck Stops With 'You'

Former US president Harry S. Truman frequently used the phrase 'The buck stops here'. In fact, he had kept a plaque with this phrase on his desk. Derived from the phrase, 'Passing the buck', which meant transferring responsibility to someone else, this particular phrase resonated with the fact that the President was the one who made the final decisions and accepted the ultimate responsibility for those decisions. Hence the phrase 'The buck stops here'.

At Mahindra Satyam, I personally believe that 'the buck' does not stop with just one person, instead 'the buck stops with each one of you'...the collective...for you are the driving force of this organization!

Here's a recent example where this trait was personified. I was in China a little while back, and was attending an IES event. As an organization, we had invested in China quite a while back, and were almost five to six years ahead of our competition. The team in China is one of our best teams—energetic, enthused, and driven by highly motivated leaders. It's really no surprise that this collaborative approach has been pushing us into a growth mode in this region.

The event per se was a hit! We had close to thirty-five customers participating in the event, and by the end of the event, every one of them went back with a renewed trust in us. Kudos to the team that worked tirelessly behind the scenes to make this event a great success. Special thanks to David Chen and Terence Wang for their commitment and leadership; and Bill Pan for working tirelessly with the excellent support from Yong Ye, Percy Pan, Crystal, and Kevin Sima. Thanks for going the extra mile Sophia and ensuring that everything was bang on target and right the first time. Congratulations Ravi Karne, Daisy, and your team for running a very tight operation with a lot of dedication. Last but not the least, I would like to specially thank Kiran and Ravi Y, who, by focusing on Engineering Services, have created a major differentiator for us in China. I am sure there are many more such individuals who have worked tirelessly behind the scenes, and I would like to take this opportunity to applaud their efforts and sincerely thank them.

I also recently visited our Bengaluru campus. I received a very warm welcome from the team there, and they took time out to walk me through some of their major activities. The team there was quite committed, motivated, and charged up. I'm sure it had something to do with the performance of their home team in IPL!

While there, I shared updates pertaining to the recent wins that we have had globally, and the current growth trajectory of the organization. My session with the associates there was quite interactive, and it was nice to see several questions being raised, especially around the requirements of associates for projects and inflow of resources. Some of the associates who raised queries included Sudharshan Shapurkar, Jagadeesh Nayak, Ganesh Rane, and Dinesh Kumar. It was also nice to see Ashutosh, one of our GLC members, address the leaders who were present and provide them with a view of how energized the organization was. At this juncture I'd like to be very frank with you all. We are an organization that has recently come out of a crisis and are on the path to recovery. We are back on the growth curve, though this growth is currently happening in pockets. All of us are working and striving hard to make this organization grow, and the leaders are putting in their 100 percent in making this transformation journey a success. If the recently launched Hyderabad Leadership Council is any indication, then I must say the leaders are very much charged up and are motivated to transform this organization to an enviable position. All I would ask for is a little patience, for all the pieces to fall into place. I can assure you, that once we take the leap to the next level, there will be no turning back! Towards the end, I also invited all who were present to participate in process improvements, for it is only with this collaborative approach and sense of ownership that we would be able to move to the next level.

While I wouldn't like to let the cat out of the bag, I would strongly urge you all to keep a keen eye on the Fun & Connect activities that are soon to take place in the organization...there is quite a lot in store!

CP

# TURNING THE TIDE
## The Story of Satyam's Turnaround

*We have been able to very successfully tide over a crisis where we would have become history but in many ways I think we made history. Tyco, Xerox, Anderson Consulting—they just evaporated.*
—Indraneel Ganguly, Serior VP, Marketing and Communications, Mahindra Satyam

*2009–12*
*Hyderabad*

By December 2010, not only was Mahindra Satyam stable at the US$1–1.1 billion revenue level but the exodus of customers had also stopped. By that time, total staff strength was 28,832 and the company had 217 customers.

The company announced in mid February, 2011 that it was on the recovery, and that its revenue and net profits grew in the third quarter ended December 31, 2010. The firm said that revenue had grown to Rs 12.8 billion (US$281 million), up by about three percent from the previous quarter, while net profit had more than doubled to Rs 590 million (US$12.9 million) from Rs 233 million in the previous quarter.[1]

Satyam's turnaround—from a scandal-hit company with an uncertain future to a company that reported a ten-time increase in its year-on-year profits—took many watchers by surprise. One Indian commentator wondered if Mahindra Satyam was the next dark horse of the Indian IT industry. With a hefty dose of good luck, he wrote, this company could become the next Cognizant—the US-based company that beat Wipro to become the third-biggest IT services company.

As the months went by, Satyam's performance became better and better. Within two years, Satyam's leadership had turned the company around—the company was not only growing, it was also making handsome profits. In November 2011, Mahindra Satyam reported growth for the fifth consecutive quarter despite an uncertain macroeconomic environment. Consolidated revenue for the quarter was US$330 million, up 3.2 percent quarter on quarter.

The company now had over 32,000 employees, though still a lot less than the 53,000 headcount that Satyam had at its peak. The attrition rate was now down to 15.6 percent from 17 percent in the earlier quarter.

On May 18, 2012, Satyam reported a net profit for the fourth straight quarter. 'For the quarter through March, the company posted a net profit of Rs 5.34 billion (US$98 million), compared with

|  | FY'09 | FY'10 | Q1-11 | Q2-11 | Q3-11 | Q4-11 | FY-11 | Q1-12 | Q2-12 | Q3-12 |
|---|---|---|---|---|---|---|---|---|---|---|
| Revenue | 1.9 Bn | 1.16 Bn | 268 | 272 | 284 | 304 | 1.13 Bn | 320 | 330 | 325 |
| EBIDTA (After Exceptional Expense) |  | 2.8% | 9% | 5.2% | 5.0% | -28.6% | -2.9% | 15.8% | 15.3% | 16.3% |
| Attrition |  | 41% | 23.8% | 25.4% | 25.2% | 21.9% | 23.8% | 17.3% | 15.6% | 15.9% |

Source: Mahindra Satyam

### Financial Highlights

| Particulars | 2011–12 | 2010–11 |
|---|---|---|
| Income from Operations | 56,643 | 47,761 |
| Other Income | 3,900 | 2,837 |
| Total Income | 65,543 | 50,598 |
| Operting Profit (PBIDT) | 13,655 | 7,263 |
| Interest and Financing Charges | 112 | 92 |
| Depreciation/Amortization | 1,494 | 1,499 |
| Exceptional items (net) | (518) | 6,411 |
| Profit/(Loss) before Tax | 12,567 | (739) |
| Tax expense | 539 | 537 |
| Profit (Loss) after Tax | 12,028 | (1,276) |
| Equity share capital | 2,354 | 2,353 |
| Reserves and Surplus | 30,788 | 19,259 |
| Earnings per share (₹ Per equity share of ₹ 2 each) |  |  |
| – Basic (₹) | 10.22 | (1.08) |
| – Diluted EPS (₹) | 10.21 | (1.08) |

Source: Annual Report 2011–12, Mahindra Satyam

a net loss of Rs 3.27 billion a year earlier when it took a Rs 5.72 billion charge to settle lawsuits in the US Sales rose 21 percent from a year earlier to Rs 16.66 billion. The sales growth was just shy of industry bellwether Infosys' 22 percent expansion and better than Wipro's 19 percent increase.'[2]

It reported annual revenues of US$1,311 million (Rs 6,396 crore) for the financial year that ended on 31 March 2012, up 24 percent year on year. Total headcount stood at 33,353 and attrition improved to 15 percent in fourth quarter (Q4FY12) as compared to 22 percent in corresponding quarter of last year.

How did this miracle happen? How did Satyam navigate through the rubble of disrepute and the loss of market confidence after the scandal and manage to come out with positive growth stories?

After Satyam's takeover by Mahindra Satyam, the major challenge before the company's leadership was to stabilize it and then put it on the path of growth. 'This can be divided into two parts at the very high end,' says Hari, the Chief Marketing Officer (CMO) and Chief People Officer (CPO) of Mahindra Satyam.[3] 'We told ourselves it is a three-year plan. We divided three years into three specific directions: first year around stabilization, second year around investments, and third year around growth. And from that corporate messaging if you may, we derived the messages that we would need to communicate and the actions that we will need to take.'

'So when we talked about stabilization, we talked about the need to be capable of sustaining the company. We talked about actions that may be painful, so as to allow the organization to take the next leap. In the second year, all our communication would have been around how we were forming the competency, how we were encouraging new innovation. We talked about the innovation clubs and allowing people to come up with new ideas. We talked about enabling Mahindra Satyam to be on the leading edge of being a mobile workforce—enabling everything on handhelds compared to other companies. So we made a lot of our messaging and programmes to the customers, and to the associates around the fact that we were now bending at the knees so that we could jump.'

'In year three now (2011), if you look at it from the last quarter, the messaging has been around how we have been able to grow. I see the traction not scaling down. What are we trying to say is that the messaging has been derived from the larger objective. The good news is people are seeing the traction in growth,' says Hari.

## Board of Directors

**Vineet Nayyar**
*Chairman*

**C. P. Gurnani**
*Whole-time Director & CEO*

**C. Achuthan**
*Government Nominee*

**T. N. Manoharan**
*Government Nominee*

**M. Damodaran**

**Ulhas N. Yargop**

---

**S. Krishnan**
*Chief Financial Officer*

**G. Jayaraman**
*Company Secretary*

## THE THREE-YEAR TRANSFORMATION JOURNEY

'The 2009 stabilization issues were around the realities of where we stand vis-à-vis the banks—realities as far as the liabilities were concerned to disgruntled investors, and some of the lawsuits that were against us,' says Indraneel Ganguly, Senior Vice President,

Marketing and Communications, Mahindra Satyam's. 'Stabilization in terms of keeping the delivery engines up and running so that customers wouldn't suffer.'

During those precarious months, Satyam was keeping an eye on numbers such as the number of customer defections, which was a two-way street: one way coming in from customers themselves (because of some of the government issues, some customers decided to part ways) and the other was, of course, the competition playing its own role.

Also, Satyam focused on keeping the teams together because a lot of people were scared, and a lot of people were unsure of the new way of doing things. Coupled with it was, in 2009, people's cautiousness. 'Although there was no perceived recession as to the global economy, people were very cautious,' he says. 'So the pipeline visibility was an issue. There was therefore a business part to it, a governance part to it, and a people part to it, if I were to just keep it kind of segregated.'

'Then from there we moved on, we moved on to fix not only these three issues, but we said we'll have to consolidate,' says Ganguly. 'Consolidation meant doing several things parallelly. 'It was almost like—there was a time when we had to keep both ears to the ground because we didn't have a choice, unlike others. We had to listen, we had to act on whatever we listened to, and we had to immediately do a few things. While a lot of other companies in the world, especially our peers, had the luxury of doing a lot of analysis and lot of thinking around a particular thing, we unfortunately didn't have because we lost a lot of time in 2009.'

'So the year of consolidation meant getting our processes right, getting our teams in place, getting our structures in place, getting our fund flow in place, dealing with the class action suits one after the other, and most importantly, getting a visibility of our own accounts because this fraud or whatever was happening across several years, and we discovered to our horror that this was happening even before what the government authorities had predicted to be. It is very difficult to get things brought back to normalcy levels if you don't have a view, and the other thing was that sometimes the view was stunted as these documents were not available to us. There were a lot of documents that were not there. They were with the government authorities, we had to plead with them, and then get a few things done.'

'Despite all this, we managed to consolidate our position not only with our systems, but also with our customers and we got our customers to start believing in us, saying that it's all about our capabilities that could take the relationship forward. Then we said to ourselves, if the engine is running, and we had taken the car out of the garage, it's time the car hit the highway because we had a mission of being seen in the rear view of our competition's mirror, and we wanted to do that. Kudos to the (internal) finance team. They managed to restate our results in record time. It was unbelievable—it is a case study by itself. By September, we had one view of the entire results—we knew where the real EBITDA levels were, we knew what our results were, and so on. And the next quarter, we were able to go across the world and flash those results.'

'Now come to the growth phase. In 2011 we said to ourselves that we would want to be among the chosen top quartile growth companies in the ICT business because Mahindra Satyam brought to the table a brilliant set of minds who were the true experts in the enterprise side of the business. And Tech Mahindra brought the mobility aspect to the business. When you join this one plus one, we wanted it to become eleven. Enterprise mobility is, of course, what my CEO very fondly says the dowry piece that we received in this entire match. So we took the enterprise mobility story to the world at large. It gained a lot of traction. People were listening to us. We were going across from city to city in US, in Europe, in APAC, and India, and we were talking about it and analysts were picking it up. In fact, a lot of advisory firms were telling us that

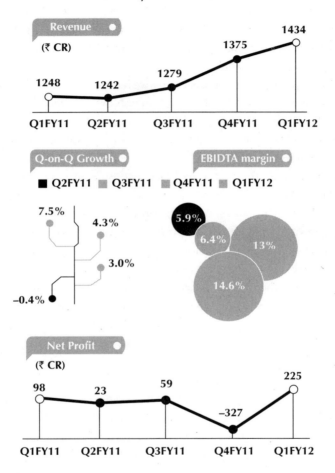

[Source: *Times of India*, September 29, 2011]

perhaps this was the way to do our business, and we found not only was it fetching us new logos, it was fetching us a larger amount of business from our existing customers. So the growth phase was about tantamount growth, not incremental growth. It meant that we were walking into accounts, we were at a consolidating level, at a delivery level, we were doing what it takes to reach those to kind of take us to those same situations of the previous years. When I say the same situation, I mean not the same financial situation but the same regard situation.'

'So from the growth phase, I think we have successfully completed our three-year transformation journey. Now, the leadership is in place. We have empowered a lot of young leaders from within the system. And we have run a lot of interesting concepts which are almost a first in the industry.'

Ganguly cites the example of the Shadow Board. 'It's a beautiful concept,' he says. 'The Shadow Board is a group of young people (average age of about 23–24) who comprise this board and their job is to constantly advise and tell our actual board what needs to be done and what needs to be done better, faster, simpler. The Shadow Board is also the elite group which is allowed to meet up with the world, so whether it is the world of Mahindras or whether it is the outside world, we always encourage the Shadow Board to go out there. Because we strongly believe that the youth power is something that is going to take this company, this industry, to the next league.'

'Then we have what we call the global leadership cadre programme where we pick up a few bright MBAs from premier institutes like IIM, XLRI, etc, and they form the global leadership cadre,' says Ganguly. 'Their job is to almost think like a CEO. For the first six months or a year, they are put in charge of, or are made a part of, a particular business unit, which they later get to lead, and it is all cross-functional stuff. So if I get a global leadership cadre in marketing, and that person shows increasing traction and increasing interest in how we are getting our revenues from a particular emerging market, in one year's time, that person is heading that market in sales. Try and push them into the deep end of the pool and we have seen that most of them have been successful. This experiment worked for us.'

'The third thing that we did was to kind of infuse a lot of pride within the system,' he says. 'This happened primarily because we ran a campaign, a way-of-life campaign in Mahindra Satyam and the Mahindra Group, called RISE.'

'RISE has three tenets to it. The first is accepting your limits, which is nothing but stretch behaviour. The second is called alternative thinking, which is nothing but innovative, out-of–the-box thinking, inside-the-box thinking, what have you. Third is driving positive change which is always creating measurable, tangible, positive value for our stakeholders.'

'You don't wake up every morning, you RISE. And we do incremental changes with RISE. So if we handled the world's largest cloud computing solution to manage the FIFA world cup during the peak of our crisis, it happened only because we decided to RISE. If we managed to get the fuel emissions of a large, global airline down by 50 percent, it's because we decided to RISE through alternative thinking. And we also never shied away from being seen or heard in the right places because we are strategic partners to the World Economic Forum (WEF)—only hundred companies in this world get or enjoy that status. Despite our issues and problems we said no, we will be with the WEF because it gives us a great platform to interact, interface with what's happening across the world. So we are slated to be in the WEF in a couple of weeks from now in Davos. And why just Davos. We participate in lot of these regional events, whether it is Dalian in China, Mumbai, India, Argentina, or Brazil, you name it and we are there as a strategic partner in the WEF.'

'So in a nutshell, we have been able to very successfully tide over a crisis where we would have become history, but in many ways I think we made history,' he says with evident pride. 'Tyco, Xerox, Anderson Consulting—they just evaporated.'

## MANAGING THE EMPLOYEES

After the crisis, managing the employees was one of the greatest challenges for Hari. How did he manage to increase the performance bar of the employees during the time of the crisis? 'One was to be able to move the sense of uncertainty and fear-neutralizing; that was as important as bringing forth transparency at where we are going,' he said.

'The first year was about being as transparent as you could, so that there was a connect (with the associates). Our Chief Executive Officer, C.P. Gurnani, used to write a blog every fifteen days. So all the messages that we wanted to share would go from the CEO's table and we had people responding to those and we would be responding to those responses. What we did was to flatten the organization in terms of the communication and connect. You had 22,000 employees in the company at that time, feeling comfortable to connect with the CEO. That helped a lot because people knew what was coming.'

'When we did take some difficult decisions, in July 2009, the uncertainty and the fear was enhanced for about almost three-four months. During that period, we said in every forum that this was a one-time activity and so, once the fear part of it was gone, and people could see what we would do three months down the line, things started to change...'

As new business came in, that became the biggest motivator for the employees. 'For us, in that turnaround phase, even a US$700,000 win was a big win,' he said. 'We would actually send a mail out and nobody cared about the revenue size. What everybody cared about was the fact that we could actually turn the tide, even if it was a small one. And with every win, there were mails exploding around in the office; people were feeling very bullish about it, and every week you had something to cheer about.'

'With senior management, we were connecting every two-three days; now, we connect every two-three months,' he said. The company's leadership council is around hundred people. Mahindra Satyam's APAC leadership council had eighteen members. 'Even two-and-a-half years later, sixteen of them are still working,' he said.

'The first few months featured massive crisis management,' agrees Rohit Gandhi, Mahindra Satyam's Senior Vice President.[4] 'There were issues of customer and employee retention, then there were legal cases to deal with, there was corporate governance to be brought back. We formed an Asia-Pacific Leadership Council and brought everyone together. It could not have been done by one or two people. We met every week and came out with a proper to-do list.'

This to-do list had thirty points. Initially, twenty-four points were about turning around the embattled tech company and six points were about growth. For illustration, some of the points from that to-do list were as follows:

1. Implementation of Employee Connect Program—one on one, in groups—ownership of 150 employees/leadership council member
2. Review implementation of executive-customer connect program—matrix of who from Mahindra Satyam will meet which customer in what frequency
3. Hire twenty salespersons across Asia Pacific
4. Sublease excess office space
5. Review bench
6. Review marketing plan—confidence building with analysts, partners, media

'As part of the crisis, we lost a number of key people,' says Gandhi. 'We started massive hiring. Initially, I thought that that would be my biggest challenge. Why would somebody want to join Satyam? Surprisingly, there were so many people in the market—good people from very good organizations—who said we want to come here just for the fun of it. They wanted to be a part of this company to see a turnaround.'

'We promoted a number of people internally to leadership positions. The rest we hired from top IT companies.'

'Employee attrition has come down dramatically. It was very high, alarmingly high. But, it has now come down to almost industry level. We definitely need to work more on this.'

'We started pulling a number of levers to improve profitability, whether it was onsite-offshore ratios, or utilization, or benchmarks, or whatever, there was a taskforce working on this. We asked ourselves: how do we get the best out of business? How do we come back to industry norms? It is not over yet but there are encouraging signs. We are almost 60 percent towards where we want to go. Now we are working on the balance.'

'These are four key issues we have been looking at: growth, profitability, customer delight, and employee delight. These are the mantras of our turn-around strategy.'

## THE SHADOW BOARD

Satyam, in Gandhi's words, embarked on a number of good strategies to maneuver the company to profitability. 'Our CEO started a Shadow Board,' Gandhi said. He explained the rationale behind setting such a unique entity. 'IT services companies are typically very young companies. The average age in such companies ranges between the twenties and early thirties. On the other hand, the average age of the board is sixty. They are very wise people but the thought leaders in the organization are younger people. So, the CEO picked up nine most promising young people. The cut off age was thirty-five. In this new arrangement, the CEO reports the quarterly results to both the main board and the Shadow Board. And the Shadow Board comes out with its own set of suggestions.'

As a turnaround strategy, a Shadow Board was constituted, drawing in younger employees. 'The thought behind the Shadow Board was to bring in unconventional solutions to unconventional problems,' says Hari. A move like this empowered the grassroots-level worker.

The Shadow Board was a parallel board comprising lower- and mid-level employees. Mahindra Satyam employees believed that the Shadow Board 'will link the senior officials with the bottom level employees—a move that will not only bring in better transparency, and motivate the employees, but also change the way they do daily business'.[5]

'The board has a team of nine young professionals to help the management with ideas on how to make the company more profitable,' said Gurnani. 'Their mandate is to function like a normal board. While we do share data on market trends, feedback surveys and so on, the Shadow Board does not have access to sensitive financial information. This board has bounced off the idea that Mahindra Satyam should be marketed as an ICT firm to focus on Tech-Mahindra's skills in the communication sector. So we will bundle IT and communication services and market it to customers as ICT instead of pure-play IT.'[6]

'It feels great to be a part of Shadow Board,' said Arathi Ponangi, a Shadow Board member. 'I always wanted to be a part of change. The Shadow Board is giving me a unique opportunity to not only be a part of change but also contribute towards change. So it's great.'[7]

Like Arathi, the Shadow Board also has Swamy Swaminathan and Sripathi Sripada as members.

Gandhi gave some examples of the ideas that originated from Mahindra Satyam's Shadow Board. 'The idea of our using social media tools for marketing, both within and outside the organization, came from the Shadow Board,' says Gandhi. 'They actually drove it. They came up with many other interesting ideas. For example, we are configuring a service in Australia which is basically a business process outsourcing service called "social media listening". This service can give daily reports to a company about the chatter on its social media activities—that is, what its customers and stakeholders are saying about it. The payment is on a per transaction basis. Our logic behind this is that when the social media monitoring volume grows, companies don't need to deploy a separate department to do this.'

'The Shadow Board at Satyam works on an annual basis. The first board has now retired and the second one is on now.'

Other measures, besides promoting new thinking and introducing fresh blood into the leadership ranks, included making the staff mobile-enabled time sheets, leave application, an NFC-enabled recognition system—the whole nine yards.

According to Hari, social media is being used extensively within the organization. Twitter is allowed in the office. There are Internet kiosks on every floor for employees to access Facebook.

## MAHINDRA SATYAM AND GROWTH IN THE ASIA PACIFIC

The Satyam brand had taken a big hit after the crisis unfolded. There was an urgent need to promote Satyam's new brand, Mahindra Satyam. One of the things that the company did for branding purposes was to hitch its wagon to Fédération Internationale de Football Association (FIFA). The tech company handled the IT for the FIFA World Cup in 2010 held in South Africa. 'For FIFA we did two things,' says Gandhi. 'One, we did the entire IT for the event. We deployed it using the cloud. It was the world's biggest sporting event with three million people watching matches every day. The entire application was built using agile methodologies. Because of cloud deployment and agile methodologies, the overall cost of ownership or running the system was pretty low. Two, we also set up a call centre in South Africa supporting seven different languages.'

**Geographic segment**

Revenue based on geography considering the location of customers/ultimate customers and compiled based on the information available with the Management is as follows:

*(Rs. in Million)*

| Particulars | For the year ended March 31, 2010 | For the year ended March 31, 2009 |
|---|---|---|
| Americas | 28,891 | 53,067 |
| Europe | 14,799 | 17,956 |
| Asia Pacific | 6,708 | 10,308 |
| India | 2,505 | 4,380 |
| Rest of World | 1,907 | 2,415 |
| **Total** | **54,810** | **88,126** |

Segment assets based on the location of customers/ultimate customers and compiled based on the information available with the Management re as follows:

**Revenues from IT services based on offshore and onsite / offsite**

(₹ in Million)

| Location | Year ended March 31, 2011 | | Year ended March 31, 2010 | |
|---|---|---|---|---|
| Offshore | 21,761 | 45.90% | 24,491 | 48.11% |
| Onsite / offsite | 25,653 | 54.10% | 26,413 | 51.89% |
| Total | 47,414 | 100.00% | 50,904 | 100.00% |

**Revenues based on geography**

(₹ in Million)

| Location | Year ended March 31, 2011 | | Year ended March 31, 2010 | |
|---|---|---|---|---|
| North America | 25,228 | 53.21% | 27,311 | 53.65% |
| Europe | 12,577 | 26.53% | 13,076 | 25.69% |
| Asia Pacific | 6,122 | 12.91% | 6,374 | 12.52% |
| India | 2,120 | 4.82% | 2,346 | 4.61% |
| Rest of the world | 1,367 | 2.53% | 1,797 | 3.53% |
| Total | 47,414 | 100.00% | 50,904 | 100.00% |

[Source: *Mahindra Satyam*]

Satyam also used social media in a big way to report the FIFA events. On Twitter, they had nearly 25,000 followers.

'We now jointly own the IT operations with FIFA,' says Gandhi. 'We were also the sponsors, so the Mahindra Satyam branding was also important at that point of time. It had a huge impact. The brand recall was amazing. After that, we have now also started a sports vertical.'

For Mahindra Satyam, there were some positive signs to begin with, at least in the Asia-Pacific region. 'Now, in the Asia Pacific, we have not lost customers,' Gandhi says. 'On the contrary, we have found twelve significant new customers, netting in large, multimillion-dollar deals. We have found a new customer in the Singapore government. We signed up with a large financial institution in Australia, a new customer in the area of platform BPO vertical. That is something people are talking about.'

Gandhi outlined Satyam's growing expectations for Japan. 'From an existing customer in Japan, we were managing certain parts of its applications. Another major player was managing the other part. With an open tender, we could significantly increase our share and grow our Japan business.'

In Singapore, Satyam has signed multiple deals with the Singapore government, said Gandhi. 'Employee strength in our office in Singapore has doubled in one year.'

This did not, however, mean that all of Satyam's woes were over.

There were reports that said that although Satyam had started focusing on select markets, these efforts had not yet translated into high revenue and profit growth for the company, although the outsourcing market was bouncing back.[8]

'The company's operating margins are still very thin, at less than 4 percent. Going by current revenue levels, the company may show a revenue drop of about 8 percent in its fiscal year ending March 31, 2011,' said an IDG report.

By that time, even though Satyam had stabilized its revenues, it remained saddled with a lot of potential liabilities and costs, including a claim by some thirty-seven companies who said they want to be repaid Rs 12 billion (US$260) they had allegedly advanced to Satyam.

The company also faced a class action suit in the US alleging violations of American federal securities laws. The company was delisted last year from the New York Stock Exchange after it failed to publish its results according to US accounting rules within a stipulated period.

Its profits in the quarter were whittled down by Rs 533 million (US$11.7 million) in exceptional items relating to restructuring costs, forensic investigation and litigation support, and erosion in value of assets in subsidiaries.

'Satyam, which was once India's fourth-largest outsourcer, is far from reaching the revenue and profit levels of its competitors, such as Tata Consultancy Services, Infosys Technologies, and Wipro,' the IDG report said. 'All these three companies reported strong revenue and profit growth in the quarter ended December 31, benefitting from a recovery in the outsourcing market.'

'On its proposed merger with Tech Mahindra, Satyam's minority shareholders have demanded that it should be delayed until the company's full recovery, and when the valuations of equity are reasonable,' the report further added.

Rohit was aware of all these challenges that Satyam faced as a company.

'Have we returned to industry-standard profitability yet? The answer is no,' admits Gandhi. 'Are we getting there? The answer is yes. Could this turnaround been done in any other fashion? I have my doubts.'

'I think it was a mammoth task, pretty well orchestrated. It has been the experience of a lifetime. When there is a crisis, you tend you work very differently. When things are stable, you actually become very lethargic.'

By mid 2011, Satyam clearly was on the road to more stability and more success and its leaders and employees were out of the woods now, but they still had some distance to go. For the moment, it seemed that they just needed to keep the faith and keep going.

Now that the company is back on its growth path, Hari is looking forward to the Mahindra Satyam and Tech Mahindra merger, which is on the cards for next year (2012). 'The combined Tech Mahindra and Mahindra Satyam will have the most mobile workforce in the world,' he says.

Two-and-a-half years after the crisis (we met in July), Hari and his colleagues at Satyam have put the crisis behind them, so much so that they don't even talk about it anymore.

After all this, has the old pride of Satyam come back?

'I think a lot of pride has come back,' says Dr Khanna. 'Many of us who have been in the organization for so long chose to stay because…personally for me, it was an emotional connection. I am sure it is the same with many other leaders in the organization.

There is something in the spirit of the organization which just holds us together.'

'Almost about two-thirds of the organization is new now,' she says. 'The remaining one-third is still the old gang. The pride is there in both categories of people. The new people don't understand what the old Satyam was and I think it is not important for them to know that. It's all right because organizations have to keep moving. But this one-third keeps referring to the calamity that one has witnessed. So the bonding with the organization is much stronger. It is very difficult to tell stories, you just have to experience the whole thing yourself to understand what one went through. Because when you read what happened to Arthur Andersen and Johnson & Johnson, you just read it as a story. But for people to really be there on the spot, just feel what the crisis at that point of time was, is a completely different game.'

'So the pride has come back. People feel good about the organization growing, and they feel good about the litigations going off. People have hope that we will move forward when they see the new infrastructure coming up. Be it in Chennai or be it here, we feel good. Yes, we have come out of it. Very few organizations come out, stand up and say, yes, we are making profits. We just finished our sales meeting in January,[9] and we said, let's grow, let's grow big hog if we can, let's come together with Tech Mahindra and become a larger organization of 80–85,000 people. If other companies can show a 25–30 percent growth, why can't we? That's the collective hope of people and I think with that hope, the pride comes automatically.'

## ANALYST VIEWS

In a report in August 2011,[10] IDC noted three major things about the company: It had returned from uncertainty to certainty, it was doing a good job of executing the integration (of Mahindra Satyam and Tech Mahindra) and it was retaining customers and re-acquiring those who had jumped ship when the Raju episode happened.

'While Mahindra Satyam has returned stronger and surer of itself, there remains the last straw of integration with Tech Mahindra and the role of British Telecom (BT) in the larger organizational context, which was left largely unaddressed at the event,'[11] the analysts noted. 'IDC believes that key to Mahindra Satyam and Tech Mahindra's growth in the long term will be the execution of its M-Cube strategy wherein the approach will be to identify and grow synergies towards co-sourcing and co-creating solutions by having Mahindra & Mahindra (M&M) group of companies provide industry expertise and Tech Mahindra/Mahindra Satyam bring through the technical capabilities. The successful execution of this will be manifested through new partnerships being undertaken (for example with Cisco) and new solution areas (such as virtual dealers) being launched.'

On the customer front, the analyst noted: 'In addition, it was encouraging to note that over the past twelve months, erstwhile clients that lost to competitors were coming back into the fold and the company was able to sustain its high levels of customer satisfaction. As such, Mahindra Satyam has done well to adopt an 'extend and accelerate' go-to-market strategy (i.e., extending existing engagements and accelerating new solutions and market presence while not compromising on margins).'

'In its true sense, the recovery of Mahindra Satyam is the return of the phoenix, yet the flight is young,' IDC analysts wrote in the report. 'How strong and swift will the flight be? That is best witnessed.'

Though so much had been achieved and Vineet Nayyar says that Mahindra Satyam's 'three-year transformation has been completed' at the company, some minor issues still bother the management of Mahindra Satyam. For example, it still faces lawsuits in the US and UK, filed by Aberdeen Asset Management PLC and some other holders of its American Depositary Receipts (ADRs) who claimed that they lost more than US$150 million due to the fraud. The company is also battling a Rs 21.13 billion tax demand at home.[11] On top of it, the company faces claims from Ramalinga Raju family-run firms to the tune of Rs 1,230 crore. But it can be argued that these are minor challenges in the flight path of the battle-hardened phoenix that is Mahindra Satyam.

# BACK IN THE BIG BOYS' CLUB
## Mahindra Satyam and Tech Mahindra Merge Into a Single Entity

*The Mahindra Satyam turnaround is a shining story of determination and grit and now comes to its most important chapter with this merger.*
—C.P. Gurnani, CEO, Mahindra Satyam

March 20, 2012
Singapore

It was a Tuesday afternoon and I was in my office on Beach Road. My phone rang unexpectedly. A Mahindra Satyam public relations (PR) representative was on the line.

'The information I'm going to give you is embargoed until tomorrow when a formal announcement will be made,' he told me, sounding cautious. 'But I wanted to give you a heads up.' I became immediately interested and pressed my ear closer to the receiver. 'What is it?' I was burning with curiosity. 'The merger of Tech Mahindra and Mahindra Satyam will be announced tomorrow morning,' he said.

As I thanked him and put the phone down, I could sense the Mahindra Satyam story coming to an end. And it was going to be a happy ending.

The funny thing is that the merger was not unexpected. It was very much on the cards. But the very fact that it was happening and an announcement had been made in this regard was a remarkable milestone for a beleaguered company like Satyam. *The news of the merger must be such a relief for the Satyamites,* I thought.

The next morning, true to the advance information, the merger of Tech Mahindra and Mahindra Satyam was announced in India. The two companies had formally applied to become one after their respective boards approved a proposal to merge the two entities. This merger, of course, is subject to government approval.[1] And with that, the ghosts of Satyam's past were laid to rest.

Last year, when I had spoken to Satyam officials, the impression was that the merger would be announced by mid-year or later. But it happened a bit early. Still, not many were taken by surprise. The merger of the two companies was always the intended end game.

I called up Rohit Gandhi, Mahindra Satyam's managing director for Asia Pacific, to get his reaction. He was in Australia.

I asked him how he felt about the merger. 'The good part is that we have done it (the merger) under three years of the acquisition,' he said. 'Overall, it is very heartening.'

He had every reason to feel glad. With the merger announcement, Satyam's tainted past was like water under the bridge and the company would be back in the reckoning.

The merger changes the game for Mahindra Satyam. Together with Tech Mahindra, it will once again be one of the top dogs in the IT services business. The merger will result in the creation of a new offshore services leader with about US$2.4 billion in revenues, more than 75,000 employees and over 350 active clients (including Fortune Global 500 companies), across fifty four countries.

'This merger will help propel the combined entity into the top tier of Indian software and services companies, achieving the group's key objective of being in a leadership role in each of our focus business areas', said Anand Mahindra, chairman, Tech Mahindra.

A report in the *Economic Times*[2] said the combined entity is now the sixth-largest India-based IT services provider with a market value of a little over US$3 billion.

'The Mahindra Satyam turnaround is a shining story of determination and grit and now comes to its most important chapter, with this merger', said C.P. Gurnani, whole-time director and CEO of Mahindra Satyam. 'As enterprises the world over look to bolster their IT strategies to keep pace in the connected world, this merged entity will provide the perfect blend of capability to address this evolving market', he added.

## KEY HIGHLIGHTS OF THE MERGER

According to the statement issued by Mahindra Satyam, the exchange ratio recommended by the valuers and approved by both the boards was two shares of Tech Mahindra (face value of Rs 10 each or US$0.19), for every 17 shares of Mahindra Satyam (face value of Rs 2 each). On a pro-forma basis, the Mahindra Group would own 26.3 percent in the combined entity, British Telecom would own 12.8 percent,[3] 10.4 percent would be held as treasury stock, 34.4 percent to be held by the public shareholders of Mahindra Satyam, and the balance 16.1 percent will be held by the public shareholders of Tech Mahindra.

### COMBINED ENTITY SHAREHOLDING STRUCTURE

| Particulars | Shareholding Swap Raio 2:17 % |
|---|---|
| Promoters Shareholding | 49.5 |
|    Mahindra & Mahindra Ltd | 26.3 |
|    British Telecommunications Plc | 12.8 |
|    TML Benefit Truxt | 10.4 |
| Tech M Public Shareholding | 16.1 |
| MSAT Public Shareholding | 34.4 |
| Total | 100% |

Source: *Hindu Business Line*[4]

Tech Mahindra said it would issue 10.34 crore (100.34 million) new shares, thereby increasing its outstanding shares to 23.08 crore and its equity capital to Rs 230.8 crore (US$4.5 billion).

It was announced that the joint entity will have a unified 'go-to-market' strategy with deep competencies and a balanced mix of revenues from telecom, manufacturing, technology, media and entertainment, banking, financial services, insurance, retail, and healthcare.

The combination of the two companies will benefit from operational synergies, economies of scale, sourcing benefits, and standardization of business processes. 'This merger is a key part of our strategy to deliver industry leading performance', said Vineet Nayyar, Vice Chairman and Managing Director, Tech Mahindra and Chairman, Mahindra Satyam.

The merged entity is expected to generate over 40 percent of its revenue from the Americas, with a further 35 percent of its earnings coming from Europe. Emerging markets would represent 23 percent of its combined revenue.[5]

'The deal works well for both Satyam and Tech Mahindra at many levels,' writes K. V. Kurmanath in the *Hindu Business Line*. 'But most importantly this marriage would reduce risk of high exposure to the US and Europe markets for both companies. While Satyam's exposure to the Americas stands at 50 percent, Tech M's exposure to Europe is very high at 45 percent. This would come down to 43 percent and 35 percent respectively after the merger, with contribution from rest of the world remaining stable at around 25 percent.'[6]

'The other major gain for the two is that their vertical spread will increase,' Kurmanath writes. 'Currently, Tech Mahindra is skewed towards telecom with 96 percent of its revenues coming from this vertical. On the other hand, Mahindra Satyam, like any other software services firm, has a relatively distributed basket, with manufacturing contributing 32 percent and BFSI and tech-media chipping in 19 percent and 21 percent respectively. Once the merger goes through, the combined entity's exposure to telecom in overall revenue would come down to 47 percent. Manufacturing would be at 17 per cent, BFSI 11 percent and technology-media at 10 percent.'

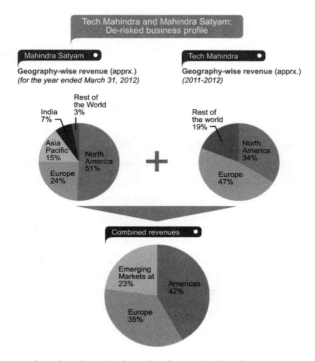

Source: Based on data from Tech Mahindra and Mahindra Satyam

## A SLIGHT SURGE IN SHARES

Just after the announcement, the Indian stock market showed some positive gains for the Tech Mahindra shares. It was still early in the day. I asked Rohit if he was tracking the market. No, he said, he was not. But he did speak to some of his clients in Australia and he received positive feedback from them. It was a small sample size but it satisfied him.

By and large, the merger of Tech Mahindra and Mahindra Satyam was seen as a positive deal by market analysts.[8] Edelweiss expected the combined entity to become a formidable competition in the scale player league with complementary skill sets and a well-balanced revenue mix.[9] MF Global said they believed that the combined entity would benefit from synergies with respect to size and mix. They, however, also said that it was too early to say whether it would result in superior growth rates in the near term. Their rating was neutral (Tech Mahindra).

'We see improved ability of the merged entity to bid for the larger projects, but the crux would be a seamless integration of the entities and reaping the benefits,' said Prabhudas Lilladher. 'We see a daunting task for the management ahead, hence would wait before flagging a re-rating. The rating that they gave to Tech Mahindra was Accumulate.

'We view the merger as a positive catalyst for creating a value accretive entity for the future,' said Sharekhan. 'However, legal hurdles pending with Satyam and slowdown in the telecom vertical (main industry exposure for Tech Mahindra) would stand to be a roadblock in the medium term. On a longer term, the new entity will have a more diversified and scalable revenue stream and operational synergies will create value for the investors.'

SPA Securities said that the combined entity will have higher margins than the two companies due to operational efficiency gains, 5 percent reduction in fixed and G&A (General and Administrative) costs, and improvement in Satyam margins, though partially offset by Tech Mahindra in the short term.

The shares of both companies closed about 5 percent higher on Bombay Stock Exchange that day.[10]

Now that the merger has been announced, the actual amalgamation of the two companies' operations will take a while to take effect. The proposed merger is subject to court approvals (courts in Andhra Pradesh and Maharashtra), and clearances from shareholders, lenders, and creditors. 'The legal formalities will still take some time,' said Rohit. 'The good part is that the merger has been announced. The swap value, exchange ratio, etc., has all been approved. So to that extent, it has become a reality. With that, now we can go and take all the necessary approvals. Once that is done, then you are up and running (as a merged entity).'

According to Rohit, now no major legal issues remain to be settled. 'We had told our customers that we will not merge till each and every issue is settled,' he said.

This is largely true but some thorns still remain in Satyam's path to glory. For example, there is still a pending class action suit from the Aberdeen Group. The company also faces tax claims of US$125 million from the income tax authorities. Satyam is contesting these claims.[11]

'I mean most of it is all sorted out,' Rohit said. 'So, the only legal issue is you have to take formal approvals. It is time consuming but we don't see frankly any significant challenges of any kind.'

'(Mahindra Satyam's) Management expects six-nine months for formal closure (of the merger). However, our view is that legal issues at Satyam are potential risks to timelines,' say Pankaj Kapoor and Apoorva Oza, equity researchers at Standard Chartered.[12]

Mahindra Satyam's CEO C.P. Gurnani is, however, quite gung-ho. 'We have been facing issues like these in our three-year journey. We will overcome these as well. We would like to consummate the marriage as early as possible,' he told a newspaper.[13]

## THE CONFUSION IS TACKLED

'Till the legal formalities are cleared, we still have to run as two different operating companies, but I think with this announcement now what can happen is that at least from the customers' point of view, the confusion is gone,' he said. 'Earlier what used to happen was when you go with the mobile solution of Tech Mahindra to a Satyam customer, he would more or less in his mind treat Tech Mahindra as a sub-contractor. Now customer looks at it as a seamless solution.'

So with the merger, Mahindra Satyam's most pain points are gone. That is a big deal in itself.

'Also, once we have officially announced it, we can now go and do a lot of informal synergies, which earlier was extremely difficult,' he said. 'We can now start selling some of the Satyam offerings like business intelligence, analytics that are very relevant for the telecom sector.'

'Earlier, it was very complicated,' Rohit said. Now, the opportunities for both the companies have expanded. 'If you look at Asia Pacific, there can be a lot of synergy in that location. For example, Tech Mahindra is very strong in Indonesia and New Zealand. Satyam does not have a significant presence there. Now we can start formally leveraging that.'

'So, go-to-market becomes much easier because in services business people don't get confidence till they feel that you are one entity. In outsourced services, they look at long-term players.'

'Also, look at Satyam's locations; we are strong in China and Japan where Tech Mahindra is not strong. So, it is very complimentary in this region. That can start right away. We don't have to wait (for legal approvals).'

## A NAME FOR THE MERGED ENTITIES

One thing that was missing from the merger announcement was the single brand name of the merged companies.

'Name will be decided once the legal formalities are through,' explained Rohit. 'Probably around that time, the name will be sort of decided and announced. Today, we didn't want to do it because it will confuse the marketplace.'

However, the new creature definitely will have a single identity. 'It will be a single entity, a single brand name, and the management structure will be a lot more formal,' he said.

On March 24, the *Times of India* reported that the Mahindra Group had hired a consultant to suggest a name for the merged entity.[14] 'We have hired a consultant to suggest a name for merged entity,' Tech Mahindra President, L. Ravichandran, said in Kolkata. He did not reveal either the name of the consultant or the deadline for renaming the merged IT company.

## IMPACT ON BUSINESS OPERATIONS AND STRUCTURE

The announced merger will not have any impact on the two companies' organizational structure for now.

'Nothing formal as yet in terms of organizational changes will take place till the legal approvals are there,' he clarified. 'I think now we will start synergizing a lot more closely. Also, there will be a lot of preparatory work for the final merger like rationalization of HR structures and things like that. Those cannot start commencing in a formal way.'

'The good news is that since we were in two separate segments, there is not any turmoil of any kind,' he said, referring to Tech Mahindra's strengths in the telecom area and Mahindra Satyam's in all the other verticals. 'Probably very complimentary.'

There have been reports about the sluggishness of the telecom sector and Tech Mahindra's performance getting a hit from that slowness in the vertical.

In a report in the *Financial Times*,[15] analysts said that the new group faced a number of challenges, especially an over reliance on telecoms revenues, part of Tech Mahindra's legacy with BT.[16] Ankita Somani, IT and telecom analyst at Angel Broking in Mumbai, told *FT*: 'Their telecom business is not growing, and while BT used to be their top client, that revenue is now declining too. They need to scale up in others areas.'

The London newspaper said that nearly half of the combined group's revenues will remain in telecoms, but it planned to expand aggressively into other areas, including business and enterprise services. C.P. Gurnani, Chief Executive Officer of Mahindra

Satyam, told the British paper: 'The Indian outsourcing industry is now US$100 billion-plus and we see plenty of room for growth. We see a big potential to get into an untapped market for IT and engineering services.'

Like Gurnani, Rohit also sees the telecom sector game play out differently. 'Telecom will also grow, in my opinion,' he said. 'Things will change; the offerings will change. Telecom companies know that voice revenues are falling, but all of them are investing big time in whole media network and machine-to-machine communications. I think the revenue mix will change. Maybe telecom's canvas will increase. Maybe Apple could become our customer. Telecom, IT, mechanical stuff, they are all merging actually. That's good from the point of view of the Mahindra's legacy. For example, car is becoming a computer, and a communication device.'

'In the Asia-Pacific market, we will go a little more aggressive,' said Rohit. 'Satyam never had any significant operation in the Philippines, Indonesia, and New Zealand. Now, we will go very aggressive on that because now we can leverage the base quite seamlessly. From Tech Mahindra's perspective, we never looked at North Asia—China, Korea, Japan—that seriously. Now, given this base of Satyam in those countries, we will go more aggressive because today Tech Mahindra, for example, doesn't utilize any of the China delivery centres of Satyam. Therefore, there is no concrete offering to China telcos from Mahindra Satyam. Now, there can be (offerings). So, we will go very aggressive now in mutual synergies.'

Post merger, will there be an expansion in Mahindra Satyam's team in the region? 'I see additions in the team,' said Rohit. 'One plus one will equal three eventually. It's difficult to forecast the exact number but in the emerging markets we expect significant growth. Some of these markets are doing exceedingly well—Australia, Indonesia, Malaysia, and Japan is obviously a little slow. Middle East is growing very well for us. Overall, we are very bullish.'

## A FORMIDABLE FORCE?

In one of its reports,[17] the *Economic Times* had Mahindra Satyam CEO C.P. Gurnani saying that the merger catapults the combine into the 'big boys club' because bigger size will mean it can compete better for larger technology outsourcing deals.

'But analysts and executives from the rival software companies were sceptical about the combine's ability to disrupt the competitive landscape—dominated by Tata Consultancy Services (TCS), Infosys, Cognizant, Wipro, and HCL—at least in the next few quarters,' the report noted.

It's not surprising to hear such talk about Satyam. TCS, the numero uno in this business, is about four times the size of the merged entity. HCL is nearly double its size.

'There is no evidence to suggest that their sales engine has what it takes to be taken seriously by the bigger players,' a senior executive at one of the 'big five' told the paper on condition of anonymity. 'We don't run into them much while competing for large deals, except in the telecom sector,' he added.

During the analysts' briefing on Wednesday (March 22), it was revealed that about twenty clients that left Satyam in 2009 after the scandal broke had returned to the fold. Of those, nearly nine were 'significant' customers.

'Even so, the new force probably has a better shot at increasing its wallet share with existing clients rather than competing with the larger players and winning new customers', said the *Economic Times* report. 'So until the new entity stabilizes, this may mean that it would have to be happy with the crumbs rather than the cream.'

In the same report, Hitesh Bhavanji Shah, director of institutional equities research at IDFC Securities, was quoted. He said that Vineet Nayyar, the chairman of Mahindra Satyam, and Gurnani, were well regarded in the industry and both have done a good job turning around the erstwhile Mahindra British Telecom five or six years ago, but the environment has changed dramatically since then.

'In terms of Satyam's sales performance, there have been no dramatic wonders during the last two years', Shah told the *Economic Times*. 'But during the same time, HCL Technologies, which will be the closest in pecking order, has leapfrogged with combination of organic growth and the Axon acquisition.'[18]

According to the report, Gurnani defended himself by saying that his aim was not to create a 'me-too' company challenging the top-tier firms across the spectrum of IT services. Instead, the focus will be on chosen verticals and service offerings.

'It is nearly three years since Indian IT services firm Tech Mahindra secured a majority stake in local rival Satyam, so the only surprise about the news that the two companies are to merge is that it has taken so long to happen,' said Ovum's Senior Analyst Ed Thomas.[19]

'That is not to say that this announcement bring the saga to an end,' he added. 'It will take the rest of the year for the merger process to be concluded and no name for the combined entity has yet been announced. On this latter point, it will be interesting to see if the Mahindra Group, which will own over one-quarter of the new operation, decides to finally rid itself of the Satyam brand, which was badly tarnished by the accounting scandal that came to light in 2009.'

'The companies will benefit from the merger through operational efficiency, which they are already seeing in their shared sales, marketing, and support functions,' Sudin Apte, Principal Analyst and CEO of Offshore Insights, a research and advisory firm in Pune, India, told John Ribeiro of IDG News Service. 'Tech Mahindra hopes to sell enterprise services from Satyam to its own clients in the telecommunications industry, but that may not play out,' he added.

Rohit Partha, Asia Pacific industry analyst for ICT practice at Frost & Sullivan, said the merger came 'right about time'.[20]

Hansa Krishnamurthy Iyengar, senior analyst of market intelligence at Ovum, told *ZDNet Asia* that the delay of three years also allowed regulatory authorities to dig into details and the extent of the scam, as well as to ensure 'all the books had been set right'. She noted that while this was completed in mid 2011, the decision on the merger was timed to coincide with the new financial year beginning April 1.

Unlike Apte, both analysts are enthusiastic about the future of the merged entity. Iyengar said the merged company would 'pose a serious threat' to rivals, including Wipro and TCS. Partha noted that the chances of success for the merged company 'looks promising', adding that the the top three players in the field—Wipro, TCS, and Infosys—'cannot sit comfortably'.

Size aside, Partha said that the combined entity also has a 'good chance' of generating deals and getting clients because it now has capabilities across the spectrum.[21] 'If they play everything right, [the new company] can easily be among the top three service providers in the next two to three years,' he said.

Partha also dismissed the idea that Satyam's past would be a barrier. 'That [tarnished] image is behind them,' he told *ZDNet Asia*. Iyengar agreed, 'It is evident from contract wins and a couple of small acquisitions that the Satyam name is no longer an issue.'[22]

## STAFF EXCITED OR WORRIED?

'For 75,000 employees of Tech Mahindra and Mahindra Satyam, the news about the imminent merger brought both excitement and a sense of fear and concern', said a report in the *Hindu Business Line* on March 21 ('Tech Mahindra, Mahindra Satyam merger: Staff excited and worried'). The report was accompanied with a photo in which a few smiling Satyam employees were seen sharing ladoos.

After the merger announcement was made, some of the employees of Mahindra Satyam and Tech Mahindra began to worry about lay-offs. The senior management of both the companies assured the employees that they would not be laid off just because these two companies are merging.[23]

The report further said: 'Excitement because they can now put the gory past behind them completely. Fear and concern because they are afraid of change of roles and loss of jobs in case of redundancies.'

The report made a reference to a new campaign that was launched to celebrate the merger news: the 'Power of One' campaign.

The report further suggested that despite assurances from C.P. Gurnani, CEO of Mahindra Satyam, a good number of Satyam employees were seen discussing their future in the merged company. Some employees told the newspaper that they were expecting a message from the management intimating them about the change of roles.

After the merger announcement, Vineet Nayyar, chairman of Mahindra Satyam and vice chairman of Tech Mahindra, wrote letters to all the 75,000 employees in the two firms and their subsidies. 'Though he has not indicated any plans to downsizing the staff numbers, he has not given any firm assurance on retaining them—a hope they have been anticipating with bated breathe,' the report said. 'Their worries are not without a reason. About 10,000 of Satyamites were put in Virtual Pool soon after the new management took over and shown the door.'

'Now that the three-year transformation journey has played out in line with our plans, we are poised for a full and formal integration and acceleration in the growth phase, going forward,' he said in his message. 'The combined entity will continue to rely on your trust and support as we scale up our operations.'

To further allay the fears of job loss, the senior management of both companies reached out to every single employee at every location.

Furthermore, in July 2012, Mahindra Satyam announced that it would be shifting its headquarters from Hyderabad to Mumbai. A senior employee with twelve years of working experience at the company expressed disappointment to a newspaper over the management's decision to move the headquarters to Mumbai. 'We were shocked. Though we were aware about the merger proposal, the fact that they now want to move the corporate office to Mumbai wasn't conveyed', he said.[24]

'We had barely come out of the accounting fraud shock and now we have to deal with the merger. It requires a mindset to accept such fast transformations', said a project leader with the company.[25]

'There's not going to be any lay-off because of the merger,' assured L Ravichandran, Tech Mahindra President, IT services. 'This is not a new marriage. It was on the cards for the last two years. So it's not a surprise. We know utilization of staff in both the places. Also, we have been jointly planning on-campus recruitment and going to management institutions,' Ravichandran said.

After the merger, both companies will merge their human resource departments. 'The challenge is not big though, as staff overlapping particularly on the operational side—a factor that always poses the biggest threat to merger disruption—is just about 1 percent,' said the *DNA* report. 'That is too good to be true, but it is true,' he said.

In the coming months, as Mahindra Satyam and Tech Mahindra realize their merger, or 'consummate their marriage', as Gurnani puts it, and moves its headquarters to Mumbai, it will enter into a new phase of its history but its past—three years of 'anguish, anxiety, and helplessness'—will always haunt its older employees like a nightmare. For others in the corporate sector, who have been witness to this story, as a searchlight of warning—of how the greed of a man could reduce a crown jewel into a speck of useless dust, as well as a beacon of hope—of how a company, infused with an indomitable spirit, could arise from its own ashes. It all depends on how you read the Satyam saga.

I see the story of Satyam's resurrection and resurgence as a story of hope and courage and as a shining example of public-private partnership—an example that every Indian should be proud of today. It would be a cliché to say that 'it happens only in India', but in this case, it is irrefutable. A story like Satyam does not exist in any other country in the world. Like many great epics, this modern-day corporate epic can only belong to the land of Kalidasa and Chanakya.

# EPILOGUE

*It is impossible to know definitely another human being, a totality that always slips through the theoretical and rational nets that try to capture it.*
—Mario Vargas Llosa, *The Dream of the Celt*

April 27, 2012
Singapore

The Satyam saga had two aspects to it. One was the corrective side of the story—of salvaging the company—where the government did well and deserves kudos for its exemplary role. The other was the retributive side of the story—of punishing those who were behind the scam—and so far, that part of the story does not pass the scrutiny.

It has been more than three years since B. Ramalinga Raju resigned as chairman of Satyam and till date the man and his methods remain an enigma. I have not met a single individual who knew him and did not have good things to say about him. Even Mahindra Satyam's current CEO, C.P. Gurnani, has repeatedly said that Raju is one of the finest persons he has ever met in his life.

When Raju confessed to his fraud, and was later arrested and jailed, folks in his native village Garagaparru, in West Godavari district, mourned for him. They cancelled Pongal celebrations, arranged rallies, posted letters to the prime minister, and plastered posters in his support on walls. They even invoked the gods to intervene in the matter. For them, their God had not fallen.

Even in jail, Raju continued to spin his magic. He had a tennis court built, courtesy the family-run Byrraju Foundation. This provided 'cheer to the 30-odd VIP prisoners, including eight former Satyam employees, bankers, and politicians' in the Chanchalaguda jail.[1]

Coming out of the jail, he 'thanked the warden and other jail staff, especially constables Ramesh and Gopal, who he said provided him with good coffee from outside shops.'[2] He asked the jail employees to visit him for job references for their children. While in prison, he used to advise staff's wards on their technology careers.

He was reportedly even going to head a jail-based business processing operations (BPO) centre, to be run by Bangalore-based Radiant Technologies. A newspaper report said: 'The company is upgrading a small jail-based call centre, opened by the government a year ago, into a full-fledged BPO manned by 1,000 prisoners. But for his release, Ramalinga would probably have headed it.'[3] The company had trained the prisoners, had created the infrastructure, and the BPO operations were to be launched soon. Talks were going on to engage Ramalinga Raju in this BPO, according to a senior jail official, but were cut short due to his release.

When Raju was released from jail in November 2011, the same villagers celebrated their hero's freedom by 'distributing sweets, bursting crackers, and praying at the local Shivalayam.'[4]

What lies behind Raju's charm? How does he manage to impress a CEO as well as simple villagers? However, I didn't want to make this book about Raju. The book is about Satyam's resurgence, about its phoenix-like rise. Nevertheless, I needed to understand this charismatic man, and for this I arranged a meeting with a person who had worked closely with him. He wishes to remain unnamed for my story. I will call him Joy.

It was a slightly warm afternoon when I arrived at the swanky Marina Bay Sands to meet Joy. We met in a bar—I had coffee and he, beer.

Joy had started working with Satyam when the company began its Asia-Pacific operations in Singapore. He saw it grow from a $5-10 million concern to a $100 million concern in the region. He left the company shortly after the Raju scandal broke out. He had lost all his money in his Satyam shares and worst, he had lost his house.

Yet, his tone didn't betray any bitterness once we started talking about Ramalinga Raju and Satyam. He spoke with the enthusiasm of a fan boy. Makes one wonder what kind of a leader Raju must have been to command such respect and loyalty from a former employee, that too three years after admitting his crime and ruining his finances?

In the pantheon of Indian CEOs, Joy puts Raju on one of the highest pedestals. Even his current CEO, who is like a superstar when placed on a podium, is no match to him in some aspects, he said.

'Raju was a thinker, a strategist,' he said. 'He was so calm and collected. He was generally soft spoken but when it came to putting his foot down on a matter, he would do it without raising his voice beyond the normal decibel level. That was an art.'

Besides Joy, I have heard many people saying the same about Raju—that he was soft spoken and unassuming. He was an outstanding gentleman and exceptionally humble—so humble that 'he would often turn up for lunch at the office cafeteria and eat with his employees.'[5] I even encountered people who had never seen him or met him such as parents of employees but spoke well of him.

Raju was very farsighted and he had the ability to see things far ahead of his time. He had the ability to take risks and then follow them through to the last detail on the execution. He was 'a tough taskmaster who always set challenging goals for his team.' Also, he worked tirelessly from morning till late at night and 'at times even checked if the service level agreements with clients were being honoured.' 'In fact, once it was decided that every incoming call should be answered in no more than two rings, Ramalinga Raju would call at midnight to confirm if this was indeed being done.'[6]

Besides remembering Raju as a soft-spoken and humble gentleman, what Joy remembers most about him is his vision. Joy talks about *The Satyam Way*—a 250-page book that contained Raju's management philosophy—which was given to the Satyam employees. He mentions several management concepts that formed the core of Raju's management style or philosophy of entrepreneurship: The TDC model, the Collaborative Index, Investor Culture, and full life cycle businesses.

'It was his unique business philosophy that allowed Satyam to assemble business teams on the fly that could deliver uniform client experiences,' said Joy.

Raju believed that business value could be created through the proper balance of three critical tasks: thinking, doing, and communicating. He called it the TDC model.[7]

Joy said that Raju asked his employees to devote 33 percent of their time to each of these three activities. Why were they important? Raju explained this in an interview to the *McKinsey Quarterly*.[8]

'... The knowledge industry operates in a dynamic environment and, in our view, it required a more refined and sophisticated business model to suit the times and the industry,' said Raju. 'For example, in the knowledge industry there is a greater coupling between strategy, operations, and stakeholder intimacy than demanded by traditional industries. To bring this all into focus, we came up with our 'TDC' model, which stands for "thinking", representing strategy and innovation; "doing", operational excellence; and "communicating", connecting intimately with stakeholders.'

'It's not rocket science, but when you look at a company like ours, you see that traditionally most of the thinking and communicating is done at the top, and most of the doing at the bottom,' he added. 'In *The Satyam Way* we expect leaders throughout our organization and at all levels to strike a balance among these three value-creating tasks.'

According to Joy, Raju insisted on his employees having effective communication skills. 'If you didn't know how to communicate effectively, you had to learn it,' he said. 'He would often test your communication skills. For example, suppose you are travelling with him in a car. He would ask you about the five things that you had done in the previous quarter. If he hadn't heard of those five things that you had accomplished, he would ask you why he hadn't heard about them. He would then ask you to work on your communication skills.'

'His own communication skills were superb,' said Joy. 'If you went to meet him, within a minute of the conversation he discerned what you wanted to communicate. Then he would switch off mentally and would be elsewhere, even though he would appear to be all ears to you. He was a great multi-tasker.'

Raju himself used to be on his mobile phone all the time, from morning until midnight. Joy recalls an incident during a press conference in Malaysia. Malaysia's then Prime Minister Abdullah Badawi himself was moderating the conference. Besides Raju, there were ten other CEOs from different companies on the stage. Raju had set up a work-related conference call and he wanted to slip out of the press conference after 15-20 minutes. Could he do it? He was advised against it. But he still managed to disappear from the press meet and take the conference call.

'Similarly, every employee, no matter how senior he was, had to devote 33 percent of his time to operational activities,' said Joy. 'If you were in sales and you were the top guy in the team, you still had to do billable operations. There was no excuse to not do it.'

Raju had developed a model of leadership that was different from other companies. It was a distributed leadership model. 'We also recognized that traditional hierarchical models will not be effective in a knowledge industry,' he said in the McKinsey interview. 'Rather than focussing the whole business on delivering value in one way, as you might see in a textile mill, at Satyam value was being delivered in many different ways, depending on the services our clients needed. To cater to these differences, we created an organizational design that distributed leadership more uniformly. Ownership of results shifted to leaders who were closest to the relevant stakeholders, which could be their colleagues, investors, clients, or even society generally. The rest of the organization supported these leaders from behind the scenes, helping to create a "One-Satyam" experience for the stakeholder. This design also sought to bring the correct balance between building the right soft assets that have lasting value and delivering reliable results for stakeholders.'

To ensure cohesion in the teams, Raju developed the concept of a Collaborative Index. 'Sometimes teams (for example, delivery and marketing teams) do not cooperate with each other,' said Joy. 'This is not good from the company's overall business perspective as it hampers the delivery of uniform and smooth client experience. To encourage cooperation between teams, Raju came up with the idea of a Collaborative Index. Part of the team members' variable pay was linked with this index—if the ratings were good, it meant better pay for the employees. Every quarter, each team had to rate the other team. You could not avoid it. If you did not participate in the survey, your pay roll would not be processed. Initially, each team rated the other low but slowly they realized they should rate each other better as it affected their salaries. This led to increased cooperation among the teams.'

Raju also came up with the concept of 'full life cycle businesses'. It meant dividing the organization into smaller business units or groups in such a way that each group takes full responsibility for creating value from a certain set of activities. 'This could be, for example,' said Raju, 'relationship management with a particular client or campus recruitment. The essential way these businesses operate, their DNA, is the same. Simply stated, whatever the nature of the activity, our model tries to balance maintaining the precepts of the TDC model, creating assets that deliver consistent results and contribute to future value, and satisfying stakeholder interests.'

Satyam had about 2,000 full life cycle businesses. Where were the leaders to run those businesses going to come from?[9]

Not from the outside. Raju believed in nurturing talent and giving people within the organization opportunities to become leaders.

'We consider ourselves in the business of building leaders,' Raju said in the McKinsey interview. 'The most effective way of realizing our goals and objectives it to grow leaders faster than the competition.'

So, Satyam created an analytical engine called the Real Time Leadership Centre in 2005. It worked with individual business leaders to identify goals and the metrics needed to track progress toward these goals. 'The centre also works with leaders to develop the knowledge and skills needed for success—for instance, by training them in management tools and sharing best practices that have worked elsewhere in the organization,' said Raju. 'And it also tracks the metrics, offering business leaders a dashboard to monitor how they are progressing. Essentially, it makes the language of metrics our first language.'

Joy said that Raju treated each leader as an entrepreneur and he fostered an investor culture to grow the company. For example, he said, 'If I wanted US$10 million to grow the Japan business, he would ask me to present a business plan as I would to any outsider (investor). If Raju was convinced after hearing the case, he would give me the money. He would also give me a target. If I succeeded in hitting the target, I would get a bonus. That's how he encouraged the leaders.'

I asked Joy if he saw the dark side of Raju when he was working with him.

'The only time I felt he had a dark side,' said Joy, 'was when he used to talk about his philanthropic activities like HMRI and EMRI.'[10] Health Management and Research Institute (HMRI) was a (free) 104 system where people could call with an ailment—physical or mental—and get immediate help over the phone. HMRI also had medical support vans that went into every village and provided scheduled medical testing and support. Similarly, Emergency Management Research Institute (EMRI) was a service that was being run in eight states, besides Andhra Pradesh. EMRI ran its popular '108' emergency ambulances service. The service involved over 1600 ambulances and attended to about 10,000 emergency calls on an average, every day. While states bore 95 percent of operational costs, the remaining five percent were borne by EMRI.

Raju had earned great respect at home and abroad because of his innovative social service initiatives like HMRI and EMRI, but Joy was not convinced.

'On the face of it, he was helping the poor and the needy of Andhra Pradesh through HMRI and EMRI which was a good thing to do,' said Joy. 'But at the same time, he used to say in behind closed door meetings that he was doing all that to collect data on millions of people. Imagine this kind of data for 80 million people in Andhra Pradesh alone! It would be invaluable for pharmaceutical countries. It was also a very low cost operation. It could find worldwide customers. "Go to a head of state in Africa and tell him we have a system that could win you the next election. He would pay any price for a system like this." When he talked like this, it struck me as odd. I found this duality in him strange. I think he was secretly aiming for the Nobel Prize.'

For a man like Raju, perhaps it was show time all the time. In his book *The Little Big Things,* Tom Peters talks about persona. He writes: 'Successful performers, for good and (sometimes) for ill, know how to play a role. They don a "persona"—a mask of leadership (for the Greeks, it was literally a mask) that commands others to follow.'

In discussing persona, Peters gives three examples: George Washington, Barack Obama, and Bernie Madoff. I think Raju's case is similar to that of Madoff's. 'It was a product of a very carefully concocted persona acted out without let-up or slip-up for decades,' Tom says about Madoff.[11] It sounds so true in Raju's case too.

'This man does not belong in jail. He belongs in a mental institution,' said D.A. Somayajulu, adviser to the Andhra government on economic affairs and policy implementation. When he was the secretary of APIRDC, he had given a young Ramalinga Raju his first loan for a spinning mill in 1982. That venture had failed. 'He was never in need of money...not even when he took that loan from us,' he said.[12]

'If anybody in the industry is capable of pulling off a scam like this, it would be Ramalinga Raju...the capability, the thinking through, the planning of such a large operation...only he had the ability to pull it off,' said Ganesh Natarajan of Zensat Technologies.[13]

Some psychoanalysts saw Raju as a 'rather remorseless person who was a control freak.' 'Though in his confessional statement he did apologize to all stakeholders, it hardly seemed as if he was sorry. Rather, he seemed to be issuing instructions on how to salvage the situation, after admitting to cooking the books.'[14]

★ ★ ★

No matter how you look at it, Satyam's is an extraordinary story.

It is the story of one of India's early startups that, just like Microsoft, started from a garage and went on to become India's fourth largest IT services company. At its peak, it had more than 50,000 employees with clients in 66 countries.

It is the story of India's biggest corporate fraud, which was perpetrated by Satyam's Founder and Chairman, Ramalinga Raju. Never before in India's history had someone inflated the company books by US$1.5 billion.

It is also the story of a company that went to hell and came back, rescued by a smaller company Tech Mahindra which had only 23,000 employees—talk of a small fish swallowing a big fish.

It is also the story of a company that showcased India's determination—the first and most successful example of a public-private partnership to save a company through the government's intervention. In India, the general belief is that when the government steps into something, it messes it up. The state of India's national carrier Air India is a living example. But in Satyam's case, it proved everyone wrong. Satyam was saved without the government spending a single rupee in bailing it out. In the US, when Enron and WorldCom happened, they just tanked. Satyam outlived that fate.

The role played by the Satyam associates is no less heroic. They went through trauma, humiliation, and uncertainty but they stuck to their guns, made sacrifices when necessary, and made sure that at no point of time they let their customers down. They showed an indefatigable spirit—the so called 'Spirit of Satyam'—and in my opinion, it was the most crucial X factor that ensured Satyam's survival.

One of the most startling facts of this journey of Satyam's survival is its acquisition by the Mahindra Group. Satyam was not saved because it needed saving—that might have been a government view and the reason for the government's intervention. At the same time, saving Satyam was not any corporate's noble duty. Nobody swooped in as the knight in shining armour to save the damsel in distress. The Mahindras came for a distress sale, to pick up the soiled jewels from the mud of controversy and scandal. There was risk involved but it made great business sense. Anand Mahindra wanted to internationalize the Mahindra brand and he wanted to use Information Technology (IT) as a lever for this expansion. He got what he wanted, and that makes him a great businessman.

The changes at Satyam were swift when the new regime took over. Satyam's nemesis in the old regime was the very way the company was organized and run, the so called 'Satyam Way'. That had to go. That system had created many hierarchies and it worked in so many different watertight compartments—in the guise of encouraging entrepreneurship—that the left hand in the company did not know what the right hand was doing. Only the almighty sitting at the top of the pyramid—Raju and his brother—knew what was going on. Gurnani dismantled that structure, and in its place, he created a leaner organization, and blew into it the ethics and the governance model of the Mahindra Group.

When Mahindra Satyam and Tech Mahindra finally merge (pending legal approval), the merged entity will be rebranded and from all indications, the name 'Satyam' will probably be dropped off for good. The Satyam legacy will live on but maybe under a different guise.

Even though Satyam's new owners have done a remarkable job of turning it around and transforming it, not everyone believes in this fairy tale of recovery. Critics of Mahindra Satyam say that the leadership of the company took a wrong approach. They first squeezed the company and got rid of 10,000 people. Only now, they are talking of growth and investment. They say that they should have started the transformation with investing in the company first, not with pruning it.

No matter what the critics say, the bottom-line is that Satyam is back in the reckoning and with the merger with Tech Mahindra, it will be back in the big boys' club.

The only jarring note in this story is what happened, or actually did not happen, to Raju. When the scandal broke out, everyone said that Raju and his accomplices deserved harsh punishment for carrying on this mega fraud. But the mastermind got out of jail on medical grounds on August 18, 2010. On November 4, 2011, Raju, along with his brother, B. Rama Raju and the former chief financial officer of Satyam, Vadlamani Srinivas, were granted bail by the Supreme Court of India. The bail was granted because charges had not been filed against them, even though they were in jail for 2 years and 8 months.[15]

The court also took into consideration the fact that the maximum punishment for the offence was seven years imprisonment and that they had fully cooperated with the trial after their bail was cancelled in October, 2010.

Perhaps, after all, Raju's calculations were correct. Perhaps, being the shrewd man that he is, he knew that by confessing his crime he would escape with light punishment. Perhaps, he knew how the system could be played.

Today, according to people who know him, Raju leads a normal life in Hyderabad. Even though he cannot travel out of India, those who have seen him recently report that at his home, there is no change in his lifestyle. The only difference, post his time in prison, is that he has been reduced in half healthwise.

How ironic it is that Raju, whose entrepreneurial fecundity was the reason for Satyam's birth, is today the only loose end in the Satyam story.

# AFTERWORD

In 2009, the Mahindra Group's largest IT services company, Tech Mahindra was highly concentrated in the telecom vertical. Tech Mahindra needed to diversify and derisk its presence within the IT sector and we felt that the strength of Satyam's competencies and people was an appealing proposition. We saw several synergies of scale, skills, delivery, capacities and most importantly, of best practices. It was a no brainer that the whole of the two companies had huge potential to be greater than the sum of their parts.

When Satyam made the Maytas acquisition move in mid-December 2008, the combination of IT services and infrastructure appeared very unusual, especially given Satyam's maturity in the IT sector. Certainly, everyone was quite intrigued by this move. When Ramalinga Raju admitted his accounting fraud on January 7, 2009, I thought it was ironic that such large scale deception had occurred in a company called 'Satyam'!

When we acquired Satyam, the deal made good business sense because of the obvious complementarities. But we also felt that our processes and reputation for good governance would be an important factor in reviving the company. So we did consider it a privilege to have the opportunity to correct an injustice.

I was delighted when, at the World Economic Forum that year, we received compliments across the board from industry leaders, all of whom hailed our decision.

Tech Mahindra won the bid for Satyam because it was able to offer the best price after considering the synergies both companies could derive. Today, three years down the road, we can confidently say that our assessment proved to be right. I think the government-appointed board deserves to be complimented for conducting the auction process in a transparent yet timely manner. The board played a crucial role and deserves a lot of credit for salvaging the company.

## AFTER THE ACQUISITION

After Tech Mahindra won the bid for Satyam it was important to manage the integration process so that we were able to leverage the synergies we had identified while managing the litigation and reputational risks we inherited. Integrating two large companies of this scale is never an easy task and we encouraged them to set out and follow some very clear principles.

- Focus on governance, and put in place policies for the future to ensure that the lapses are corrected
- Ensure an environment of inclusivity, fair play and trust
- Create a culture of a courageous, connected and agile organization, where ethical conduct is valued.
- Manage reputation risks by meeting customers and demonstrating our commitment to stay invested in critical 'go to market' opportunities
- Restore faith within our customers through new found business models of delivery and engagements

The team has done a tremendous job on all these fronts.

Vineet, CP, and the leadership team was very experienced and knew what they were doing. I had complete confidence in them. I was, of course, available for the team if they required my guidance or any intervention, especially with customers and associates.

Of course we were aware of the many risks involved including litigation issues, the possibility of customer flight, associate attrition and so on. But we had confidence in the inherent strength of the company, its people and capabilities and I think our leap of faith has paid off. There wasn't a single inflexion point. Rather, it was a sequence of events that gave us the confidence that we were on track.

Customer attrition stopped in July, 2009, providing us much needed validation of the inherent strength of the business. When we restated financials as per plan, we knew the exact magnitude of the problem we were dealing with. Soon thereafter, we embarked on the growth trajectory, when it became clear that we had turned the corner completely. As soon as the litigation issues were resolved we were ready to consider the merger with Tech Mahindra.

## LESSONS FROM THE TURNAROUND

The Mahindra Satyam story has been a challenging yet exciting three year transformational journey. Not only has it been a successful one, but it has also been an inspirational one.

The entire experience of the Mahindra Satyam turnaround taught me that crisis can always be turned into an opportunity, that when you have the courage to take challenges head on, you are always rewarded with results. It also taught me that engaging hearts and minds and giving people reason to hope, brings out the best in them. Today, Mahindra Satyam is back in the reckoning. It has recovered lost ground and is raring to go as a refreshed, recharged and revitalized organization.

I certainly think the turnaround reflects the resilience of the company, the spirit of corporate governance in India and the deftness with which the Indian system can act when confronted with a challenge. Hopefully, this has created a global impression.

I am very optimistic about the future of the Tech Mahindra and Mahindra Satyam merged entity. We see it as fuelling our ambition of becoming the No. 1 Indian IT company. The merged company will create a new offshore services leader with approximately US$ 2.4 billion in revenues, a 75,000+ workforce and 350 active clients.

The combined entity will be able to better leverage Tech Mahindra's depth of expertise developed in telecom to penetrate the opportunities within Mahindra Satyam's diverse set of clients across multiple verticals. Likewise, Mahindra Satyam's expertise in enterprise solutions will offer a more complete value proposition to Tech Mahindra's clients.

Companies with larger scale in the IT industry have a demonstrated track record of deeper penetration into the client's wallet share, lower volatility in earnings and higher growth. We hope to achieve all of these through the merger.

Anand Mahindra<br>
September 5, 2012<br>
Mumbai

*(This afterword has been adapted from Mr Anand Mahindra's interview with the author. Mr Mahindra is the Chairman and Managing Director of one of India's largest enterprises, Mahindra & Mahindra.)*

# ACKNOWLEDGEMENTS

To keep things simple, I will begin from the beginning.

The idea of this book sprouted from my discussions with Rohit Gandhi of Mahindra Satyam. From day one, he gave me his unwavering support and opened doors for me wherever I needed to go and introduced me to whoever I needed to meet to fulfil my dream of writing this book. Without his constant encouragement and support, I wouldn't have pursued this idea for long. So, thanks Rohit for the inspiration.

The second most important link in this chain is not one but actually two people who form the literary agency, Jacaranda. They are Jayapriya and Priya—the warmest and friendliest agents one could ever find. They have always believed in me; and in the case of this book, they strongly backed it from the get-go and made it happen.

As the project moved forward, many people held my hand and helped me in various ways in the research and writing of this book and made it what it is. My greatest debts are to Hari T. and Indraneel Ganguly of Mahindra Satyam for their assistance in the entire project and for their spirit of generosity. I am also enormously indebted to the executives at Mahindra Satyam who contributed their time and insights to this book, including (in no particular order) C.P. Gurnani, CEO; A.S. Murthy, Chief Technology Officer; Rakesh Soni, Chief Operating Officer; B.K. Mishra, Senior Vice President, Energy and Utilities; Hari Babu, Lead Manager of Operations, HR Department; and Dr Renu Khanna, Asst. Vice President, Leadership Development, Mahindra Satyam Learning World. Special thanks are also due to

Anand Mahindra, Chairman and MD of Mahindra & Mahindra; Anant Rangaswami; Shantanu Rege; Som Mittal, President of NASSCOM; and P.N. Balji for their kindness and extraordinary help.

Other folks I am thankful to, who are directly or indirectly associated with Mahindra Satyam and provided critical help on this project, are (in no particular order) Upasana, Ashish, Shruti, Uday, Vikram, Chatts, Reshma, and Lai K.K..

I also had insightful conversations with many people who wish to remain unnamed on these pages. I thank them for sharing their candid stories about their time at Satyam.

I am also thankful to my friend Mirza Rizwan and his brother Mirza Faizan, who hosted me in Bangalore while I was working on this book.

I am grateful to my colleagues at Fairfax Business Media, Singapore, especially Teng Fang Yih and Mark Hobson for their moral support and tolerating my broodiness while this book was being hatched.

The final product that you are holding in your hands became possible because of the passion and expert inputs of my wonderful editor, Milee Ashwarya. A huge thanks to her, Radhika Marwah, and the entire team at Random House India.

I am also thankful to my extended family and friends who kept me going with their encouragement and kind words, especially my father who would ask me every few weeks when the book was coming out. Thanks Papa and Ma for just being there for us.

Finally, I don't have adequate words to thank my wife Shabana and my daughter Zara for fervently believing in me and for enduring those absences from home and hearth when I was working on the book. A zillion thanks anyway and let me tell you that you are the light of my life and your smiles illuminate even the darkest caverns of my soul. God bless you!

# NOTES

## Prologue: In Search of Satyam (Truth)

1. Raju acknowledged his culpability in hiding news that he had inflated the amount of cash on the balance sheet of India's fourth-largest IT company by nearly US$1 billion, incurred a liability of US$253 million on funds arranged by him personally, and overstated Satyam's September 2008 quarterly revenues by 76 percent and profits by 97 percent. Source: Kripalani, Manjeet. 'India's Madoff: Satyam Scandal Rocks Outsourcing Industry.' *Bloomberg Businessweek*, January 7, 2009. http://www.businessweek.com/globalbiz/content/jan2009/gb2009017_807784.htm
2. Yet, interestingly, unlike in Enron's case, the Satyam scandal was not unearthed by a journalist. It was Satyam's Founder and Chairman Ramalingam Raju himself who admitted to the accounting fraud that brought his company down. Many in the financial circles are dismayed that the biggest-ever corporate fraud in the country could have escaped unnoticed for so many years. Source: Vaswani, Karishma. 'Satyam Scandal Shocks India.' BBC.co.uk, January 8, 2009. http://news.bbc.co.uk/2/hi/business/7818220.stm
3. Before the shocking confession from Raju, there was a long list of reported suitors for Satyam. They included HCL Technologies, Wipro, IBM (IBM), Hewlett-Packard (HPQ), Larsen & Toubro Infotech, Cognizant (CTSH), Cap Gemini (CAPP.PA), and even private equity players KKR and TPG. Source: Kripalani, Manjeet, Op. Cit., http://www.businessweek.com/globalbiz/content/jan2009/gb2009017_807784.htm

4. Tech Mahindra made a public statement that it would not be interested in acquiring Satyam 'in the current environment'.
5. On November 15, 2010, Mahindra Satyam announced its unaudited Indian GAAP results for Q1 & Q2 of FY 2010–11. Under Indian GAAP consolidated basis, the company reported revenue for Q1 and Q2 which was Rs 1,248 crore and Rs 1,242 crore respectively. Operating profit for Q1 and Q2 was Rs 114 crore and Rs 65 crore respectively. Headcount stood at 27,722 and 28,068 for Q1 and Q2 respectively. 'Our performance over the last two quarters clearly reflects the stability that has been brought in,' said C.P. Gurnani, CEO, Mahindra Satyam. 'We have retained our traditional strengths and leadership in areas like Enterprise Business Solutions (EBS) and Integrated Engineering Services (IES). Our uninterrupted service delivery has helped us to expand on existing relationships, resulting in multiple order renewals.' *Mahindra Satyam Press Release.* http://www.mahindrasatyam.com/media/Msat-results-q1-q2-fy2011.asp
6. HITEC City stands for Hyderabad Information Technology Engineering Consultancy City. It is a major technology township which is at the centre of the information technology industry in Hyderabad, Andhra Pradesh, India. HITEC City is spread across 151 acres (0.61 km$^2$) of land under suburbs like Sharthpur, Kondapur, Gachibowli, Nanakramguda, Manikonda, Thellapur etc. http://en.wikipedia.org/wiki/Hyderabad,India
7. Mahindra managers are more likely to end work on time and go out for a beer with colleagues—the former culture was more formal, with colleagues calling each other 'sir', said the current Mahindra managers at Satyam. Source: Bellman, Eric. 'Mahindra Satyam's New Owner Tries To Move Beyond Disgraced Founder.' *Wall Street Journal*, January 23, 2009. http://online.wsj.com/article/SB124830819046274189.html
8. In January 2011, Mahindra & Mahindra launched a new brand positioning spanning all group industries, companies, and geographies. This new brand positioning, expressed by the word 'Rise' is an articulation of values the group has always held dear. The idea of 'Rise' rests on three brand pillars: Accepting no limits; Alternative thinking; and Driving positive change. 'Rise' captures a sense of optimism about the future and a determination to shape one's own destiny. It means that our products and services empower our customers to achieve their aspirations. *Mahindra Satyam Annual Report*, 2010-11.

9. Excerpted from http://online.wsj.com/article/SB124830819046274189.html

## The Birth of a Scandal

1. The NASDAQ Stock Market, or simply NASDAQ, is an American stock exchange. NASDAQ stands for National Association of Securities Dealers Automated Quotations and, after the New York Stock Exchange, is the second-largest stock exchange by market capitalization in the world.
2. Maytas Properties was incorporated in 2005 as Maytas Hill County Ltd to carry out real estate development. It became Maytas Properties, a public company, in 2007. Raju's elder son, Teja Raju, and his younger son, Rama Raju Jr, and Suryanarayana Raju sat on the company's board.
3. Maytas Infra, incorporated in 1988 (as Satyam Constructions Pvt. Ltd) and converted into a public company in 2007, was in the business of infrastructure development. It raised Rs 327.45 crore from an IPO. The company's vice chairman was Ramalinga Raju's son, Teja Raju. The Raju family had about a 36 percent stake in the company.
4. US Securities and Exchange Commission website, Government of United States. http://www.sec.gov/Archives/edgar/data/1106056/000114554909000025/u00107exv99w3.htm
5. Kumar, Nagesh S. 'Fall of an Icon.' *Frontline*, vol. no. 26, issue 03. January 31–February 13, 2009. http://www.hindu.com/fline/fl2603/stories/20090213260300900.htm
6. Bhandari, Bhupesh. *The Satyam Saga*. New Delhi: BS Books, 2009.
7. Jafri, Syed Amin. 'Brand Hyderabad Takes a Hit in Indian Unrest.' *Telegraph*. UK, January 5, 2010. http://www.telegraph.co.uk/expat/expatnews/6935514/Brand-Hyderabad-takes-a-hit-in-Indian-unrest.html
8. Kripalani, Manjeet. Op. Cit. http://www.businessweek.com/globalbiz/content/jan2009/gb2009017_807784.htm
9. Mahindra, Anand and Vir Sanghvi. *Tycoons with Vir Sanghvi*. CNBCTV18, August 10, 2009. http://www.youtube.com/watch?v=eP5OJ96HChI&feature=related

10. Gombar, Vandana. *The Satyam Saga*. New Delhi: BS Books, 2009.
11. Natarajan, Ganesh and Manjiri Gokhale. *Inspired,* 2006.
12. He was enrolled in the executive owner/president management program (OPM) at Harvard Business School.
13. Gombar, Vandana. *The Satyam Saga*. New Delhi: BS Books, 2009.
14. Ibid.
15. Kumar, S.Nagesh. Op. Cit. http://www.hindu.com/fline/fl2603/stories/20090213260300900.htm
16. Ibid.
17. Bhandari, Bhupesh. *The Satyam Saga*. New Delhi: BS Books, 2009.
18. Reuters. 'Satyam Stunner: Highs and Lows of Raju's Career.' *IBNLive.com,* January 7, 2009. http://ibnlive.in.com/news/satyam-stunner-highs-and-lows-of-rajus-career/82183-7.html?from=rssfeed
19. At the time when the scandal broke, EMRI was running its 108 emergency ambulances service in eight other states besides Andhra Pradesh, where it ran over 1,600 ambulances and attended to about 10,000 emergency calls on an average every day.

    PTI. 'Satyam Led EMRI Continue Operations Despite Scam.' *Mid Day,* January 18, 2009. http://www.midday.com/news/2009/jan/180109-Satyam-NGO-EMRI-to-continue-operations.htm
20. Krishnamoorthy, Suresh. 'Responsive Saviour for People in Distress.' *Hindu,* January 27, 2006. http://www.hindu.com/thehindu/thscrip/print.pl?file=2006012714280200.htm&date=2006/01/27/&prd=th&
21. The Byrraju Foundation has taken up development work in a number of fields including education, health, drinking water, and several others in hundreds of villages in the coastal districts of West Godavari, East Godavari, Krishna, Visakhapatnam, and others. Source: Agencies. 'Ramalinga Raju's Village Still Blesses Him.' *Indian Express,* January 9, 2009. http://www.indianexpress.com/news/ramalinga-rajus-village-still-blesses-him/408725/
22. Bhandari, Bhupesh. *The Satyam Saga*. New Delhi: BS Books, 2009.
23. Ibid. 12.
24. Ibid. 12.
25. Ibid 13.
26. Ibid. 15.
27. Nag, Kingshuk. *The Double Life of Ramalinga Raju.* New Delhi: HarperCollins India, 2009.

28. Kumar, S. Nagesh. Op. Cit. http://www.hindu.com/fline/fl2603/stories/20090213260300900.htm
29. Though, Satyam had forecast 33–35 growth in business less than two months earlier. Bhandari, Bhupesh. *The Satyam Saga*. New Delhi: BS Books, 2009.
30. Nag, Kingshuk. *The Double Life of Ramalinga Raju*. New Delhi: HarperCollins India, 2009.
31. Bhandari, Bhupesh. *The Satyam Saga*. New Delhi: BS Books, 2009.
32. Wang, Tina. 'Investors Slap Down Satyam.' forbes.com, December 17, 2008. http://www.forbes.com/2008/12/17/satyam-controversy-india-markets-equity-cx_twdd_1217markets2.html
33. Ibid. 31.
34. Wang, Tina. Op. Cit.
35. Wang Tine. Op. Cit.
36. Kumar, S. Nagesh Op. Cit. http://www.hindu.com/fline/fl2603/stories/20090213260300900.htm
37. Kriplani, Manjeet. 'India's Madoff: Satyam Scandal Rocks Outsourcing Industry.' *Bloomberg Businessweek*, January 7, 2009. http://www.businessweek.com/globalbiz/content/jan2009/gb2009017_807784.htm
38. Chapman, Siobhan. 'Satyam Fraud Scandal: Timeline.' *Computerworld UK*, January 13, 2009. http://www.computerworlduk.com/how-to/outsourcing/1982/
39. Ibid.
40. Bhandari, Bhupesh. *The Satyam Saga*. New Delhi: BS Books, 2009.
41. Satyam Computer Services is up for grabs. Founder and Chairman B Ramalinga Raju is set to exit a company that he has built over 21 years after his failure to repair its tarnished image... Would Ramalinga Raju's voluntary exit from Satyam be a low watermark on his career or is it inevitable anyway? Source: 'Satyam Board to Discuss Dilution of Raju's Stake.' *Economic Times*, December 18, 2008. http://economictimes.indiatimes.com/tech/software/satyam-board-to-discuss-dilution-of-rajus-stake/articleshow/3902043.cms
42. The promoter, that is Raju, and his family held an 8.5 percent stake in the company.
43. 'Satyam Board to Discuss Dilution of Raju's Stake.' *Economic Times*, December 18, 2008. http://economictimes.indiatimes.com/

tech/software/satyam-board-to-discuss-dilution-of-rajus-stake/articleshow/3902043.cms

44. 'Billionaire Kills Himself Over Financial Crisis.' *msnbc.com*, January 6, 2009. http://www.msnbc.msn.com/id/28522036/ns/business-world_
45. Raju was the not the first businessman to have confessed his crime of fraud through a letter. In the famous Dalmia case, unraveled in 1956, Ramakrishna Dalmia, then chairman of Dalmia-Jain Airways and owner of Bharat Insurance Company, admitted in a written confession, much like Satyam chief B. Ramalinga Raju, that he had embezzled funds to the tune of Rs 2.2 crore from his insurance company. He faced trial and was sentenced to two years in jail. More importantly, the scandal led to the nationalization of the insurance sector. Source: Ramakrishnan, Venkitesh. 'Pliant Systems.' *Frontline*, vol. no. 26, issue 03. January 31–February 13, 2009. http://www.hindu.com/fline/fl2603/stories/20090213260302200.htm
46. 'Wife Says Raju Was Trying to Save Satyam.' NDTV Profit, March 29, 2009. http://www.youtube.com/watch?v=eWQb0VcX9rc&feature=relmfu
47. Nag, Kingshuk. *The Double Life of Ramalinga Raju*. New Delhi: Harper Collins India, 2009.
48. Nandini Raju said to an *NDTV* reporter in March 2009: 'He (Raju) knew that the company would go completely bankrupt and whatever is happening with Satyam, now they say it is exactly what he wanted—to have a stable board and ensure that employees were secure and clients would stay.' Source: 'Wife Says Raju Was Trying to Save Satyam.' NDTV Profit, March 29, 2009. http://www.youtube.com/watch?v=eWQb0VcX9rc&feature=relmfu
49. Nag, Kingshuk. Op. Cit., 47.

## Shock, Anger, and Betrayal

1. Priscilla Nelson was global director of people leadership and her husband, Ed Cohen, was chief learning officer at the Satyam School of Leadership. They have described their experiences at Satyam in a book. *Riding the Tiger: Leading through Learning in Turbulent Times*. United States: American Society for Training and Development, 2010.

2. 'Satyam Chairman Ramalinga Raju's Letter.' Reuters, 7 January, 2009. http://uk.reuters.com/article/2009/01/07/satyam-text-idUKBOM 36807220090107
3. 'None of the board members, past or present, had any knowledge of the situation in which the company is placed. Even business leaders and senior executives in the company, such as, Ram Mynampati, Subu D., T.R. Anand, Keshab Panda, Virender Agarwal, A.S. Murthy, Hari T., S.V. Krishnan, Vijay Prasad, Manish Mehta, Murali V., Sriram Papani, Kiran Kavale, Joe Lagiola, Ravindra Penumetsa; Jayaraman, and Prabhakar Gupta are unaware of the real situation as against the books of accounts. None of my or Managing Director's immediate or extended family members has any idea about these issues.' Reuters, 7 January, 2009. http://uk.reuters.com/article/2009/01/07/satyam-text-idUKBOM36807220090107
4. Ibid. 3.
5. NASSCOM (the National Association of Software and Services Companies) is a trade association of Indian Information Technology (IT) and Business Process Outsourcing (BPO) industry.
6. Excerpted from http://www.docstoc.com/docs/75456797/Mahindra-Satyam-company-background
7. Back in 1996 to 2000—the golden era for the Y2K problem.
8. 'Learning lab has always played a very critical role in terms of building capabilities of people be it in the area of domain or technology or project management'—Dr Khanna.
9. Cohen, Ed, and Priscilla Nelson. *Riding the Tiger: Leading through Learning in Turbulent Times.* United States: American Society for Training and Development, 2010.
10. Excerpted from http://www.docstoc.com/docs/75456797/Mahindra-Satyam-company-background
11. Ibid. 9.
12. Ibid. 9.
13. Bhandari, Bhipesh. *The Satyam Saga.* New Delhi: BS Books, 2009.
14. 'Unedited Open Letter from Satyam Interim CEO Ram Mynampati.' *Economic Times*, January 7, 2009. http://articles.economictimes.indiatimes.com/2009-01-07/news/28481369_1_satyam-ceo-ram-mynampati-leadership-bandwidth
15. Satyam receives letter from chairman tendering resignation and detailing financial irregularities, Mahindra Satyam Media centre

(company website). http://www.mahindrasatyam.com/media/pr2jan09.asp
16. Nag, Kingshuk. *The Double Life of Ramalinga Raju*. New Delhi: HarperCollins India, 2009.
17. Ibid. 13.
18. Ibid. 16.

## A Bomb Explodes in New Delhi

1. Goswami, Omkar. 'Nuts and Bolts of Satyam Saga.' *Mint*, January 8, 2009. http://www.livemint.com/2009/01/08205554/Nuts-and-bolts-of-Satyam-saga.html
2. An internal Satyam report, 'Getting the Word Out', says the fax went out at 9.32 am at Satyam Computer Services headquarters in Hyderabad.
3. Goswami, Omkar Op. Cit.
4. 'Ex-Corporate Affairs Secretary Reveals How Government Saved Satyam.' *Moneycontrol.com*, January 8, 2010. http://www.moneycontrol.com/video/business/ex-corporate-affairs-secyreveals-how-govt-saved-satyam_434437.html
5. Bhandari, Bhupesh. *The Satyam Saga*. New Delhi: BS Books, 2009.
6. Ibid. 6.
7. Ibid. 6.
8. Ibid. 5.
9. Narendranath, K.G. 'Right Decisions on Time Saved Satyam.' *Economic Times*, May 5, 2009. http://m.economictimes.com/opinion/interviews/right-decisions-on-time-saved-satyam/articleshow/msid-4484587,curpg-3.cms
10. Howlett, Dennis. 'Satyam Scandal—The Fallout.' *Guardian*, January 15. 2009. http://www.guardian.co.uk/technology/2009/jan/15/satyam-computer-services
11. Mahindra, Anand, Nandan Nilekani, and Rajdeep Sardesai. 'Satyam Computer Scantal Part 1.' IBN Live footage on Youtube. http://www.youtube.com/watch?v=9Kg7gpFjd2c&feature=related
12. Maindra, Anand, Nandan Nilekani, Narayana Murthy, and Rajdeep

Sardesai. 'Satyam Computer Disaster.' IBN Live footage on Youtube. http://www.youtube.com/watch?v=1XHcUCJI0nY

13. Murthy, Narayana. 'Satyam Case is a Warning for Other Managements.' *Economic Times*, January 8, 2009. http://articles.economictimes.indiatimes.com/2009-01-08/news/28468342_1_satyam-case-biggest-corporate-scam-managements

14. 'Raju's Letter on Shareholding Misleading.' *Times of India*, January 8, 2009. http://articles.timesofindia.indiatimes.com/2009-01-08/india-business/28056927_1_cr-shares-ramalinga-raju-promoters

15. Ibid.

16. 'System Failure.' *Frontline*, vol. 26, issue 03, January 31–February 13, 2009. http://www.hindu.com/fline/fl2603 stories/ 20090213260300400.htm

17. 'Satyam Mega Fraud 5.' CNN IBN Footage on YouTube, January 7, 2009. http://www.youtube.com/watch?v=g3ubFpsnzsY&feature=relate

18. 'Satyam Mega Fraud 6.' CNN IBN Footage on YouTube, January 7. 2009. http://www.youtube.com/watch?v=JUt7EqDsuCc&feature=related

19. Kripalani, Manjeet. 'India's Madoff: Satyam Scandal Rocks Outsourcing Industry.' *Bloomberg Businessweek*, January 7, 2009. http://www.businessweek.com/globalbiz/content/jan2009/gb2009017_807784.htm

20. Nag, Kingshuk. *The Double Life of Ramalinga Raju*. New Delhi: HarperCollins India, 2009.

21. According to his family, he was depressed for the past few days after losing money, but on Wednesday when the Sensex dipped further after the Satyam shock, all his hopes crashed. A teacher of mathematics at Guru Har Rai Public Senior Secondary School in Dosanjh Kalan, Harsh Kumar, 35, was a resident of Urban Estate area. Source: 'I P Singh, Rs 14–15 lakh Loss in Stocks Drives Teacher to Suicide.' *Times of India*, January 10, 2009. http://articles.timesofindia.indiatimes.com/2009-01-10/india-business/28009352_1_stock-market-extreme-step-celphos-tablets

22. Trading on Satyam ADRs was suspended on January 7 after it plunged by over 90 percent to US$0.85 in pre-market trade in US following Satyam Founder and Chairman B. Ramalinga Raju's confession to a Rs 7,800

crore fraud in the company. NYSE in a statement yesterday (January 7) had said, 'NYSE Regulation is currently evaluating the news relating to Satyam and will closely monitor further developments. The security will remain halted until further notice.' Source: 'Satyam Faces Class Action Lawsuit in US.' *Indian Express*, August 31, 2012. http://www.indianexpress.com/comments/satyam-faces-class-action-lawsuit-in-us/408266/

23. Nag, Kingshuk. The Double Life of Ramalinga Raju. New Delhi: HarperCollins India, 2009, 31.
24. Paljor, Karma. *IBN Live*
25. Nag, Kingshuk. Op. Cit.
26. Nag, Kingshuk. Op. Cit., 32.
27. Narendranath, K.G. 'Right Decisions on Time Saved Satyam.' *Economic Times*, May 5, 2009. http://articles.economictimes.indiatimes.com/20090505/news/27643120_1_ministryprocess-partnerships
28. Ibid.

## Hyderabad Blues

1. Bhandari, Bhupesh. 'Salvaging Satyam.' *The Satyam Saga*. New Delhi: BS Books, 2009.
2. Ibid.
3. Ibid.
4. Ibid.
5. Ibid.
6. 'Raju May Face 10 yr Jail, Rs 25 cr Fine.' *Indian Express*, January 8, 2009. http://www.indianexpress.com/news/raju-may-face-10-yr-jail-rs-25-cr-fine/408321/
7. Mishra, Pankaj. 'Tesco Could Move Satyam Projects to Rivals.' *Economic Times*, January 8, 2009. http://articles.economictimes.indiatimes.com/2009-01-08/news/28414779_1_hindustan-service-centre-third-biggest-retailer-satyam-computer-services
8. 'Satyam Faces Class Action Lawsuit in US.' *Indian Express*, August 31, 2012. http://www.indianexpress.com/comments/satyam-faces-class-action-lawsuit-in-us/408266/

9. 'Satyam's Top Leaders Commit To Stay Despite Disclosures By Founder on Financial Irregularities.' *Mahindra Satyam press release*, January 8, 2009. http://www.mahindrasatyam.com/media/pr4jan09.asp
10. Ibid.
11. 'U S Securities & Exchange Commission, Form 6-K.' http://google.brand.edgar-online.com/EFX_dll/EDGARpro.dll?FetchFilingHTML1?ID=6339769&SessionID=-EI6WWvvg9pqow7
12. Rajiv, M., S. Nagesh Kumar. ,Ramalinga Raju Surrenders to Police.' *Hindu*, January 10, 2009. http://www.hindu.com/2009/01/10/stories/2009011060330100.htm
13. Ibid.
14. 'Satyam CFO Srinivas Arrested.' *India Today*, January 10, 2009. http://indiatoday.intoday.in/story/Satyam+CFO+Srinivas+arrested/1/24970.html

## The League of Extraordinary Gentlemen

1. Mathew, George, and P. Vaidyanathan Iyer. 'Salvaging Satyam.' *Indian Express*, April 19, 2009. http://www.indianexpress.com/news/salvaging-satyam/448585/0
2. Ibid.
3. Bhandari, Bhupesh. *The Satyam Saga*. New Delhi: BS Books, 2009.
4. 'India Steps in to Save Satyam.' NDTV footage on YouTube, January 12, 2009. http://www.youtube.com/watch?v=ME3flXuhuzw&feature=related
5. Timmons, Heather, and Jeremy Kahn. 'Satyam Founders Interrogated; Government Appoints New Board.' *New York Times*, January 11, 2009. http://www.nytimes.com/2009/01/11/business/worldbusiness/11iht-11satyam2.19246500.html?_r=1
6. 'Inside Story: How They Saved Satyam.' *Money Control, CNBC TV 18*. http://www.youtube.com/watch?v=Npu1iHDnYho&feature=relmfu
7. 'Satyam Shares Rebound as New Board Meets.' *Times of India*, January 12, 2009. http://timesofindia.indiatimes.com/home/specials/Satyam-shares-rebound-as-new-board-meets/articleshow/3969599.cms
8. Ibid.

9. Ibid.
10. Meanwhile, on January 13, the board received a letter from Satyam's statutory auditors, PricewaterhouseCoopers, stating that PricewaterhouseCoopers performed audits of Satyam from the quarter ended June 30, 2000 until the quarter ended September 30, 2008 (the 'Audit Period'). The auditors also notified the board that in view of the contents of the resignation letter of B. Ramalinga Raju, PricewaterhouseCoopers's audit reports and opinions in relation to Satyam's financial statements for the Audit Period should no longer be relied upon.
11. 'Govt Appoints 3 New Directors on Satyam Board.' *India Today*, January 15, 2009. http://indiatoday.intoday.in/story/Govt+appoints+3+new+directors+on+Satyam+board/1/25403.html
12. Ibid.
13. Ibid.
14. Ibid.
15. Ibid. 6.
16. Ibid. 6.
17. Mathew, George, and P. Vaidyanathan Iyer. 'Salvaging Satyam.' *Indian Express*, April 19, 2009. http://www.indianexpress.com/news/salvaging-satyam/448585/0
18. Ibid.
19. Ibid.
20. 'Commonwealth Connects Programme' http://www.commonwealthconnectsprogramme.org/partners/cc-steering-committee/mr-kiran-karnik-chairperson-of-strategic-advisory-committee-2/
21. Surendar, T. 'A Person of the Year: Deepak Parekh.' forbes.com, December 29, 2010. http://www.forbes.com/2010/12/29/forbes-india-person-of-the-year-deepak-parekh.html
22. 'Former Securities Appellate Tribunal Chief C. Achuthan Passes Away.' *Economic Times*, September 20, 2011. http://articles.economictimes.indiatimes.com/2011-09-20/news/30180259_1_sabarimala-temple-c-achuthan-sterlite-industries
23. 'Executive profile of Tarun Das.' *Bloomberg Businessweek*. http://investing.businessweek.com/research/stocks/private/person.asp?personId=5910769&privcapId=5911494&previousCapId=74877366&previousTitle=Physician%20Advantage,%20Inc.

24. 'Executive profile of S.B. Mainak.' *Bloomberg Businessweek.* http://investing.businessweek.com/research/stocks/private/person.asp?personId=52286755&privcapId=8033827&previousCapId=8033945&previousTitle=General%20Insurance%20Corporation%20of%20India

## The Healing Begins

1. These figures are according to Raju's letter of confession.
2. Mitra, Moinak. 'Satyam Crisis: Leadership Lessons.' *Economic Times*, October 9, 2010. http://articles.economictimes.indiatimes.com/2010-10-09/news/27592664_1_satyam-crisis-satyam-case-satyam-founder-and-chairman
3. 'Saving a Crisis-Ridden Company by Priscilla Nelson and Ed Cohen in Strategy + Business.' http://m.strategy-business.com/article/00065?gko=4fc3d
4. One year after the Satyam crisis, both husband and wife returned to the US. Now, they run their own consulting business. Priscilla is president and CEO of Nelson Cohen Global Consulting while Ed is executive vice president.
5. Ibid. 2.
6. Ibid. 3.
7. Based on interview with the author.
8. According to Encyclopaedia Britannica, the Y2K bug, also called Year 2000 bug or Millennium Bug, was a problem in the coding of computerized systems that was projected to create havoc in computers and computer networks around the world at the beginning of the year. Satyam's business grew as it helped companies tackle the so-called Y2K bug. http://www.britannica.com/EBchecked/topic/382740/Y2K-bug
9. Monga, Deepshikha, and Joji Thomas Philip. 'Satyam Fallout: US Staff Lose Health Cover, Credit Cards.' *Economic Times*, January 14, 2009. http://articles.economictimes.indiatimes.com/2009-01-14/news/27648059_1_credit-cards-health-insurance-medical-insurance
10. 'Satyam Employee Commits Suicide Fearing Job Loss.' *Economic Times*, January 15, 2009. http://articles.timesofindia.indiatimes.com/20090115/chennai/28010375_1_satyam-employee-extreme-step-suicide

## An Unlikely CEO

1. 'Satyam Names CEO and Special Advisers, and Secures Financing.' *Mahindra Satyam Press release*, February 5, 2009. http://www.mahindrasatyam.com/media/pr2Feb09.asp
2. Hari T. is currently the chief people officer and chief marketing officer of Mahindra Satyam.
3. Ibid. 1.
4. Ibid. 1.

## A Marriage Made in Heaven

1. Leahy, Joe, and Varun Sood. 'Satyam's Saviour Has a Mountain to Climb.' rediff.com (a *Financial Times* story reproduced by rediff.com), April 14, 2009. http://www.rediff.com/money/2009/apr/14satyams-saviour-has-a-mountain-to-climb.htm
2. Bhandari, Bhupesh. *The Satyam Saga*. New Delhi: BS Books, 2009.
3. Mathew, George, and P. Vaidyanathan Iyer. 'Salvaging Satyam.' *Indian Express*, April 19, 2009. http://www.indianexpress.com/news/salvaging-satyam/448585/0
4. Bhandari, Bhupesh. Op. Cit.
5. Ibid.
6. 'Satyam Announces Renewed Customer Confidence; Wins New Business of Over USD 250 Mn. in Last Seven Weeks.' http://www.mahindrasatyam.com/media/pr5Feb09.asp
7. Ibid 4.
8. Ibid. 4.
9. Ibid. 4.
10. Ibid. 4.
11. Ibid. 4.
12. Ibid. 4.

13. Mathew, George, and P. Vaidyanathan Iyer, Op. Cit. 'Retired justice S.P. Bharucha was roped in to monitor the bidding process. The six new directors met week after week in Hyderabad, Mumbai, and Delhi to finalize the sale process. Tarun Das, with his phenomenal clout in the government, helped move files quickly.' http://www.indianexpress.com/news/salvaging-satyam/ 448585/0
14. Some newspaper articles quote the figure as Rs 49.50.
15. Mathew, George, and P. Vaidyanathan Iyer, Op. Cit. http://www.indianexpress.com/news/salvaging-satyam/448585/0
16. Leahy, Joe, and Varun Sood, Op. Cit. http://www.rediff.com/money/2009/apr/14satyams-saviour-has-a-mountain-to-climb.htm
17. 'Tech Mahindra Wins Bid for Satyam at 2,900 cr.' *Times of India,* April 14, 2009. http://articles.timesofindia.indiatimes.com/2009-04-14/india-business/28028861_1_bidding-process-satyam-board-techma
18. Ibid.
19. 'Is Tech Mahindra Best Satyam Suitor? Experts React.' *moneycontrol.com,* April 13, 2009. http://www.moneycontrol.com/news/business/is-tech-mahindra-bestsatyam-suitor-experts-react_393085.html
20. Ibid
21. Ibid.
22. Timmons, Heather. 'Indian Group Wins Big Stake in Outsourcing Company.' *New York Times,* April 13, 2009. http://www.nytimes.com/2009/04/14/business/global/14outsource.html
23. Ibid.
24. Leahy, Joe, and Varun Sood, Op. Cit. http://www.rediff.com/money/2009/apr/14satyams-saviour-has-a-mountain-to-climb.htm
25. Mathew, George, and P. Vaidyanathan Iyer Op. Cit. http://www.indianexpress.com/news/salvaging-satyam/448585/0

## The Camel Rider

1. All unreferenced quotes are sourced from the author's interview with C.P. Gurnani.
2. Mahindra Satyam's C.P. Gurnani on Opportunity, Innovation and Uncertainty, India Knowledge@Wharton, 3 November 2011,

available at http://knowledge.wharton.upenn.edu/india/article.cfm?articleid=4657
3. Gurnani, C.P. 'Integration and Positioning for Growth.' *QSAdvisory*. http://www.qsadvisory.com/opinion_details.php?oid=269
4. Ibid.
5. Ibid.
6. Annual Report, 2008–2009 & 2009–2010, Satyam Computer Services Limited.
7. Virtual Pool Programme; a layoff exercise of benched staff of Mahindra Satyam.

## Turning the Tide

1. *IDG News Service*.
2. Machado, Kenan. 'Satyam Posts A Profit' *Wall Street Journal*, May 18, 2012. http://blogs.wsj.com/dealjournalindia/2012/05/18/satyam-posts-a-profit/?mod=google_news_blog
3. The author met Hari in July, 2011 in Singapore. Hari has over two decades of experience in the IT industry. He has been with Mahindra Satyam for the past 11 years, playing vital roles in the organization's growth and during its turbulent phase in the recent past. He was in town to collect an award for Satyam's people practices.
4. The author interviewed Rohit Gandhi in February, 2011.
5. Reddem, Appaji, and Sandeep Srikant. 'Mah-Satyam Sets Up Shadow Board to Resurrect Firm.' *moneycontrol.com*, November 14, 2009. http://www.moneycontrol.com/news/cnbc-tv18-comments/mah-satyam-setsshadow-board-to-resurrect-firm_424962.html
6. 'Satyam Aims to Put in Place Robust Corporate Governance System: CEO.' *Economic Times*, October 27, 2009. http://articles.economictimes.indiatimes.com/2009-10-27/news/27647055_1_mahindra-satyam-ict-firm-customers
7. Ibid. 5.
8. Ibid. 1.
9. The meeting being referred to here occurred in January 2012 in Hyderabad.

10. 'Insight: Mahindra Satyam: Rise of the Phoenix'. *IDC (Asia/Pacific Consulting and Integration Services: Insight)*, August 2011, IDC #AP2577413T, Volume: 1
11. Machado, Kenan Op. Cit. http://blogs.wsj.com/dealjournalindia/2012/05/18/satyam-posts-a-profit/?mod=google_news_blog

## Back in the Big Boys' Club

1. In a filing to the Bombay Stock Exchange on March 21, Tech Mahindra said that its board has approved the amalgamation of its subsidiaries with the company, including wholly owned unit Venturbay Consultants which acquired a 43 percent stake in Satyam in 2009.
2. 'Mahindra Satyam, Tech Mahindra Merge to Create $2.4-billion Company.' *Economic Times*, March 22, 2012. http://articles.economictimes.indiatimes.com/2012-03-22/news/31224979_1_mahindra-satyam-cp-gurnani-vineet-nayyar
3. Crabtree, James. 'Satyam and Tech Mahindra to Merge.' *Financial Times*, March 21, 2012. http://www.ft.com/intl/cms/s/0/8fe6eb94-733f-11e1-9014-00144feab49a.html#axzz1pvem5KQF
4. Kurmanath, M.V. 'Making Their Way through the Merger.' *Business Line*. http://www.thehindubusinessline.com/features/eworld/article3412624.ece?ref=wl_smartbuy
5. Scott, Mark. 'Tech Mahindra to Merge With Satyam.' *New York Times*, March 21, 2012. http://dealbook.nytimes.com/2012/03/21/tech-mahindra-to-merge-with-satyam/
6. Kurmanath, M.V., Op. Cit. http://www.thehindubusinessline.com/features/eworld/article3412624.ece?ref=wl_smartbuy
7. Ibid.
8. 'How Do Analysts View Tech Mahindra-Satyam Merger?' moneycontrol.com, March 22, 2012. http://www.moneycontrol.com/news/market-outlook/how-do-analysts-view-tech-mahindra-satyam-merger_683897.html
9. Ibid.
10. Tech Mahindra's shares rose 5.6 percent on news of the merger, to close at Rs 685.10, while Mahindra Satyam rose 4.7 percent to Rs 77.65.

11. Satyam agreed to pay US$125 million to settle one American suit in early 2011, but another case for a further US$68 milliom brought by the Aberdeen Group, an asset management company, remains outstanding. The second case relates to a claim for about US$125 million which India's tax department says is due on revenues stated before the 2009 revelations. The company disputes the claim, arguing that these revenues were subsequently proved to be fictitious. *Financial Times*, London.
12. Ibid. 6.
13. Ibid. 6.
14. 'Mahindra Group Hires Consultant to Suggest Name for Merged Entity.' *Times of India*, March 24, 2012. http://articles.timesofindia.indiatimes.com/2012-03-24/strategy/31233258_1_tech-mahindra-mahindra-satyam-president-l-ravichandran-mahindra-group
15. Crabtree, James, *Op. Cit.* http://www.ft.com/cms/s/0/8fe6eb94-733f-11e1-9014-00144feab49a.html# axzz1pvem5KQF
16. BT called Tech Mahindra a 'key strategic supplier', but also reiterated that it could consider further share sales 'at some point in the future'. *Financial Times*, London.
17. 'Open to Acquisitions if They Serve a Strategic Purpose: Vineet Nayyar, VC, MD & CEO, Tech Mahindra.' *Economic Times,* March 21, 2012. http://articles.economictimes.indiatimes.com/2012-03-21/news/31220073_1_tech-mahindra-mahindra-satyam-vineet-nayyar-cp-gurnani
18. Compared with about 17 percent revenue growth for Mahindra Satyam since 2010, HCL has expanded its top line by 44 percent. Nayyar and Gurnani have both worked for HCL Technologies.
19. Excerpted form http://www.computerworld.com.sg/tech/industries/tech-mahindra-and-mahindra-satyam-merger-announced/?page=2
20. Yap, Jamie. 'India's Satyam-Mahindra Poses "Serious Threat" to Rivals.' *ZDNet.com*, March 22, 2012. http://www.zdnet.com/indias-satyam-mahindra-poses-serious-threat-to-rivals-2062304266/
21. 'While Tech Mahindra is predominant in the telecommunications sector, the merger would give it access to other verticals including manufacturing and enterprise management services in which Satyam is a major player,' he explained. 'The merged entity can now offer a

"full lifecycle of solutions" from business process outsourcing (BPO), to application development and management (ADM), infrastructure management, and enterprise business solutions,' he added.
22. In March 2012, Mahindra Satyam acquired BPO company vCustomer's international operations for US$ 27 million, and in February, had bought a 15 percent stake in software company Dion Global Solutions. Mahindra Satyam Press Release, March 7, 2012. http://www.mahindrasatyam.com/news/Mahindra-Satyam-acquires-vCustomers-International-Operations.asp
23. Moitra, Sumit. 'Satyam, Tech Mahindra Talk to Staff, Allay Job Loss Fears.' *DNA India*, March 26, 2012. http://www.dnaindia.com/money/report_satyam-tech-mahindra-talk-to-staff-allay-job-loss-fears_1667389
24. Mahalakshmi. 'Mahindra Satyam's Headquarter Shift News Fuels Fear of Job Losses.' *Financial Express*, March 23, 2012. http://www.financialexpress.com/news/mahindra-satyams-headquarter-shift-news-fuels-fear-of-job-losses/927340/1
25. Excerted from http://www.financialexpress.com/news/mahindra-satyams-headquarter-shift-news-fuels-fear-of-job-losses/927340/1

# Epilogue

1. Radhakrishna, G.S. 'Raju Out of Jail and a "Job".' *Telegraph*, November 6, 2011. http://www.telegraphindia.com/1111106/jsp/frontpage/story_14714800.jsp
2. Ibid.
3. Ibid.
4. Ibid.
5. Bhandari, Bhupesh. *The Satyam Saga*. New Delhi: BS Books, 2009.
6. Ibid.
7. Sengupta, Joydeep, and Prashant Gandhi. 'Spurring Value Creation in IT Services: An Interview with the Chairman of India's Satyam Computers.' *McKinsey Quarterly*, September, 2007.
8. Ibid.
9. According to Joy, when Satyam was founded, it was staffed with three

people, including Raju himself and his brother. When it became a US$10 million company by 1992, it had 7 leaders. When Satyam reached the US$100 million revenue mark, it had 16 leaders running the company. When it became a US$1 billion company, it had 40 top leaders, and when it became a US$2 billion company, it had a top leadership of over 100 people.

10. 'Satyam Led EMRI Continue Operations Despite Scam.' *Mid-Day*, January 16, 2009. http://www.mid-day.com/news/2009/jan/180109-Satyam-NGO-EMRI-to-continue-operations.htm
11. Peters, Tom. *The Little Big Things: 163 Ways to Pursue Excellence*. New York: HarperStudio, 2010.
12. Gombar, Vandana. 'Jekyll and Hyde?' *The Satyam Saga*. New Delhi: BS Books, 2009.
13. Ibid.
14. Ibid.
15. 'Bail for Ramalinga Raju, brother and another.' *Hindu*, 4 November, 2011. http://www.thehindu.com/news/national/article2597752.ece

# A NOTE ON THE AUTHOR

Zafar Anjum is a Singapore-based Indian journalist and writer. He has been writing fiction and essays since 2000. Over the years, his writing has appeared in periodicals and websites in India, US, UK, Hong Kong, Singapore, and other countries.

Zafar is a cineaste, an avid blogger (dreamink.blogspot.com), and editor of Kitaab.org, a website dedicated to Asian writing in English. An award-winning journalist—Zafar works as the Asia Online Editor for Fairfax Business Media's technology publications including *Computerworld Singapore*, *Computerworld Malaysia*, *CIO Asia and MIS Asia*.

To find out more about *The Resurgence of Satyam*, log on to resurgenceofsatyam.wordpress.com

# A NOTE ON THE TYPE

Dante was created in the mid-1950s by Giovanni Mardersteig who wanted to develop a typeface that was easy to read and whose italics worked harmoniously with the roman. Special care was taken with the design of the serifs and top curves of the lowercase to create a subtle horizontal stress, which helps the eye move smoothly across the page. The font was first used to publish Boccaccio's *Trattatello in Laude di Dante*—hence the name.